THE DAM BUSTERS

ABOUT THE AUTHOR

W. B. Bartlett is a writer and historian. He is the author of ten history books including *Titanic: 9 Hours to Hell*, *The Survivors' Story*, *Why the Titanic Sank*, *The Mongols: From Genghis Khan To Tamerlane* and *Islam's War Against the Crusaders*. He lives in Bournemouth.

Praise for W. B. Bartlett

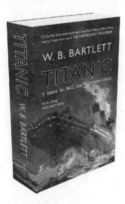

'So enthralling that you can almost hear the ghosts of the drowned, pressing to share their memories of that night of terror'
THE DAILY MAIL

'Quite the best and most level-headed telling of the whole story I have ever read' *THE INDEPENDENT ON SUNDAY*

'Bartlett is the first to concentrate on the treatment of the third-class passengers... well worth a read' *NAUTICAL MAGAZINE*

THE DAM BUSTERS

In the Words of the Bomber Crews

W. B. BARTLETT

AMBERLEY

Cover illustrations: Detail from the 1955 film *Dam Busters*. Canal + Image UK Limited. *Back*: © Martin Bowman.

This edition first published 2013

Amberley Publishing
The Hill, Stroud,
Gloucestershire, GL5 4EP

www.amberleybooks.com

British Library Cataloguing in Publication Data.
A catalogue record for this book is available from the British Library.
ISBN 978 1 4456 1193 8
Ebook ISBN 978 1 4456 1200 3

Typesetting and Origination by Amberley Publishing

CONTENTS

Preface

Britain and the British people were, in 1943, in much need of a boost. It was true of course that much had changed since the darkest days of 1940. The heroic triumph of the RAF in the Battle of Britain had helped remove the imminent threat of invasion and by now the country also had two great powers as her allies, because the German leadership had decided to launch unprovoked attacks on the Soviet Union as well as declaring war on the United States of America in the aftermath of the Japanese attack on Pearl Harbor.

It was also true that a great victory had been won by the British Army at El Alamein in November 1942, a triumph that famously caused the British Prime Minister Winston Churchill to remark that 'this is not the end. It is not even the beginning of the end, but it is, perhaps, the end of the beginning.' But, although church bells had been rung in recognition of the defeat of Rommel in the Egyptian desert, it would only look like a fork in the road to victory with the benefit of hindsight.

The clue was in the 'perhaps' in the Prime Minister's famous phrase, for Churchill would only remark later on that El Alamein was a definitive turning point for the British people, after which 'we never had a defeat'. For Britain, a long, hard slog still lay ahead. Between the beginning of 1942 and March 1943 a potentially crippling 7 million tons of British shipping had been lost to enemy action, mainly through U-boat activity. On several occasions during this period, over a hundred ships had been lost in a month. Rationing continued to bite, strengthening the entirely accurate perception that this was an age of real and grim austerity. Neither was the news from abroad universally good; 16 May 1943, the very day of the raids, marked the formal conclusion to the brutal suppression by the Third Reich of the rebels in the Warsaw Ghetto, an act that sentenced thousands of Jews to death.

Luftwaffe activity had nevertheless sharply reduced since the Battle of Britain, though occasionally attacks would be launched which would create significant damage, most famously the so-called Baedeker raids (named after the famous tourist guides) launched in 1942 against a number of culturally significant cities: Bath, Exeter, Norwich, York and Canterbury. These raids came about in response to vastly increased RAF activity over Germany which had led in that same year to the first '1,000 bomber' raids against the enemy.

Despite the massive upsurge in the intensity of British air raids against Germany in 1942, Bomber Command still needed a major victory to convince its critics that it was headed in the right direction. Bomber Command's formidable Commander-in-Chief, Sir Arthur 'Bomber' Harris, had adopted a strategy known as 'area bombing'. This argued that the best approach was to attack key targets such as factories, towns and cities with heavy and, if necessary repeated, raids. However, there were many critics who did not agree with the strategy. A fierce argument had raged in the British High Command about how to best use the RAF during 1942 and, although Harris had won it in the short term, he needed a convincing victory to boost his standing and that of his Command. Only then would he feel secure in the knowledge that his Command enjoyed the confidence of the British leadership.

He would get such a victory on the night of 16/17 May 1943. At 0730 on the morning of the 17th, Squadron Leader Gerry Fray of 542 Squadron left RAF Benson in his Spitfire to fly towards the Ruhr to assess the impact of raids carried out there a few hours before. When he was about 150 miles from the Möhne dam (which was some 25 miles east of Dortmund), he could see industrial haze over the Ruhr area.

> On flying closer I saw what had seemed to be cloud was the sun shining on the floodwaters. I was flying at 30,000 feet and I looked down into the valley, which had seemed so peaceful three days before, but now it was a wide torrent with the sun shining on it.[1]

He could in fact see an inland sea where there was none marked on the map. Fray was well placed to comment; he was the last British pilot to see the dam before it was breached on a reconnaissance flight on 15 May, and now he was the first to see it afterwards. He had flown the same reconnaissance missions frequently over several months and had got to know the area well. Now he could barely recognise it.

Shortly after this mission confirmed the success of the activities of the previous night, the news of a great victory was broken to the British people. Whilst the delivery may have been dry, the broadcast hinted at the fact that something extraordinary had taken place:

> This is London. The Air Ministry has just issued the following communiqué. In the early hours of this morning, a force of Lancasters of Bomber Command led by Wing Cdr G. P. Gibson DSO DFC attacked with mines the dams of the Möhne and Sorpe reservoirs. These control over two-thirds of the water storage capacity of the Ruhr basin. Reconnaissance later established that the Möhne dam had been breached over a length of one hundred yards, and that the power station below had been swept away. The Eder dam, which controls the headwaters of the Weser and Fulde valleys and operates several power stations, was also attacked and reported as breached. Photographs show the river below the dam in full flood. The attacks were pressed home from a very low level with great determination and coolness in the face of fierce resistance. Eight of the Lancasters are missing.[2]

Churchill followed this up with a message that asked that the following greeting should be passed on:

> Please convey to the crew of the Lancasters of Number 617 Squadron who attacked the Möhne, Eder and Sorpe Dams my admiration and my congratulations on this outstanding and very gallant action. They have struck a blow that will have far-reaching effects.[3]

It is highly unlikely that most people in Britain had any idea where the Möhne, Eder and Sorpe dams actually were. Even if they did, because of wartime censorship they would not know for years to come the full story of the extraordinary nature of the attack that had taken place. So secret were some of the details that when a major movie was made about the raids in 1955, some crucial details were incorrect. This included the shape of the bomb, which was still a classified secret.

This was somewhat ironic as the Germans had a live working example in their possession on the morning after the raid.

There was of course much euphoria in Britain in the wake of this victory. Harris was ecstatic; this too was ironic as for some time he had been one of the biggest potential obstacles to the raids ever being launched at all. Churchill's delight was not just because of the impact on morale or the practical effects on German war production. Britain was in an increasingly problematic strategic situation. The Soviet Union, in the shape of its fierce leader Josef Stalin, was scathing about the lack of a meaningful 'second front' in Europe to distract the German armies from the bitter war that was still being fought in the East. Britain's main role as far as he was concerned was as a source of supply through its Arctic convoys. The British Empire, he felt, was otherwise increasingly an irrelevance in the modern world.

The daily meeting of the War Cabinet on 18 March 1943 offered up a case in point. Premier Stalin had sent two telegrams to Churchill. The first of them (both were sent on the 15th) was in response to a telegram from the Prime Minister which appeared to postpone any attempt to launch a 'second front'. In reply, the Soviet leader had noted that the 'uncertainty' of Churchill's comments aroused 'grave anxiety'. The second telegram was much more placatory, congratulating the British on the 'successful bombing' of Essen and other German cities. Clearly Bomber Command's efforts were not going completely unnoticed, even on the international scene.[4] Such positive news was welcome, especially as Britain was on the verge of postponing the North Atlantic convoys to the Soviet Union because of heavy German warship concentrations in the region. Anything that might help placate the formidable 'Uncle Joe' was to be welcomed.

Stalin's more dismissive views were shared by many in the US. There was frequent debate about whether the British were a 'busted flush' or not. Few Americans doubted the bravery of the British people but the record of the British Army in the early years of the war had been far from positive: Dunkirk may have been a gallant action but it was, when all was said and done, a retreat from the continent of Europe. An attempt to re-announce a return, albeit in a small-scale operation, in a raid on Dieppe in August 1942, was an unmitigated disaster with 60 per cent casualties and no significant objectives achieved.

Now Churchill had the victory he wanted in order to restore British pride and, more importantly, credibility. In contrast, *der Führer*, Adolf Hitler, had a headache. In the early hours of the 17th, his Armaments Minister, Albert Speer, had been woken by the news of an incredibly audacious attack. Shortly after, he had set off for the town of Werl – a few miles to the north of the Möhne valley and protected from the flood by a belt of higher land in between – in a Fieseler Storch light aircraft. As he approached the area, he could barely believe his eyes.

Speer witnessed the aftermath of one of the most incredible acts of daring of the entire war. The details when he started to establish them seemed unbelievable, but in this case fact was almost as strange as fiction. Most pertinently of all, had it not been for the genius and perseverance of an engineer and the bravery and skill of an RAF wing commander and his squadron, not to mention the talent of an often overlooked aircraft designer, the raid would never have happened in the first place.

The raids soon entered the realms of legend. Some details would appear in the press within a few days of the mission, though key facts would be suppressed in the interests of security. A decade later, the film would further add to the status of the raids in popular consciousness. Although not a complete distortion of the truth, rough edges were smoothed off, partly for the sake of artistic continuity perhaps but misleading nevertheless (Gibson's rather acerbic personality, for instance, was significantly played down in the movie). Attacks on two dams were shown but there were in fact four targets bombed (two unsuccessfully, hence their omission from the storyline). Other facts were plain wrong; Gibson is shown as having a flash of inspiration regarding how to work out the height at which his plane was flying while he's watching a West End show in London; in fact, it was from the rather more mundane source of an engineer's brain that the inspiration came.

And of course history is written by the victors, and this influenced the presentation of the film too. Nothing is said of the impact on human life of the chaos unleashed when the dams were burst. At the time, the loss of civilian life was larger than in any other raid. A large number of the dead were not even Germans but slave labourers in a camp in the path of the floods. This does not make for good material in a film perhaps, but it is as much a part of the true story as Gibson and his pet dog, 'Nigger', or the heroic (and very real) sacrifice of the British aircrews.

This is not meant as a carping criticism. Rather it is said to emphasise that there is little that is black or white in history; instead a rather large helping of grey is normally thrown in. Neither is it to moralise; the key lesson learned from wars is perhaps that people ought to be rather more careful about starting them because when they do it is not only the 'enemy' and his civilians that suffer but also one's own people too. The comments serve to make the point though that the raids were a source of great pain, both to the aircrews who suffered very heavy losses and to the civilians caught up in the effects.

A visit nowadays to the region where the raids took place, known as the 'Sauerland', holds rather pleasant surprises for the uninformed visitor. It is an area of great natural beauty (60 per cent of the area is currently part of a national park), and with the gently flowing Möhne river below the great dam it is a region of peace and tranquillity. With rolling hills around the stream (in a number of places it seems barely big enough to be called a river) rather than rugged mountains, it might easily remind a British visitor of the Wye valley. Some miles to the east, the Eder valley (in which the water flows in a different direction to that of the Möhne) is steeper and rockier, but the hills are still shrouded in pine trees and again it is a place of beauty. It is hard to imagine that these placid streams were turned into raging torrents as a result of what took place during the raids.

This book began as a tribute to the brave crews who took part in the raids. It ended, without diminishing the achievements of the courage and skill of the aircrews one jot, also as a journey into a place of beauty and tranquillity turned into one of terror and heartache. The paradox could not be more exquisitely painful, for war too takes some of the finest of human emotions – dedication, loyalty, devotion – to the point of death itself, and distorts them into a warped and deviant reflection of terrifying intensity. More than anything, at the end of my journey, the message was one of the futility and brutality of war and how, in the end, there are no real winners and losers but those who are left alive (often haunted by memories of terrible scenes witnessed or loved ones lost) and those who are not.

I have relied as much as I am able on the words of those who took part in the raids, as well as those on the receiving end, in the account that follows. Some, like Gibson, wrote their own books; many others were interviewed and their words then published. I have also trawled through the official records in an attempt to piece everything together and give a convincing narrative of these extraordinary raids. Only where there is evidence that contradicts some of the accounts have I introduced it. I do not do this lightly, nor do I insinuate any deliberate deception on the part of those whose detailed versions may sometimes be questioned. It is just that so much happened in such a short time that it is very easy to become confused by it all.

The events of that fateful night were telescoped into a few short hours. Between the time that the first plane took off at about 2130 on the evening of 16 May 1943 to the moment that the last surviving aircraft landed eight hours later, what was in fact a series of air raids was launched unlike any that had ever been seen before, or for that matter have ever been seen since. Now that the memories are receding, the story of sacrifice, suffering, bravery and resilience (not all of it from the British aircrews) deserves another telling if only as a reminder of the horror and tragedy of war and the very real dangers of complacency after decades of peace. There was plenty that was heroic and self-sacrificing in the raids and much to admire from that perspective, but in truth very little glory. We forget that particular lesson at our peril.

Wayne Bartlett
Bournemouth
16 May 2011

I

The Rationale for the Raids & Early
Preparations

It was not long after dawn on Monday 17 May in 1943. Another fine day was hoped for over the skies of eastern England after the glorious sunshine experienced on the day before. At Scampton airbase in Lincolnshire there were some unusually important people scanning the horizons at this unearthly hour, just after 4 a.m. Amongst them was one of the most important figures in the RAF, and one of the most controversial figures of the entire Second World War, Sir Arthur 'Bomber' Harris.

The tired group gathered around him, who had been up all night, looked hopefully into the early morning sun, expectant and excited. A magnificent result had been achieved and there was every hope that a decisive blow had been struck against the German war effort. Now it was time to welcome back the heroes and pray that all nineteen planes that had been counted out would return.

A few pilots had returned already. Some had come back early because of damage caused either by accident or enemy action. Others had delivered their bombs and had arrived back with glorious confirmatory news that one major target at least had been breached. But the man that the welcoming party really wanted to see was the one who had directed the attacks, Wing Commander Guy Penrose Gibson, DSO, DFC.

Just about 0415, a plane appeared on the horizon, a small dot at first, growing bigger by the second, the imminent arrival of the returning

Lancaster heralded by the heavy throb of its four engines. It began its descent, dipping ever lower, until it made contact with the grass runway at Scampton. It taxied into position and came to a halt, its power off. After the throbbing of the engine, only the sound of the morning chorus interrupted the subdued chatter of the small group waiting.

From the rickety steps that led down from the plane, a slight, boyish-looking figure emerged: the hero of the hour. Gibson was greeted warmly by Harris, who had marked him out as a special pilot a long time before, and by Barnes Wallis, the bespectacled scientist whose deadly invention had been successfully delivered over Germany. They congratulated each other on the brilliance of the invention, the success of the mission, the bravery and determination of the pilots. Gibson had not just made history; he had become part of it.

Some hundreds of miles away to the east, morning was also breaking over the Möhne valley. This too was normally a place of quiet at this time of day, broken only by the occasional farmer going to work or shift workers on their way in and out of their factories further down the valley. At the furthest recess of the valley, just below the massive concrete walls of the Möhne reservoir, the Porto Coeli convent had stood for hundreds of years, a beautiful building much ornamented over time since its humble beginnings, an eternal beacon of certainty and continuance that had survived defiant despite the huge changes that had reshaped the world since it was first established.

It had been loved by the local people who lived nearby as much as anything for its comforting stability – emotions that were strengthened now that the great war seemed to be running on and on without an end in sight. But now it was gone and where it had stood for all those centuries there was just a vast, muddy river that stretched without end into the far distance. Not even the bell tower stood above the waters. The church, the symbol of peace, of hope and of permanence, had itself become a graveyard of the newly dead. In the process, it too had died.

The pace of change that marked the twentieth century was phenomenal. Technological change, however, is usually a two-edged sword with the power for positive or negative impacts. The Porto Coeli convent had just paid the price for technological 'progress' with its extinction as all but a melancholy ruin.

It was air power that made this possible but, just four decades before, air travel in anything but a balloon had only existed in a Jules Verne novel. Even by the beginning of the First World War, the concept of conflict in the air was in its infancy. It was only eleven years since the Wright brothers had made their first pioneering flight in 1903 for a distance travelled of 120 feet at an altitude of 10 feet above the ground. It was only five years since Louis Bleriot had become the first man to cross the English Channel, travelling the 22 statute miles in 37 minutes.

When the war broke out in 1914, the only role envisaged for aircraft was that of reconnaissance, in the same manner that hot-air balloons had been employed in the Franco-Prussian War of 1870 (though the first such use of the balloon can be traced as far back as the Battle of Fleurus in 1794). The First World War was the era of the biplane, so fragile that it looked as if it might fall out of the sky at any minute. At the outbreak of war the British military – there was as yet no such dedicated air service as the RAF – had access to a sum total of 110 planes and six airships.

But it did not take long for strategists to see the potential for far more destructive duties, an insight that would bring death and devastation to many, not just military personnel but civilians too. War was no longer confined to the battlefield; in reality it never had been but civilians who had been hundreds of miles from the front line had felt safe in the past. Not for much longer. By 1915, Zeppelins were flying ponderously over London and the first civilian deaths from air-bombing were suffered. This was not one-way traffic: German cities were targeted, as was Istanbul. Two thousand civilians died because of air raids by the time that the Armistice came into force on 11 November 1918.

In the Second World War, individual raids would eclipse this number of deaths in a terrifying inflationary pattern that would culminate on an August day in the atomic bombing of the Japanese city of Hiroshima, where conservative estimates reckon that 100,000 people died. Whilst this was in the future in 1918, by the end of the First World War the shape of future conflicts, and of the part that airpower would play in them, was already becoming apparent though no one could envisage the sheer scale of the awesome terror they would bring to towns, cities, factories and other industrial installations all over the world.

When German Gotha planes flew over London on 13 June 1917, civilians crowded the streets, full of curiosity and unbothered by any sense of imminent danger. The main threat before 1917 had come from airships and airplane raids were still a novelty. The innocent naivety of the Londoners was soon exposed and in the raid that followed 162 people were killed and 432 injured. Amongst the dead were forty-six children in a kindergarten. Twenty-one years later, Air Commodore Lionel Charlton would describe the raid as 'the beginning of a new epoch in the history of warfare'.[1]

This raid helped to shock Britain out of its complacency. At the time there were two bodies responsible for military aircraft: the Royal Flying Corps (RFC), which operated in support of the army, and the Royal Naval Air Force. It was realised that a force was now needed to defend the skies as well as attack the enemy. And so on 1 April 1918, what would be known as the Royal Air Force (RAF) was born, the first independent air force in the world. Its first commander would be Hugh Trenchard, who had recently resigned from leadership of the RFC.

Trenchard would resign from command of what was then known as the Independent Air Force shortly before the end of the war in October 1918. The very next year, he returned. When he did so, he remarked that 'there can be no doubt that we must be prepared for long distance aerial operations against an enemy's main source of supply'. This indirectly confirmed that in the future civilians might not just be innocent victims of war but that they would be deliberate targets.

Two decades later, as the world moved towards catastrophe once more, Trenchard's vision was drawing increasingly closer. The bombing of civilian targets was undertaken ruthlessly by the Japanese in China in 1932. Four years later Mussolini's Italian air force attacked defenceless towns in Ethiopia. Strategists such as the Italian General Giulio Douhet argued that the deliberate targeting of civilians would have a beneficial effect in breaking the morale of the enemy. A slippery downhill moral slope was being travelled. No military power in the world would be immune from such thinking.

The bombing of the northern Spanish town of Guernica by the German Condor Legion and the Italian Aviazione Legioniari on 26 April 1937 served for many as striking evidence of the horrors of modern war and the use of terror tactics against civilian targets as an unavoidable facet of it. When Pablo Picasso was inspired to produce a painting as a memorial to the hundreds of non-combatants who lost their lives as a result of the bombing, he created one of the most iconic images of the twentieth century. After its unveiling at the Paris Exhibition of 1937, the painting then toured Europe before crossing the Atlantic to the USA. It seared the soul of many viewers and helped to spread terror amongst civilian populations as the haunting spectre of a worldwide confrontation loomed.

When raw emotions are exposed as a result of such terrible events, objectivity is also a victim. It mattered not that there were a number of military thinkers even in Germany who were not yet advocates of terror tactics in war. A document adopted by the Luftwaffe in 1935 entitled 'The Conduct of the Aerial War' rejected the concept of terror as a legitimate and effective instrument of war. Despite this uncertainty, to many the events of Guernica, alongside the wider conflicts in the Far East and Ethiopia, seemed to prove that the arguments for the bombing of civilians had been decisively proved as an authentic military strategy.

Whatever the sincerity of those whose sentiments inclined them to argue for the protection of non-military targets against attack, it would soon become apparent with shocking clarity during the Second World War that the protection of civilians as innocent victims had little if no priority at all. It would become even clearer that the targeting of civilians involved in the war effort of an enemy, such as those working in factories, would become a legitimate objective.

And it was not just the Germans or the Italians that were planning heavy strikes against civilian targets should a conflict begin. In October 1937, the RAF's Air Staff identified forty-five industrial plants in the Ruhr, the Rhineland and the Saar region as vital to the German war effort. These were highlighted as targets. An Air Targets Sub-Committee would later suggest that the direct destruction of these would be difficult as it would require a level of bombing accuracy that did not presently exist and it would instead be sensible to concentrate on bombing the Möhne and Sorpe dams and unleash indirect destruction on these targets. And so an idea was born.

It was easy to understand why these regions were considered to be so important, for the Ruhr valley in particular was crucial to the German war effort. During the late nineteenth century it had been the crucible in which a new superpower was forged, literally, in the steel furnaces that were dotted all over it. A German fleet, constructed out of the Ruhr's end-products, had been built to rival that of Britain, whilst German industry had powered ahead, taking on Britain, the USA and others across the globe. After the First World War had ended in humiliation,

Germany slowly but surely rebuilt her shattered armies and navy throughout the 1920s and 1930s, again substantially on the back of the Ruhr industries.

Not only was the German steel industry hugely reliant on supplies from the Ruhr, the area was also liberally blessed with supplies of coal to drive the blast furnaces. There was naturally a massive infrastructure supporting all this: roads, railways, bridges, canals – all prime targets for RAF attempts to strike a crushing blow against the German war effort.

The so-called Western Air Plans had been drawn up by the Air Staff in October 1937. These identified nineteen power plants and twenty-six coking plants in the Rhine, Ruhr and Saar areas that should be knocked out if German industry was to be crippled; but this turned out to be overambitious. The Air Target's Sub-Committee, which was subordinated to the Prime Minister's Committee of Imperial Defence led by Sir Maurice Hankey, felt that major blows could be struck against German industry in the Ruhr by instead breaching the Möhne and Sorpe dams.

Widespread flooding would occur if this could be successfully achieved. The loss of water to the power industry would also be substantial. It would take many conventional raids to achieve the same impact as could be delivered by just two successful attacks against the dams, making it a very enticing proposition. The fact that there would inevitably be large numbers of civilian casualties when the dams were breached did nothing to stop the enthusiasm of supporters of the plan growing significantly over time.

Discussions were held by the British Air Ministry in 1937 considering the possibilities for attacking dams in the event of war. Minutes from the Ordnance Committee in October of that year led to a response from the Chief Superintendent of the Research Department at Woolwich considering the possibilities for aerial attack on dams. These were not altogether encouraging in considering the possibility of success.[2]

The Air Ministry Bombing Committee further considered attacking the dams in 1938. At the meeting held on 26 July the potential for attacks on them was discussed and three objectives were agreed:

- To cut off essential supplies of water for industrial and domestic purposes.

- To cause flooding and damage to industrial plants, railways, waterways, etc., in the Ruhr valley.
- To prevent the maintenance of sufficient water for navigation in the inland waterways system.[3]

At this meeting, Squadron Leader Burge noted that he had 'been informed by experts that the destruction of this dam [he was referring at this point to that at the Möhne reservoir] would result in enormous damage … the Ruhr Valley, which was low-lying, would be completely flooded, with the result that railways, important bridges, pumping stations and chemical plants, would be destroyed or rendered inoperative'.[4]

In these objectives can be seen the great prize that enticed the British to develop plans to attack the dams. It was not just the most obvious element, namely the destruction that the breach would cause. Depriving German industry of water was also very important. To produce just one ton of steel required 100,000 tons of water.[5] Clearly, destroying the dams would, it was hoped, strike a decisive blow against the German war effort.

This initial meeting concluded with a summing-up that stated that low-level bombing would be the best way of achieving the desired results and that a torpedo would be the most effective way of breaching the dam. However, even at this early stage there was some discussion about whether or not such a weapon would be capable of breaching any defensive netting that had been deployed to resist attack.

It was one thing to recognise that the breaching of the dams would cause significant damage but quite another, given the technology then available, to manage to do it. There were several major problems. First of all, a massive volume of explosive would need to be delivered against the targets, far beyond the capability of the RAF in the late 1930s. It would also need to be delivered with great accuracy, again far beyond what could realistically be expected. And even then there was no guarantee that the dams could be destroyed.

The dams were massive structures and their very scale and method of construction helped to protect them. The two major dams in the Ruhr region, at the Möhne and the Sorpe, were in fact of different types. The first was of a type known as a gravity dam, a large masonry structure held in position by its own weight. Such dams were either straight or curved inwards (as was the one at the Möhne) with emergency sluices to allow rapid draining if it was needed. Water was normally drawn out through sluice towers so that sludge could be filtered out. It was important in any attack to breach the dam low down so that most or all of the water would filter out (though it could not be too near the base as the walls became more massive lower down, making them harder to breach). It was also important to damage sluices and water pumps too if maximum chaos were to be caused.

The statistics concerning the Möhne dam were impressive. Built between 1909 and 1913, it had a capacity when full of 134 million cubic metres. Its masonry wall was over 130 feet in height, 112 feet wide at its base and 2,100 feet long. Located to the south-east of Dortmund, it supplied water for industrial and domestic purposes and hydroelectric power.

The nearby Sorpe dam was built between 1929 and 1933. It held 72 million cubic metres of water and its wall was 58 metres in height. Together the two dams held 75 per cent of the total reservoir capacity in the Ruhr catchment area with two-thirds of that being held by the Möhne dam.

The Sorpe dam was of a different construction to that of the Möhne, and that would later prove to be significant. It was an earth dam, a type which has a vertical concrete or clay core (the Sorpe dam had the former). A sluice was once more used to take away excess water – this was especially important so as to avoid erosion of the earth covering. It was triangular in cross-section, as was a gravity dam, but had a much broader base. This made it a much tougher nut to crack in practice than a gravity dam. The Sorpe was not as important as the Möhne dam but widespread disruption to hydroelectric power with a knock-on effect on industry would occur if it were to be breached. If both could be breached together then the impact on the Ruhr could be crippling.

A third target would also be identified, though in practice it would be much less important than the other two. This was at the Eder, to the south-east of the Möhne and the Sorpe. It was also a gravity dam, 139 feet high, 115 feet wide at the bottom and 1,309 feet long. It had a capacity of 44,400 million gallons – about 168 million cubic metres, even bigger than the Möhne. Its location, however, meant that its breaching would not create so much collateral damage as would the breaching of the dams at the Möhne and the Sorpe as its water supplies did not flow into the Ruhr region. However, it still had local significance. Before the dam, the winter flooding of the Eder had been notoriously unpredictable. Now the Eder dam provided drinking water and also water for industrial and agricultural purposes. Its breaching would be a bonus if it could be delivered alongside the other targets.

Some German authorities were aware of the threat, such as Justus Dillgardt, the mayor of Essen and chairman of Ruhrtalsperrenverein, the organisation responsible for the dams. In August 1939 he predicted that bombs exploding below the surface of the water in the reservoirs would cause more damage than a direct hit because of the compressed effect of the water, which could cause the wall to collapse. This was a remarkably prescient piece of scientific analysis as this was exactly what would happen in practice. The attraction of the bombing of dams and the resultant collateral damage was not just attractive to the British either; the Luftwaffe considered bombing the Derwent and Howden dams near Sheffield but lacked the means to do so and the idea was not developed.

Just how to breach the dams remained the key problem to be solved as far as the British were concerned. At one stage, what sounds a very futuristic idea was considered but not developed further, namely the use of unpiloted drones against the Möhne dam. Yet despite the challenges, the possibilities of launching a raid against the dams continued to grow. In 1940, Sir Charles Portal, Air Officer Commanding-in-Chief of Bomber Command, wrote to the Under Secretary of State for Air, Harold Balfour: 'The time has arrived when we should make arrangements for the destruction of the Möhne dam.'[6]

He had been encouraged to do so by Air Vice-Marshal Norman Bottomley, Senior Air Staff Officer (SASO) at Bomber Command. However, when writing to Balfour, Portal confessed that before this could be done the right weapon needed to be available and it did not yet exist. It also needed an appropriate method of delivery and it was debatable whether that existed either. Portal's suggestion was that Handley-Page Hampden twin-engined bombers (an aircraft so dangerous to its pilots that it was sometimes known as 'the flying coffin') should be modified into torpedo carriers for the purposes of attacking the dams.[7]

But the performance of the RAF in the early days of the war was far from encouraging. The pre-war maxim that 'the bomber will always get through' was proved to be false, at least as far as the British were concerned (though German bombers also suffered heavily in the Battle of Britain). There were heavy losses amongst RAF bombers for little tangible return.

Nevertheless, on 2 May 1940, Wing Commander C. R. Finch-Noyes of the RAF's Research Department was instructed to work out what payload would be needed to shatter the dams. The reply four months later was a not altogether encouraging 20,000 lb of explosive, far bigger than anything yet in use by the RAF and far beyond the delivery capacity of any bombers currently available to them (though Finch-Noyes felt that the 20,000 lb could be made up of a number of bombs of 2,000 lb each).[8]

Several methods of delivering the payload were investigated. Torpedoes were a popular suggestion but the dams were defended by torpedo nets and this therefore did not augur well for a positive result. Another suggestion promised more: a 'hydroplane skimmer' to be delivered by Wellington bombers using a 'glide-bombing approach'. This device would fill with water when it struck the dam wall and then sink. When it reached a certain depth, a hydrostatic device would set the explosive off. It was hoped that the cumulative effect of a number of these devices would do the trick. This was by no means dissimilar in many respects to the solution that was finally adopted. It should also be noted that, despite the crucial contributions of Barnes Wallis, a number of other scientists were also looking at the problems and experimenting before him.

But despite continued interest, by 1941 there was still widespread scepticism within the RAF that the means could be developed to deliver an explosive device of the size required to breach the dams, though the attraction of bombing such targets was reinforced when, on 2 February that year, the hydroelectric Santa Chiara dam on the Tirso River in Sardinia was attacked by eight Swordfish torpedo bombers from HMS *Ark Royal*, though the raid was unsuccessful.

However, the technical problems appeared insurmountable. On 2 June 1941, Sir Richard Pierse, the Air Officer Commander-in-Chief of Bomber Command (who had also been involved in discussions with Finch-Noyes the year before) rejected proposals to attack the Möhne dam as being currently impractical, noting in particular that the huge volume of explosive required to force a breach was way beyond the scope of anything then available. But the idea refused to go away.

The involvement of an engineer by the name of Barnes Wallis would prove to be crucial. Wallis was originally an airship designer amongst whose achievements was the design of the R100 airship. Although he would come to be regarded as something of a kindly natured, mild-mannered English middle-aged gentleman (he was born in 1887), this was not a view that was shared by all those who worked with him. Some have suggested that Wallis gained 'a reputation for being technically competent and imaginative, but arrogant, unwilling to delegate and difficult to get on with'.[9] Wallis had worked for Vickers next to the famous Brooklands racetrack since 1930. Seeing that the airship industry was effectively finished, he had switched to aircraft, working first of all on the Wellesley monoplane and later the Wellington bomber.

He then started working on two other bombers, the Warwick and the Windsor. However, in his 'spare time' he started to study bombs and also to think about the possibility of attacking key German dams which could be used as a target for them. He sketched out designs for a 22,400-lb bomb, over 19 feet long and nearly 4 feet in diameter, something that if developed would at least offer the possibility of a weapon that could be used against the dams in the Ruhr.

Wallis came from a relatively humble background (his father was a doctor in Derbyshire) and was a driven and determined man. Stereotypes of him (fostered, for example, by Gibson's accounts of him and the 1955 film *The Dam Busters*) portray Wallis as an absent-minded professor type, something of a paternalistic figure. Yet he was a complex individual. There is no doubting his genius – without it the dams could not have been breached. But he did not suffer fools gladly and had an arrogant disdain for a number of individuals whom he considered his intellectual inferiors, particularly senior Air Staff officers, some of whom he considered to be 'singularly stupid'.

As the idea of launching an attack refused to die, testing on possible destruction of the Möhne dam began at the Road Research Laboratory at Harmondsworth, Middlesex. Wallis later met some of those working on this scheme and discussed the possibility of attacking the Möhne and Eder dams and another, the Santa Chiara di Ula multiple-arch dam in Sardinia, which had already been unsuccessfully attacked. However, a report in February 1941[10] stated that severe damage was unlikely to occur unless a 15,600-lb bomb was exploded within 50 feet of the wall, something that appeared very fanciful given the notorious inaccuracy of RAF bombing at the time.

The Butt Report in August 1941 showed that only one in ten RAF bombers was getting within 5 miles of the target. To further depress those who wished to attack the dams, it was calculated that two in every three bombers attacking the French ports achieved this target but only one in ten of those attacking the Ruhr did so. Nearly 50 per cent of all bombs dropped, claimed David Bennison-Butt (who had prepared the report for Lord Cherwell, Chief Scientific Adviser to the Cabinet and a close confidant of Churchill), landed in open countryside.

Wallis was very dismissive of current RAF tactics of attacking targets with 500–1,000 lb of explosive, regarding the process as extremely inefficient. He planned to develop a massive 'earthquake bomb' carrying nearly 16,000 lb of explosive which would have to be dropped from 40,000 feet to be effective. To deliver this he suggested the development of a six-engined bomber, the 'Vickers Victory', which would be huge and a major advance on anything then available to the RAF. He was encouraged in this plan by Lord Beaverbrook, Minister of Aircraft Production. The 'Victory' was planned to have a range of 4,000 miles and be able to fly at 40,000 feet carrying a 20,000-lb bomb load.

Wallis presented a paper entitled 'A Note on a Method of Attacking the Axis Powers', in response to which the Air Attack on Dams (AAD) Committee was set up. Wallis's original plans for a 10-ton 'earthquake bomb' were not considered practical. He therefore had to find an alternative way of delivering the charge to the dam.

His opening maxims in the paper reveal his thinking on war. In so doing they demonstrate that not only did Wallis have an excellent scientific brain but he also understood a lot about modern warfare. His main strategic maxims were that:

- Modern warfare is entirely dependent upon industry.
- Industry is dependent upon adequate supplies of power.
- Power is dependent upon the availability of natural sources of energy such as coal, oil and water ('white coal').

He also recognised an important scientific principle behind his approach to the weapon he needed to develop, namely that a bomb would create more damage if exploded in the earth, air or water around a structure. This eventually inspired him to think about his 'bouncing bomb'. The fact that the bomb would bounce would be its most famous attribute but, in terms of its effectiveness, an equally important facet was that it would sink to 30 feet below the water and then explode right up against the dam wall. However, some of his ideas were considered so outlandish that it was even suggested in some quarters that he could have been a German sympathiser deliberately wasting government effort on impractical ideas.[11]

Indeed, despite Wallis's enthusiasm 1941 proved to be a frustrating year for him. On 21 May, Sir Henry Tizard, Scientific Adviser to the Ministry of Aircraft Production (MAP), informed Wallis that there was no interest in developing a large bomber. By the end of the year Wallis also temporarily gave up on the idea of developing his massive bomb and looked for other ways of achieving his objectives.

It was 'early in 1942' according to his own recollection that Wallis had the idea of a ricocheting bomb to breach the dams (though as noted already the idea of a 'hydroplane skimmer' device had already been thought of). His daughter, Mary Stopes Roe, was later reminded of holidays in the Isle of Purbeck in Dorset when they would skim stones across the surface of the sea. He would later famously experiment with his children's marbles before developing spherical devices at Vickers to prove that a bomb could be developed. He wrote up his ideas in a paper called 'Spherical Bomb – Surface Torpedo'.

There was though something of the archetypal British eccentricity in his early experiments; when he catapulted wooden spheres across Silvermere Lake at Byfleet, they were recovered from the water by his formidable secretary, Amy Gentry, who would row out in a rowing boat to pick them up. Despite what could be his very dominant personality, she did not hesitate to berate him when he occasionally stood up in the boat during an overexcited reaction and threaten to sink it.

Wallis approached Professor P. M. S. Blackett, Scientific Adviser to the Admiralty, with his ideas about the 'bouncing bomb' as he considered the weapon would be well suited to the Fleet Air Arm, but Blackett also saw its uses for the RAF and forwarded it to Tizard, who visited Wallis shortly afterwards. They got on well. Within days, Wallis had moved his testing to the rather more formal surroundings of the ship-testing tank at the National Physical Laboratory (NPL) at Teddington.

Here it was proved that spinning the prototype bomb before release would make it more effective. The idea of using backspin rather than topspin came from a Vickers aircraft engineer, George Edwards, who as a cricketer felt that it would be more appropriate. Forward spin would tend to sink the bomb before it reached the target, whereas back spin would encourage it to be propelled until it hit the dam wall and rolled down it before exploding, thus making it much more effective.

Wallis was now starting to attract important supporters and Sir Henry Tizard's support was particularly significant. His conversion from a potential obstacle to Wallis's plans to a supporter of them was very helpful. Wallis also had a visit from Air Vice-Marshal Sir Ralph Cochrane, a senior RAF officer, who would in February 1943 be made commander of 5 Group, which would be responsible for the dam raids. At Teddington, experiments with 2-inch spheres were made and considered very promising by Tizard, who considered a full-scale trial using a Wellington bomber. Vice-Admiral Edward de Faye Renouf, who was also involved in experimental work, became a big supporter too. Renouf enlisted the support of other senior officers and from this the development of Highball, a smaller weapon for use against enemy ships, was developed.

Air Vice-Marshal Frederick Linell, the Ministry of Aircraft Production's (MAP) Controller of Research and Development, also became a strong and very influential sponsor. On 25 June he ordered a Wellington bomber to be modified to drop a mock-up sphere. However, there were already doubts about the capacity of the Wellington to do this and Tizard was soon advising 'that Wallis be instructed straight away to submit an opinion as to whether a bouncing bomb of [the required size] could be fitted to a Stirling or a Lancaster'.

But Wallis in the meantime was becoming increasingly frustrated at the lack of definitive universal commitment to his ideas, remarking that 'there is no doubt that the Air Staff have been singularly stupid over this point'.[12] Nevertheless, authority to test out twelve of these 4-foot, 6-inch spheres was given and the Oxley Engineering Company was given approval to build them.

There had been a crucial development when, in February 1942, Air Marshal Arthur Harris was appointed as Commander-in-Chief of Bomber Command, replacing Richard Pierse. His superior officer, Air Chief Marshal Charles Portal, Chief of Air Staff, directed Harris on his appointment that 'we should concentrate our efforts against a limited number of objectives and aim at sustaining our air attack on them. Even during the period of the short summer nights, suitable objectives are to be found in the densely populated and industrially important Ruhr area.'[13]

In the same month, the Air Ministry issued an Area Bombing Directive to the RAF. It stated unambiguously that 'the primary objective of your operations should be focused on the morale of the enemy civil population and in particular the industrial workers', making it clear that all-out war was to be waged against German civilians. The RAF was also told that 'you are accordingly authorized to employ your forces without restriction', which lifted constraints placed late on in the previous year when aircraft losses had been so great that limitations had been placed on the RAF in order to conserve bombers. These constraints had been imposed by Churchill himself after the loss of 37 out of 392 bombers in a raid on Berlin on 7 November 1941.[14]

The relationship between Portal and Harris would remain throughout much of the rest of the war as a sometimes complicated one. It was as well that the personalities of the two men complemented each other. Harris was always direct, sometimes acerbic, and he could rub his fellow officers – and even his superiors – up the wrong way without caring a jot that he did so. Portal in response was usually placatory but this did not make him weak. He defended his position, if such a stance was on reflection merited, with politeness but firmness. He managed to pander to Harris's ego without always giving in to it. Such would be the case with the dam raids.

At the time of Harris's appointment, the position of Bomber Command was far from secure. Initial bombing efforts in the war had been largely unsatisfactory. Early attempts to bomb Wilhelmshaven and Heligoland in daylight led to heavy losses and a change to bombing at night, but these alterations achieved little tangible result. Apart from deficiencies in accuracy already referred to, the aircraft available to the RAF were incapable of performing to the level required if bombing missions were to make a significant contribution towards the outcome of the war. Even the newest planes, such as the Manchester, failed to deliver significant improvement. So problematic was this two-engined aircraft that of 1,200 of these ordered only 200 were ever delivered before the Lancaster bomber finally became available.

Nor were the initial efforts of Harris particularly successful in changing the fortunes of Bomber Command. During Harris's first year in charge of Bomber Command, a great deal of the RAF's bombing efforts were directed in a largely unsuccessful attempt to damage the

U-boat pens at Brest in France or their construction yards in Hamburg. But Harris did decide that the bombers should in future resort to more mass attacks against enemy targets, resulting in the first '1,000 bomber raid' on Cologne in May 1942. The ground had been truly laid for the campaign for which he would later be nicknamed 'Bomber' Harris, then and now one of the most controversial figures of the Second World War.

To his more caustic critics, he would be known as 'Butcher' or 'Butch' Harris (though he was called this primarily by his own RAF personnel because of his apparent indifference to aircrew losses rather than his attitude to enemy civilian casualties. The term, however, appears to have been one awarded with dark humour in mind rather than any feeling of contempt).[15] As such, Harris was probably the most controversial British military figure of the Second World War. He was ruthless in his prosecution of British war aims and the arch-proponent of strategic bombing against enemy industrial targets. He had joined the Royal Flying Corps in 1915 and, after the war, served in – amongst other places – Mesopotamia, where he developed bombing tactics against enemy tribesmen. During a later period at Army Staff College he found himself increasingly irritated by the outdated paradigms of many of his colleagues – amongst the few people he met during this time that he respected was (the later Field Marshall) Bernard Montgomery.

At the start of the war, Harris had been appointed commander of 5 Group, from where he had moved to the then little-respected Bomber Command via an appointment in the USA. Harris's role here would be made considerably easier with the appearance in 1942 of the four-engined Lancaster bomber (its first flight had taken place on 8 January 1941 but it was not until the following year that it became operational). This would help him to deliver on his bold statements about the role of bombing in winning the war, perhaps most famously typified by his comment that 'the Nazis entered this war under the rather childish delusion that they were going to bomb everybody else and nobody was going to bomb them. At Rotterdam, London, Warsaw, and half a hundred other places, they put their rather naive theory into operation. They sowed the wind, and now they are going to reap the whirlwind.'

These were brave and inspiring words but at the outset Harris lacked the materiel to make good on them. The Avro Lancaster would completely change the terms of engagement as far as Bomber

Command was concerned. Its extensive bomb-bay allowed it to carry a heavy load, vital in terms of the dam raids. Its speed and ceiling were also a substantial improvement on what had previously been available, vastly increasing the possibilities for the RAF in terms of what could be achieved. It would be universally considered the best British bomber of the war.

Critical to its development, and an unsung hero of the 'Dambusters' mission, was Roy Chadwick, the designer of the plane. Born in 1893, the son of a mechanical engineer, Chadwick was a quiet and humble man who nevertheless was owed a great deal by his country. He had joined Avro in its factory at Woodford in 1928 and had proved himself a superb designer. In contrast to many of his colleagues, including Wallis, he was unassuming and slow to take the limelight, which meant that his role in developing the Lancaster, without which the raids on the dams could not have been made, has often been overlooked.

One of the key ingredients for success was the installation of the new mark of Rolls-Royce Merlin engines instead of the unreliable Rolls-Royce Vulture engine that had been fitted to the Manchester (though even these had their problems; in April 1943 it was noted that a Merlin 20 engine failed once in every 96 aircraft flying hours, as opposed to one every 268 flying hours for the Merlin 28, which would be suggested as a replacement).[16]

To add two extra engines Chadwick inserted a new central section to the wings of what had been the Manchester design, a masterpiece of engineering in that it was extremely strong but comparatively light. Further, with a range of 1,650 miles (with a 14,000-lb bomb load), the dams of the Ruhr were easily in range. Harris was unstinting in his praise of the Lancaster and later boldly stated that 'I believe the Lancaster was the greatest single factor in winning the war'.[17] It was substantially Chadwick's achievement and the accolades belonged more to him that to anyone else.

However, the Lancaster was only one piece in the jigsaw; another – still missing – was a bomb that could breach the dams. Development of a viable weapon to use against the dams continued. A scientific officer, A. R. Collins, at the Road Research Laboratory in Harmondsworth, made the crucial discovery that if a charge were exploded directly in contact with the target then the effect of the resultant explosion would be massively magnified.

Experiments were held on the redundant Nant-y-Gro dam near Rhyader in Wales, for which permission was received from Birmingham City Corporation. The device used at the Nant-y-Gro dam on 24 July was a 500-lb submarine mine with 279 lb of explosive. It was spectacularly successful and punched out the centre of the dam wall after earlier experiments, with a bigger payload exploded further away from the wall, had been disappointing.

Scaling up the results of this suggested that a dam of the size of the Möhne could be breached with about 6,000 lb of Torpex – with its casing this would weigh about 10,000 lb, which would be within the capacity of the Lancaster bomber to deliver. Although still a very large weapon, this was considerably smaller than some other previous predictions and potentially within the capability of existing aircraft to carry.[18] The development of Torpex (**Torp**edo **Ex**plosive) was also an important part of the dam raids' success and the timing of this was fortuitous. It was available from 1942, having been developed the year before by S. J. Pooley. Given that it was 50 per cent more powerful than TNT by mass and especially effective in underwater explosives, its production was a major breakthrough.

Following these encouraging results, further experiments were carried out. On 23 August, depth charges were dropped with a view to seeing the effect of ricochet near Troon.[19] Two days later at Vickers House in London, approval was given to trial a prototype bomb off the coast of Dorset. By December full-blown tests of the weapon that Wallis had developed were theoretically possible. The weapons he had developed had an outer spherical casing within which the explosive charge was contained. The idea was to spin the device before releasing it and then have it ricochet across the water until it reached the target. It would then sink down the side of the dam and hydrostatic pistols would cause it to explode when 30 feet below the surface and adjacent to the wall.

This would maximise damage, but to achieve this optimum result great accuracy was needed both in terms of the height from which the weapon was dropped and also the distance from the dam it was when it was released. Problems would soon become apparent though initial trials on 2 December at the Queen Mary reservoir near Weybridge, with test pilot Mutt Summers and Wallis on board, were encouraging: Summers did not notice the spinning of the large device before he released it, which was reassuring as some had predicted that the motion would be so violent that it would potentially destabilise the plane.

But tests two days later at the picturesque Chesil Beach in Dorset, an inland lagoon separated from the sea by a bank of pebbles, were anything but satisfactory. A Wellington took off from nearby RAF Warmwell. It carried two spheres as well as Wallis on board as bomb-aimer. Both bombs shattered on impact with the sea. So too did two others tested soon afterwards. After these initial failures, Wallis found that by strengthening the casing of the bomb, adjusting the height and speed of the aircraft and correcting the rate of spin, he could partially compensate for these deficiencies. There was, however, much trial and error to go through before he could be remotely confident of success.

The Navy continued to be supportive of the idea and believed that it could be used by Mosquito bombers to attack German capital ships such as the *Tirpitz*. Progress was continuing in the development of the bombs. On 19 January 1943, two further devices were dropped: one shattered on impact and the other was accidentally dropped on land, but next day a repaired cylinder was dropped and bounced to a height of 55 feet before shattering.

Then on 23 January a real breakthrough was made with the successful release of a mock-up sphere dropped at a height of 40 feet with the carrying plane at an airspeed of 283 mph: it bounced thirteen times. These developments were very timely, for on 24 January the Casablanca summit ended, the first Anglo-American strategic meeting of its type during the war. As a result of it, bombing objectives were changed and it was emphasised to Harris that 'your primary objective will be the progressive destruction of the German military, industrial and economic system, and the undermining of the morale of the German people to a point where their armed resistance is fatally weakened'.[20] This fitted in perfectly with the idea of the dam raids.

On 30 January, Wallis wrote to Cherwell arguing that the results of the Nant-y-Gro tests demonstrated that the dams could be breached and urging that the raids should take place in May or June when the reservoirs were at their fullest. He also wanted both Upkeep (the code name for the weapon against the dams) and the smaller Highball (for use against ships) to be developed and did not wish the impact of the former to be compromised by premature use of the latter. Cherwell's support would be crucial, for he was essentially Churchill's 'filter' who would eliminate any madcap ideas before they landed on the Prime Minister's desk.

Wallis believed that he would be ready to produce a usable bomb in the very near future and that any Lancasters converted would be able to switch back to conventional design shortly after the raids; both declarations proved to be very optimistic, the latter especially so. He also thought that the Sorpe could be successfully attacked based on the example of the Dale Dike dam near Sheffield, which had collapsed without warning in the previous century. However, the two were not comparable as the Dale Dike had a clay core but the Sorpe dam's core was constructed of concrete.

On 5 February there were two more successful tests, as a result of which Wallis produced his 27-page paper 'Air Attack on Dams', which discussed the effects of destroying the dams as well as the means of doing it. Twenty-one copies were distributed over the next three months, the first to Air Marshal Sir Ralph Sorley, Assistant Chief of the Air Staff. A week later, Sorley passed an assessment on to Linnell, saying that all the tests done suggested that 'the Upkeep project is technically feasible'.[21] However, a short time previously Linnell had been cautious and had recommended that Highball should be given precedence over Upkeep – Vickers was already some weeks behind in a project to develop a new bomber, the Windsor, and Linnell wanted no further delays on it because Wallis's attentions were elsewhere.

On 13 February there was a key meeting of thirteen representatives of the Air Ministry, Bomber Command, the Admiralty and MAP to discuss the project. It was agreed that Upkeep should be developed further with stronger links to Bomber Command. However, it was noted that the earliest possible time of production for the weapon was six months ahead and it was 'out of the question to consider its use before that time'.[22] In the event, it would be produced in half that time.

The moment was now at hand when a new factor would be introduced firmly into the equation, one that could have sunk this particular project before it had even, metaphorically speaking, got off the ground. After all, the early indications were that, despite the efforts to involve Bomber Command, Harris was simply not interested in what he believed was a far-fetched idea with little prospect of success.

Photographs of Arthur Harris create the impression of a man who has been chiselled out of granite, with a personality to match. In this instance, appearances do not deceive. The day after the meeting at the Air Ministry, he was quick to give his typically forthright views on the scheme in response to a copy of Wallis's paper passed on by his Senior Air Vice-Marshal Robert Saundby:

> This is tripe of the wildest description. There are so many ifs and ands that there is not the slightest chance of it working ... I don't believe a word of its supposed logistics on the surface ... At all costs stop them putting aside Lancasters and reducing our bombing effort on this wild goose chase. Let them prove the practicality of the weapon first ...

He concluded his analysis with the words that 'the war will be over before it works – and it never will'.[23]

It was perhaps just as well that the final decision was not his. On 15 February, Harris's negative reaction was effectively ignored. It was decided to develop a working Upkeep and modify a Lancaster to test it. Portal was informed but Harris immediately sent a note telling him that 'I hope you will do your utmost to keep these mistaken enthusiasts within the bounds of reason and certainly to prevent them setting aside any number of our precious Lancasters for immediate modification'.[24]

This was not the last of it. On 18 February, Harris wrote even more vehemently to Portal concerning the weapon (which he misnamed Highball in the missive), saying that he would bet his shirt '(a) that the weapon itself cannot be passed as a prototype for trials within six months; (b) that it's ballistics will in no way resemble those claimed for it; (c) that it will be impossible to keep such a weapon in adequate balance either when rotating it prior to release or at all in storage; and (d) that it will not work when we have got it'.[25] He was also dead set against low-flying missions which had, he said, been almost without exception unmitigated disasters.

Portal replied in conciliatory terms on the following day. He told Harris that 'I have the greatest respect for your opinion on all technical and operational matters and I agree with you that it is quite possible that the Highball and Upkeep projects may come to nothing'. However, he was inclined to go ahead with trials in a suitably limited fashion with no 'more than three of your precious Lancasters' until full-scale experiments had proved the case for Upkeep definitively. He explained that 'we know that the full size mock-up of Highball does what is claimed for it' (adding, in handwritten scrawl to the typed memo, 'unless the cinema lies!' – Portal had just seen a film of the trials).[26]

It was still by no means certain that Wallis would get the final go-ahead with such high-level opposition to his ideas, but the case for his weapon was rapidly starting to develop. A week later Avro – A. V. Roe and Co. (aircraft engineers) – and Vickers-Armstrong, who would design the weapon, were briefed. It had by then been decided to have a full squadron involved; a further twenty-seven planes were to be modified and 150 Upkeep weapons manufactured. According to the Air Ministry's director of bomber operations, Group Captain J. W. Baker, they were to be ready for 1 May.[27] Much had happened in a week.

Following Portal and Harris's exchange of views, the scene had been set for the meeting that could have even now derailed the entire plan. Although Harris did not have the final say on whether to proceed or not, his powerfully expressed views could be hard to resist. It was arranged that, on 22 February, Wallis would show the trial films to Harris. Given Harris's formidable temperament and vehement opposition this would be an extremely intimidating moment for Wallis (though most of those who were close to Harris insisted that he rarely, if ever, raised his voice – he did not need to; his icy temperament was far more unnerving). First impressions on the day would have done nothing to set Wallis's mind at rest; Harris's initial comments were, 'What the hell do you damned inventors want? My boys' lives are too precious to be thrown away by you.'[28] Despite this frosty beginning, Harris watched the film, dismissing the projectionist before he did as he did not wish to compromise security.

Much has been made of the fact that Harris did not like inventive types whom he saw as timewasters and it is true that there was a bewildering pace of technological change during the early way years that was hard to keep up with. Much of it proved important and useful: planes such as the Lancaster or navigation devices such as Gee. But some of it also proved frustrating. Most significantly, Harris distrusted anything that threatened to divert his Bomber Command from his main tactic, strategic area bombing. He was as a rule not at all welcoming to anyone who came up with any suggestion that might divert bombing resources from this particular tactic.

But on the other hand there was something in Wallis that would have been of interest to Harris: his desire to create massive weapons, packed with high explosives. There was an ongoing debate in Britain about whether incendiary devices, used successfully by German bombers over Britain, or high explosive was better. Harris undoubtedly saw the potential of high explosive, though he also well aware of the efficacy of using incendiaries in the right circumstances. Incendiaries were widely used in practice; orders from September 1942 recommended that bomb loads should be two-thirds incendiary, one-third high explosive and this remained the standard ratio a year later. But Harris's views of the potential effectiveness of high explosive were summed up in this rather chilling quote from him:

> The moral effect of HE [high explosive] is vast. People can escape from fires, and the casualties on a solely fire-raising raid would be as nothing. What we want to do in addition to the horrors of fire is to bring the masonry crashing down in top of the Boche, to kill the Boche and to terrify the Boche, hence the proportion of HE.[29]

There were also, despite obvious differences in some aspects, in others remarkable similarities in personality between Harris and Wallis. Neither man had particular respect for those in authority, and both were quick to air their views when they came across what they regarded as official stupidity. They were determined and persistent when faced with a challenge. And, as one of Harris's biographers remarked, 'between them they had as much diplomacy as a circus prize fighter'.[30]

The following day though, everything appeared to be off. Wallis was summoned to Vickers House to see the company's chairman, Sir Charles Craven. Craven told him that work on Upkeep was to stop; Wallis was making a nuisance of himself and had been rude to certain members of the Air Staff. Surprisingly, this had come about partly from pressure on Craven from Linnell, formerly a supporter: he had told Craven to halt 'this silly nonsense about destruction of the dams'. He apparently felt that development of the Windsor was suffering. Wallis offered to resign, at which Craven slammed his fist on the desk, shouting 'Mutiny!'

Although there is no conclusive evidence, the timing is suggestive. It seems likely that Harris's concerted pressure was beginning to have an impact. But then, just as everything appeared to be over, there was another volte-face. At a meeting on 26 February at the Ministry of Aircraft Production, the Chairman, Air Marshall Frederick Linnell, said that the Chief of the Air Staff had requested that every priority should be given to the project, thus marking out Portal as the chief decision-maker and supporter of Wallis in the process. Portal had clearly decided to ignore any objections from Harris and push ahead.

This was the breakthrough that Wallis had been longing for, but a sudden realisation now dawned on him; the weapon needed to be ready in three months and as yet no full-sized version of it had been dropped and no pilots had been trained in how to conduct the mission. There was very little time left to finish design and start production of the weapon. In fact, there were not even any drawings of the weapon that was to be used.

The very next day, work began at Burhill on full-size Upkeep drawings. It was not though until 8 March that orders were given to convert 464 Provisioning Lancasters as the carriers for the weapon. The 'Provisioning' nomenclature refers to the initial concept that the modifications would only be temporary and at some stage the changes would be undone and the aircraft would return to a 'conventional' Lancaster bomber, though this did not in fact happen to all of them. These planes would have four Packard-built Merlin 28 engines, the bomb-bay would be removed to allow for the fitting of the bomb underneath and eventually the mid-turret would be removed to help streamline the plane. Twenty-three planes were taken off Avro's production line at Woodford, Manchester, and set aside for conversion at a cost of £6,274.[31]

Now, at last, things were beginning to drop into place. The weapon was being developed and trials had been encouraging. The planes had been made available to deliver the weapon against the dams and work was in train to adapt them accordingly. All that was now needed was to find some pilots to fly a night-time mission into the heart of the Ruhr at ridiculously low levels on the night of a full moon when they would be completely visible from the ground. They then had to deliver a completely untried weapon using meticulous navigation to decide on the optimum moment to release it. Someone quite extraordinary was needed to take on such a task.

That man was Guy Penrose Gibson. He was born in India in August 1918, the younger son of a British official. Brought up whilst the power of the Raj was still dominant, surrounded by servants and living a pampered life, Gibson had a privileged background that gave him a strong sense of the hierarchies of the British class system, which later sometimes revealed itself in his leadership of 617 Squadron.

The family returned to England when Guy was six (his parents later separated and he had a generally difficult childhood with a distant father – for most of the time literally so – and a mother who later developed a fondness for alcohol). Guy made his way through prep school and an independent school at Oxford before joining the RAF almost as soon as he had completed his education. His time at boarding school merely reinforced the tendencies towards class-consciousness that his early years in India had already fostered. It came across markedly early on in his career when the ground crew who worked with him referred to him as 'the Bumptious Bastard'.[32] He perhaps improved a bit with experience, but even in 1942 he was given the uncomplimentary nickname of 'the Boy Emperor'.[33]

He graduated from flight training with average marks (his first attempt to join the RAF before the war had been unsuccessful) and was posted to 83 Squadron, where he flew Handley-Page Hampdens. When war broke out, he flew and survived thirty-nine missions. He also spent some time flying night fighters, then in an early stage of development, though his record was not exceptional: three confirmed kills, one probable and three other enemy planes damaged in ninety-nine flights.[34] He later said that he became a fighter pilot 'for fun'.

But if his piloting skills were considered average, there was no doubting his courage or his ambition to succeed. He was awarded the Distinguished Flying Cross (DFC) and was promoted to Flight Lieutenant. He proved himself to be possessed of almost incredible bravery, which was offset by a dismissive attitude towards those who did not share his characteristics as a warrior. Harris had quickly marked him out for rapid promotion but had lost the power to do anything about it due to changing his role.

Now Harris was back at Bomber Command, within three weeks Gibson had been moved from the stagnation, as he saw it, of a training unit and back on to the front line. He was given command of 106 Squadron, which he led with distinction despite having to put up – in the early days at least – with the largely ineffective Manchester bomber. Early in 1943 he also had exposure to wider public recognition when he flew with the famous BBC broadcaster Richard Dimbleby on a raid to Berlin.

Gibson also showed a strong appreciation for new technology and fully equipped his aircraft with cameras so that the accuracy of bombing missions could be assessed. He liked the company of officers, men of his own class, and had little time for NCOs or ground crews, a prejudice that a number of men from 617 Squadron would later allude to directly or indirectly. But he was difficult to gauge, as one of his biographers noted when writing of him that he was 'complicated, contradictory and vulnerable'.[35]

Yet there was no doubting his bravery, his attention to detail or his suitability to lead a raid that some thought would be equivalent to a suicide mission. Regardless of whatever social prejudices he might have had, which were anyway symptomatic of the times in which he lived, he was a good choice to lead a raid on the dams. With his arrival, a further piece of the jigsaw had been added – which was just as well, for there were now just two months to go before the deadline to launch the raids in 1943 had passed.

2

The Formation of Squadron X
11 March – 31 March 1943

On 11 March 1943, Gibson flew as commanding officer of 106 Squadron for the last time after eleven months of his leadership. He was glad of the rest coming up: he had flown 173 sorties (a mixture of night fighter and bomber missions, forty-six of them with 106 Squadron) without much of a breather. Now he could look forward to a holiday in Cornwall with his long-suffering wife Eve, an actress and dancer whom he had met in Coventry in 1939, and his beloved jet-black Labrador (strictly the dog was a mongrel but his Labrador heritage was very prominent) 'Nigger'.

Cornwall held a special place in Gibson's heart; his middle name, Penrose, was Cornish and his grandparents had a home at Porthleven, almost as far south-west as Land's End, where he had spent a number of happy childhood days before going off to school or when returning home in the holidays. His mother, Nora, was of Cornish stock but it seems that Gibson's happiest early times were spent in the company of her parents.

Gibson would develop a reputation as a tough commander. Several of his own crew who had not met his high standards when he first flew with them were quickly moved on, but when a visiting Air Ministry team considered that his rear gunner, Pilot Officer John Wickens, was too tall he quickly told them to forget the rules. Here was a man who very much liked doing things his own way.

He did not have a straightforward mission on his last flight with 106 Squadron as on the way out to bomb Stuttgart the outer port engine gave up on him. There was no option but to lose height. However, he did not want to return to base for this would mean that he would have to fly out once more when the problem was fixed. At its worst, if the weather was bad, this would mean a delay of four days in taking his leave, something that he could not stomach the thought of.

To avoid this unwelcome prospect, Gibson flew on, his plane dropping low in the sky: he described it as if she were a 'wounded bird'. The flak was heavy as they flew over Germany, directed from the angry defenders of Mannheim, Frankfurt and Mainz. However, it was ironic that at his low height he was not picked up by the searchlights that were seeking out marauders far above him. He was in as much danger from the bombs and incendiary devices dropped from above him as he was from the Germans. He dropped his bomb load and as he did so his Lancaster, free of the heavy burden it had been carrying, shot upwards before heading homewards.

He arrived back at base without further alarm. The next day Gibson woke up late, his eyes bleary from the exertions not just of the night before but also of the months preceding that. He was also already unwinding, thinking of Cornwall and the sea, the cottage in which he would relax and recharge his batteries, the time with his wife and his dog. He was a hard taskmaster, not least with himself, but he was also sufficiently self-aware to appreciate that the extended period of activity he had been through had started to wear him out. He also did not always enjoy good health – he had a long history of migraines and was already demonstrating symptoms of arthritis despite his lack of years. There was no doubt that a break would do him good.

He was surprised to be awoken by his adjutant with news that his posting had come through. He was even more surprised when he was told that he was to go to 5 Group. A Headquarters posting: he had been told that he was due a breather but this was not exactly what Gibson was cut out for. He was yet more surprised when he was told that he was to write a book for the benefit of future bomber pilots. Then the shattering news: he must start at once and his leave had been cancelled. Cornwall would have to wait.

So it was off to Grantham, where 5 Group HQ was based, after a warm and drink-fuelled send-off from his squadron at the local pub. He did not find it easy to adapt to his new surroundings when he arrived: WAAFs scurrying backwards and forwards with cups of tea, officers always in meetings, weary men trundling along the corridors with files under their arms. It was a long way from what Gibson regarded as the real action.

Unknown to Gibson, on 15 March Harris had directed Air Vice-Marshal the Honourable Sir Ralph Cochrane, who was the Air Officer Commanding 5 Group, to form a new squadron when the two men met at Bomber Command HQ in High Wycombe. Harris recommended that Gibson should lead it: Cochrane did not yet know him (he had only been the Air Officer Commanding 5 Group for less than three weeks and had only met him briefly as Gibson was coming towards the end of his stint at 106 Squadron), but Gibson was well known to Harris. Harris would later describe him as 'as great a warrior as this island ever produced'. Barnes Wallis wrote of him after his death that he was 'a man born for war ... but born to fall in war'. Harris had long admired his gung-ho attitude and had marked him out for promotion some time before. They had many similarities, including an upbringing in India before returning to lead lonely adolescent lives in boarding schools in England, and this no doubt helped to foster a similar outlook on life.

The same day that Harris and Cochrane met, Senior Air Staff Officer Air Vice-Marshal R. D. Oxland wrote two important memos. One was to G/C Ops at Bomber Command, Air Commodore S. U. Bufton, telling him that the squadron was to be formed. This information was passed on to Cochrane. Oxland also passed on the information about the new weapon that was being developed for the task ahead, telling Cochrane that 'it is proposed to use this weapon in the first instance against a large dam in Germany which, if breached, will have serious consequences in the neighbouring industrial area'.[1] It was felt that the operation against the dam would not 'prove particularly dangerous' (a somewhat complacent view as it turned out) though specialist skills would be called for and the crews involved would therefore have to be carefully selected.[2]

Cochrane, newly in charge of 5 Group, was someone who in Gibson's view had 'a lot of brain and organising ability'. Not everybody agreed with the assessment; Air Vice-Marshal Donald Bennett, a renowned commander of a Pathfinder Group, reckoned that 'his knowledge of flying and of operations was nil'. Although Harris called him 'a most brilliant, enthusiastic and hard working leader of men', others found him dour and lacking in humour.[3]

It was not long before Cochrane sent for Gibson. He first of all congratulated him on his recent award of a Bar to go with his Distinguished Service Order. However, he quickly turned to another subject with a question: how would Gibson like to go on one more trip?

Gibson, never a man to say no, nevertheless attempted to probe more to find out what was involved; but whatever this mission was, it was clearly sensitive, for Cochrane would tell him nothing. When he left soon afterwards, Gibson felt that it was something important (and therefore by definition probably dangerous).

Harris, however, had given the proviso that only three Lancasters should be converted until the weapon they were to carry had been proven. This would subsequently be increased substantially when it was agreed that the raids should go ahead. On 18 March, the Ad Hoc Committee established to develop Highball and Upkeep held its first meeting. However, it was not clear to everyone what all the targets should be. The committee, chaired by AVM Norman Bottomley, the Assistant Chief of the Air Staff, agreed that the Möhne and Eder dams should be the first priorities but ruled out the Sorpe dam as being unsuitable for tactical and technical reasons.[4] This latter opinion turned out with the benefit of hindsight to be well founded.

However, not everyone agreed with this initial analysis. An independent Ministry of Economic Warfare assessment argued that the destruction of the Sorpe dam would have a huge impact if achieved in conjunction with a successful raid at the Möhne reservoir, which was probably true but conveniently ignored the fact that it might not be technically possible. In contrast, the Eder dam was of little economic significance. Bottomley was convinced by the argument put forward by the Ministry and now recommended to Portal that the Sorpe dam should take precedence over the one at the Eder. This reflected the economic significance of the dams well enough; but recognising that the Sorpe dam was an important target was one thing, actually breaching it quite another.

On 19 March, Gibson held his second meeting with Cochrane and this time he would discover much more about his new posting, though many items of detail would remain obscure to him for a while yet. RAF Scampton's base commander, Wing Commander (later Air Commodore) J. H. N. ('Charles') Whitworth, was there with Cochrane. The latter offered Gibson a Chesterfield cigarette and then began to expand on the previous conversation the two men had had.

He confirmed that this mission was important and could not be done for two months. Gibson's inward reaction was to groan. 'Hell, it's the *Tirpitz*,' was the thought that immediately struck him. Germany's greatest surviving battleship exerted a powerful influence over the minds of Britain's military planners. The thought that she might break out into the Atlantic and create havoc amongst British shipping was a major worry. But the Germans were also well aware of her importance. She was heavily guarded and the anti-aircraft defences surrounding her were daunting. This would be no picnic.

Cochrane still did not expand though on the nature of the target, so Gibson was left guessing. But Cochrane did tell him that it had been decided that a special squadron should be set up for this raid; this was why Whitworth was in the room – it was to be quartered at his base at Scampton, Lincolnshire.[5] 49 Squadron had recently left the base to allow concrete runways to be constructed. There was therefore a lot of space available to accommodate a newly formed squadron. For Gibson, it would be returning to familiar territory; he had been stationed there before the war with 83 Squadron.

Cochrane told Gibson to prepare a list of those who he wished to fly with him, giving the impression that this would be a hand-picked squadron. There would be a lot of training. However, when Gibson pushed to know what the target was, Cochrane met him with a straight bat. He could not yet tell him.

Cochrane bent down back to his work, a sure sign that the interview was over. However, just as Gibson was about to leave, Cochrane looked up again. 'Let me know when you are ready,' he said, 'and remember not a word to anyone. This is just an ordinary new squadron. Secrecy is vital.'

Gibson's introduction to Whitworth would prove propitious too. With a polished English accent, Whitworth had the right pedigree as far as Gibson was concerned. But he was also the 'right type' of senior officer that Gibson approved of, someone who even when his position gave him the potential to avoid any dangerous missions, actively sought out opportunities to fly a plane into battle. This made him the kind of senior officer that Gibson particularly respected. (Harris too liked men of fighting spirit though he as a rule prohibited his very top commanders from accompanying their men on missions.) It was easy for the two men to warm to each other and this would enable them to work closely together.

When Gibson arrived at Scampton, he first of all started to assemble a list of his chosen aircrew. However, this list was far from definitive. It was the pilots that he knew best but he needed help with the crews. Then it was time to worry about the equipment. Ten aircraft were initially required along with all their gear. There would be more planes to come later. Then on to ancillary equipment: the crews' kit, beds, blankets, typewriters – one hundred and one mundane details that were crucial to a squadron's existence.

The next day it was off to the personnel officer to sort out the ground crew, the unsung worker bees without whom the aircrew could not function. This was followed by a trip to the WAAF Officer to sort out drivers and cooks. By the end of two gruelling days the preparations were in full swing, though the new unit did not yet have a name and was simply referred to as 'Squadron X'.

Even then, Gibson did not choose all the pilots and crews based on his own first-hand experience; far from it. Some were transferred to 617 Squadron as much for convenience as for anything else. On one occasion he was forced to send back two 'duds' who had been sent to him from a squadron that he had formerly served in and who he had already tried to get rid of previously. They were sent back to 106 Squadron from whence they had come. Two pregnant WAAFs were similarly summarily despatched.

Gibson gave the impression in his later book on the raids that this was a crack squadron with many of the crew his own personal selection. Harris wanted this to be the case too. Bomber Command at one stage suggested that crew members should be at least into their second tour of thirty sorties as a minimum. In the event these criteria would not be adhered to. There would, however, be an unusually high number of officers in the squadron, which can only have added to speculation as to what such a high-powered unit might be preparing for.

The process of forming the squadron with a full complement of staff in fact took weeks to complete. One example of the new crew members was pilot Melvin 'Dinghy' Young, so called because he had been forced to ditch in the sea twice but had been rescued on both occasions. Young, once a rower in the Oxford team that won the University Boat Race in 1938, had only recently joined 57 Squadron at Scampton when he was posted across with his crew to the new unit.

Young had indeed only just got back from the USA (his mother was an American, as was his wife, whom he had only recently married), where he had spent some months working for the RAF in various 'PR' and training tasks though he was awarded a Bar to his DFC in September of that year in recognition of the fifty-one sorties he had flown before leaving.

Gibson can have known very little about Young other than by reputation. Perhaps Group Captain Whitworth made a recommendation as he had helped teach Young to fly – although he was not completely complimentary, remarking at the time that Young was not a natural flyer.[6] However, Young would take a leading role in the training of the new squadron and possibly his reputation as a solid organiser may well have gone before him.

Young also came from a wealthy background; his American mother came from a socialite Los Angeles family and they had later lived in California though his English father had returned home to England when Young was still growing up. He would later be educated at Kent College, Connecticut, before returning to Westminster School in England to complete his education. This prestigious upbringing may also have endeared him to Gibson.

Other pilots came across, including Flight Lieutenant Bill Astell, Pilot Officer Geoff Rice and Flight Sergeant Ray Lovell, who had not flown previously with Gibson. Rice protested the decision to transfer him from 57 Squadron but unsuccessfully. Yet Gibson would soon come to rely on at least some of the men transferred over, both Young and Astell in particular. Young's ability to down a pint quicker than anyone else he knew may have helped endear him to Gibson. Ground crew member Vic Gill regarded Young as being 'very officious' and 'a little aloof from some of us' but thought that Bill Astell was 'an exceptionally friendly fellow' and that 'some ... of the pilots were more like one of the lads'.[7]

Most squadrons had two flights but 57 Squadron had a third, 'C' Flight. The creation of a third flight was often the precursor to the formation of a new squadron and this would be the case with 617 Squadron where the 'C' Flight of 57 Squadron provided Young, Astell, Rice, Lovell and Sergeant Lancaster (though the last two would not remain in the new unit for long). 106 Squadron, Gibson's former unit, also provided a number of crew members.

Squadron Leader Henry Maudslay came across from 50 Squadron. Pilot Officer Les Knight, an Australian, transferred from this unit too. Maudslay had been a middle-distance runner and was also well acquainted with the water, having been Captain of Boats at Eton. This revealed something of the social background of some of those in 617 Squadron, in common with many other contemporary units in the RAF. A number of pilots came from top-quality educational backgrounds, which meant that most of them came from the higher echelons of British or colonial society. On the other hand, other members of the crew, such as flight engineers, wireless operators and gunners, came from other less exulted parts of society and were typically sergeants. There was a clear delineation between officers and other ranks in the RAF at the time which represented the way society as a whole was in the 1940s.

But no one could doubt Maudslay's credentials as a pilot. He had spent some of his career as an instructor and was particularly experienced on the Lancaster. He had been involved in three thousand-bomber raids in 1942, against Essen, Cologne and Bremen. Knight on the other hand was something of an exception to the general rule: according to his bomb-aimer Edward Johnson, 'he didn't drink or smoke and was a bit religious' – the rest of his crew were quite different but Knight would always join them and have a lemonade when they went out.[8] He was hugely popular with his crew, a quiet disciplinarian who would quietly but firmly tell his crew if they were out of line. His front gunner Fred Sutherland said that 'we respected and admired him. He was just a wonderful person.'

Canadian Flight Sergeant Ken Brown was with 44 Squadron. Just after being briefed for a raid on Berlin, he was summoned to his C/O. He was told that he was being transferred to a new squadron but he did not want to go, preferring to complete his tour with his current unit. His C/O bluntly told him that he had no say in the matter as he was a 'named transfer'.

Flight Lieutenant Les Munro on the other hand said that he volunteered for the operation along with his crew. Wireless operator Flight Sergeant Robert Kellow recalled that they were offered a role but they discussed it before accepting. Munro was a New Zealander and had only flown his first operational sortie on 3 January 1943. He had also been involved in an operation over St Nazaire along with Joe McCarthy, one of Gibson's 'picks', a bear of a man and a New Yorker who had circumvented his country's early neutrality in the war by enlisting in the Royal Canadian Air Force (RCAF).

Some came with their crews, others as individuals. Flight Sergeant George Chalmers, another wireless operator, was bored with his current role and was posted to 617 Squadron. Many of those posted to Gibson's new unit came as crews but Chalmers came as a singleton and would eventually team up with Bill Townsend.

Gibson, however, did play a key role in choosing some of the pilots, contacting 'Mick' (or 'Micky') Martin,[9] Joe McCarthy and Dave Shannon. But Flight Sergeant Leonard Sumpter, a bomb-aimer, summed it up by saying that 'there wasn't all this selection of crews – that's a load of eyewash. Gibson might have picked a few pilots that he knew – but the crews themselves got together. We didn't get a wireless operator until almost the end of April.'[10]

Martin was an Australian, though he was a member of the RAF rather than the Royal Australian Air Force (RAAF). He had flown thirty-six missions on a combination of Hampdens, Manchesters and Lancasters. He had bumped into Gibson at a medal ceremony at Buckingham Palace, where they had conversed intently over the merits of low-level bombing. He brought an experienced crew over with him – one of them, Bob Hay, would become 617 Squadron's bombing leader. Martin had initially been turned down as a pilot as he suffered from asthma. This was ironic as he would earn himself a reputation as one of the finest low-level fliers of the war.

Another hand-picked man was Flight Sergeant David Shannon, an Australian who had flown with Gibson in 106 Squadron. He had recently been offered a job as a trainer but he did not want this and instead applied to join 83 Squadron. He had hardly arrived when Gibson phoned him and offered him a role flying with him in a new unit. Shannon and Gibson had first met in June 1942 and developed an almost telepathic understanding of each other: to Shannon Gibson was 'a fantastic leader … very strict on duty, and one of the boys off duty'. When off duty, Gibson was, he said, a 'great boozer' with 'an eye for the ladies'[11] (unlike Shannon who seemed to have a little bit of trouble coping with too much alcohol).[12] The two men had worked well together; Shannon does not seem to have been overawed by Gibson's strong personality. However, only one man from his former crew, navigator Danny Walker, came across with him to 617 Squadron.

Gibson was probably closest of all to Flight Lieutenant John 'Hoppy' Hopgood, a Cranwell graduate and despite his relative youth – he was just twenty-two – already a veteran bomber commander. He had flown thirty-five missions in Manchesters and Lancasters with 106 Squadron, having earlier flown Hampdens. He had actually helped teach Gibson to fly Lancasters and in the process had greatly impressed him with his fighting spirit.

By 21 March elements of 'Squadron X' had begun to assemble at Scampton though the aircrews did not start to arrive there until the 24th. Over the course of the next ten days more men arrived, including for example five crews transferred across from the co-located 57 Squadron.

The ruthless streak in Gibson quickly showed itself. He soon got rid of his adjutant, Flight Lieutenant Pain, whom he described as 'a last war man'. Pain had blotted his copybook by asking to live off the base with his wife; he was moved on the same afternoon that his request was made. (Gibson himself believed that the war and family life should be kept separate and rarely saw his wife – 'living out' with a wife was in his book strictly taboo.) Gibson replaced Pain with Harry Humphries, whom he knew from his previous base at Syerston. Humphries was young but had experience in business before the war. He loved flying but his eyes were not good enough to enable him to be a pilot, so he had devoted himself enthusiastically to supporting those who were able to fly. He would be a perfect man for the job.

On 24 March, Humphries arrived at Scampton. Humphries had his initial interview with Gibson, quite a long discussion in which the Wing Commander spelt out exactly what he wanted from his new adjutant. When it was over and Humphries was about to leave, Gibson concluded with a final remark: 'this Squadron will either make history or it will be completely wiped out'.[13] At times during the subsequent raids, either outcome was possible.

Humphries later provided valuable insight into the character of Gibson, whom in his memoirs he called 'the little man' – despite possessing very good looks, Gibson was not very tall. Despite his affiliation with Gibson, Humphries was also balanced in his appraisal of his Wing Commander, saying of him that 'when he was at his business commanding a bomber squadron he could be ruthless and, while never sparing himself, did not spare others either. Inefficiency he could not or would not tolerate and many that came to our Squadron departed as quickly as they had come.'[14] He could also, Humphries noted, be very tactless and possessed a strong temper that could come to the surface with fairly minimal encouragement.

George Chalmers regarded Gibson as a strong disciplinarian, suggesting that 'perhaps because he was a man of small stature [Gibson] tended to be on the aggressive side rather than be complacent about anything. Everything had to be right, and he let everybody know that too.' But in Chalmers' view, 'he was the right man for the job'.[15]

Pilot Ken Brown was one man to suffer from Gibson's disciplinarian streak; he was late for a briefing and, even though he was not last in the room, he was put on a charge by Gibson for this. Given the choice of a court martial or Gibson's own punishment, he chose the latter, which was to wash all the windows inside and outside the briefing room. He had to do this after he had finished his work for the day. The fact that Brown was a Flight Sergeant provides further ammunition to those who believe that Gibson looked down on pilots who were junior in rank. However, he was certainly not alone in his attitude – it was also remarked of Sir Arthur Harris (he was awarded his knighthood on 11 June 1942) that he never socialised with his junior staff, something that was also said of Gibson.[16]

Les Munro felt that Gibson was 'always rather caustic' about anyone who made a mistake. Bomb-aimer 'Johnny' Johnson felt that Gibson 'was a little man – with quite a big opinion of himself', whilst Chalmers thought the man had a personality which he would say was 'zero' and stuck to his own company. The only other creature that spent much time with Gibson socially most of the time was his dog, Nigger (whom, despite some popular misconceptions, was not universally liked). To ground crew member Beck Parsons, Gibson was 'a snob' – but he was also 'the right man for the job'.[17]

His driver Eileen Strawson liked Gibson very much but felt that few others did. She thought he was too clever for most people. However, he was very egalitarian in his treatment of her. Harold Hobday, a navigator, said though that Gibson could be 'the life and soul of the party' during social events. But drinking before going on operations was absolutely taboo; any offenders would be torn off a strip in front of the rest of the squadron, making anyone on the receiving end 'about two inches high'.[18] Johnson also felt that he came to the squadron with a reputation as 'an almost brutal squadron commander' but that he had calmed down quite a bit, perhaps because of the quality of people he was with at 617 Squadron.

The final word should perhaps go to his wife Eve, some eight years his senior, who said that 'I never really knew him. He kept his innermost thoughts to himself. His first love was the Air Force and he was married to whatever aircraft he happened to be flying at the time. I only came second.'[19]

In the background, a frantically hard-working group of administrators did their best to get the squadron into shape as quickly as possible. The effort involved in doing so in double-quick time was Herculean and the achievement is one of the often overlooked successes in the story of the dam raids. Gibson had no interest in administrative matters and left it all to others to do. He was well blessed with those he had around him.

Gibson was ably assisted in his task of setting up the new squadron by several other key individuals. There was Flight Sergeant 'Chiefy' (George) Powell who interviewed all 700 men when they arrived, allocating them their beds and bunks, making sure that equipment was unloaded properly and taken to the right place. Then there was Sergeant Jim Heveron, in charge of the Orderly Room. He was adept at begging, stealing and borrowing the office equipment and the people to use it, of whom the squadron was desperately short. He organised a filing system and started to respond to the letters that streamed in. Until people started to arrive to help him, he was working eighteen hours a day. Unglamorous work it may have been but it was essential to the smooth running of the unit.

A third person Gibson mentioned in the book that he wrote after the dam raids was referred to merely as a WAAF. He did not know her name for sure but thought it might be Mary. He referred to her as being 'plump and fair and the type that would make someone a very good wife one day'. She knew that the squadron was short-staffed and had volunteered to come over from another satellite base to help with the typing. These three plus Gibson formed the initial administrative and organisational backbone of the new squadron.[20] Gibson meticulously vetted new arrivals as they came in as many were unknown to him. There were two crews that he did not warm to and they were soon moved on. Efficiency took precedence over feelings.

The squadron continued to take shape, though still in a piecemeal fashion. A WAAF Officer, Fay Gillon, was called over one day from 57 Squadron. Gibson's first question to her was 'Can you keep a secret?' Convinced that she could and would, Gibson took her on with the very important practical role of liaising between the organisers of the intensive training programme and 5 Group HQ. She would prove herself to be a popular appointment.

24 March was also the day that Gibson met Barnes Wallis for the first time. Gibson was driven down the Great North Road, passing London and then on to a quiet railway station in the country. There was so much emphasis on secrecy that even his driver was not allowed to know where he was going, so Gibson caught a train for the last part of his journey. On disembarking he was met by Vickers' chief test pilot, Captain Jo 'Mutt' Summers. Summers got into his small Fiat car with Gibson and they drove off; neither man said much despite the fact that the two men had first come into contact some years before when Gibson had approached Summers for advice on how to become a civil test pilot.

At last they reached a small country house at Burhill in Surrey. This was a Georgian mansion, built in 1726 and once a regular haunt of the British aristocracy. It was now set within the grounds of a golf course and had been commandeered by the Ministry of Aircraft Production in 1940. Design engineers had been moved here after a Luftwaffe attack on the Vickers factory at Weybridge on 4 September 1940.

When Gibson and Summers arrived, security guards inspected their passes intently before the men were allowed in. Wandering through dimly lit corridors, they came at last to a room that looked like a laboratory. In contrast to the dingy areas of the house through which they had travelled, it was so bright that it caused Gibson to blink as his eyes readjusted to the light.

Facing him was a bespectacled, grey-haired, mild-mannered man who greeted him; Wallis and Gibson had at last come face to face. It quickly became apparent that Gibson still had no idea what his new squadron's targets were. Wallis was embarrassed as he had assumed that Gibson would have been fully briefed, but of course he could not breach security by taking it on himself to add to Gibson's knowledge on this particular subject.

But he did take Gibson into his confidence about the weapon that was being developed. Several things soon came out. Firstly the weapon needed to be dropped at a low level. This was dangerous as if the bombs exploded on impact then the blast upwards could seriously compromise the aircraft that had dropped it. Wallis also acknowledged the danger of flak at this low level as well as the difficulties involved in flying over water. The last point in particular seemed to hint again that something like the *Tirpitz* was the objective though it might also be U-boat pens, which were a popular target for British bombing raids.

Wallis showed Gibson the films of the trials. Gibson watched in disbelief as on the screen he saw a plane flying at about 200 feet dropping a bomb. Expecting the cylindrical object to blow up on impact, taking the plane with it in the process, he saw that it did not but bounced instead. More pictures followed and Gibson at least knew something about the weapon his squadron was expected to deliver. Wallis continued to explain that what was needed was for the aircraft to be able to fly at 240 mph at an altitude of 150 feet over clear water; the latter specification was to change significantly before the raids were launched.

As Gibson returned to Scampton, he went for a walk with Nigger and mulled over the challenges posed by the method of attack; the dog was more concerned about catching some of the rabbits that scampered around. Gibson now knew more about the forthcoming mission and had also been impressed by Wallis (a feeling that was reciprocated by the engineer). The next day Gibson briefed his men (though details of the weapon itself remained a secret for now), telling them that night flying would be needed. 'Dinghy' Young mentioned a potential problem in that it would be hard for the men to practise by moonlight, which by definition would only be possible at certain times of the month when the moon was at its fullest and the clouds were not blanketing it out.

The planned operation now had a name. On 25 March a meeting was held in the Air Ministry in King Charles Street, London. Minutes issued after the meeting noted that the two types of bomb were to be called Highball and Upkeep. Operations using the Highball weapon ('Special Operations against enemy ships') were to be called 'Servant' whilst those for use in 'Operations against enemy dams' were to be called 'Chastise'.[21]

There was ongoing inter-service tension between the Royal Navy and the RAF as to which weapon was to take precedence in terms of both development and deployment. A note from the Admiralty on 24 March summarised the problem neatly as well as giving a clear intimation – albeit in the most politely worded terms – of their view of the Air Ministry's stance on the matter:

> The real crux of the problem is the synchronisation of the attack on enemy warships, to which the Adm. attach great importance and the attack on the Möhne dam, to which the A.M. apparently attach great importance, but the results hoped to be achieved by the destruction of the latter are not clear.[22]

Further correspondence from around this time suggests something not far short of a full-blown spat between the two services, with meetings described in some official documents as 'controversial'.

Towards the end of March, there was also the start of a campaign to generate misinformation about the new devices to confuse any enemy spies who might be interested in them. It was to be said that it was a special type of mine and the wooden casing around it was to enable it to be easily used by 'native labour' when used outside of Europe. The cover story was to be that their main targets were submarines.[23]

By now 617 Squadron had officially come into existence: Air Ministry Secret Organisation Memorandum 338/43 'Expansion of Bomber Command – Formation of No. 617 Squadron' formally dates it to 23 March.[24] It was to be given the marking letters 'AJ' which were soon being painted in big red letters on the side of the planes. On the next day, the first 617 Squadron flight took place. Bill Astell was sent on this first mission to photograph lakes and reservoirs though he was not told why.[25]

The squadron was now developing into something closer to a potential fighting unit. On the evening of 26 March, Gibson and Whitworth walked together into the officers' mess and met the officer members of the crew who had arrived. The next day Gibson called everyone together for a first briefing. His instructions were clear and precise – or at least as clear and precise as they could be. He could not tell them what the target would be, but if they were successful then the results of their actions, he said, would be startling. What he did tell them was that they would be practising low-flying day and night. He emphasised that 'if I tell you to fly to a tree in the middle of England, then I will want you to bomb that tree. If I tell you to fly through a hangar, then you will have to go through that hangar, even though your wing-tips might hit either side.'

The men were told firmly that when they went into a pub at night, they should keep their mouths shut. Rumours would start and the men should do nothing to fuel them. If anyone asked what they were up to, then they should be brusquely told to mind their own business. Secrecy was everything. Mail would be censored and telephone calls monitored. Visiting senior officers were to avoid wearing their more ostentatious uniforms so as not to attract undue attention.

Whitworth also spoke, making a positive impression on Gibson as he did so. His intention, he told the assembled crews, was to run a 'happy ship' and if they didn't bother him, he would not bother them.

Despite the intensity of the training that was ahead, there would also be time for relaxation, important in bonding the new squadron together. When men were faced with mortal danger every time they took to the air, it was understandable that alcohol became a crutch for a number of them; it offered relief and escape from the very real threat of death in the near future. On one occasion, McCarthy and Jack Buckley, Shannon's rear-gunner, had a drinking competition. This started at lunchtime and, after a kip in the afternoon, resumed in the bar at six with McCarthy carrying Buckley to bed at half past seven.

As new arrivals continued to turn up, they were immediately sat down and made to read the Official Secrets Act thoroughly in order to impress on them the importance of maintaining absolute secrecy. There was clearly something special about this squadron; George Chalmers, a wireless operator with Flight Sergeant Townsend, recalled that there were no aircraft in the hangars when he arrived, but the structures were still heavily guarded.

A 'most secret order' was prepared for Gibson on 27 March telling him that the squadron would be attacking a number of lightly defended targets at night at low altitude travelling at 240 mph. Accuracy in bomb-dropping would be required to a margin of error of no greater than 40 yards. It would be advisable to practise the approach over water and Gibson should aim to ensure that all crews were able to fly to meet the necessary criteria by 10 May. Training routes were also suggested covering areas of land south-east of the Wash extending to the north Midlands and the high hills of North Wales.[26]

This order was received from Group Captain Satterly, SASO at 5 Group, who was responsible for developing the details of the plan. The fact that the targets would be lightly defended would have helped to put Gibson's mind at rest; it would not be the heavily defended *Tirpitz* they were attacking after all.[27]

By this date, all the ground crew for the new squadron were in place, all 382 of them, each one from 5 Group. They were very much the unsung heroes of the raids that were about to happen. Without them, nothing could have been achieved but not one of them would be decorated for their actions. Some of them enjoyed good relations with their aircrews but others felt that they were completely ignored by the flyers. No one could doubt though their hard work in making sure that all the planes that were to fly on the raid were in as good a condition as was possible to face the ordeal ahead of them.

As the squadron continued to come together, a number of sites were identified for training purposes. These included the Derwent reservoir near Sheffield, Bala Lake in Wales, the Abberton reservoir near Colchester and the Eyebrook reservoir (also known as Uppingham Lake) near Corby. The Derwent reservoir was perfect for training purposes. It was surrounded by high ground which made it difficult to get to – just like the targets in Germany. However, it was protected from the wind so the surface of the water was always calm.

On 28 March, Gibson took Hopgood up with him to see what the sensation of flying at 150 feet over the Derwent reservoir would be like. They dropped a bomb, which fell short (it should be noted that this was not yet full training, which would formally start on 31 March). Then they twisted their way up out of the valley, with high hills on either side of them.

This was a very straightforward exercise in daylight but they tried it again the same evening at dusk, with fog already creeping up the valley and making the approach far more difficult. The water was now as black as jet. Bomb-aimer 'Spam' Spafford muttered 'Christ! This is bloody dangerous!' Gibson, who agreed (which given his normal blasé approach to such matters shows how dangerous it was), decided there and then that if they could not devise a way of judging their height above water, then the attack was a non-starter.[28]

A number of set cross-country routes were now developed and allocated to the crews. There were mixed reports about the impact of low-level flying on the crews. George Chalmers' recollection was that 'none of them, as far as I could make out, had done any low-level flying before'. Flight Sergeant Grant McDonald, Rear Gunner AJ-F, remarked that 'low-level flying was a bit worrying and quite a bit different from what we are used to'. But Les Munro felt that 'once we started the low flying in training, it was exhilarating'. Most of the crews, he said, enjoyed it because it was normally a court-martial offence.[29]

Dave Shannon remembered that 'in the early days there was nothing but complaints and confusion coming in to Bomber Command Headquarters – everybody was sighting Lancasters flashing all around the country at very low level – and what the hell was going on?' Sergeant George Johnson, a bomb-aimer, flew with Joe McCarthy and they occasionally used to fly below pylon lines in training. On one occasion they were flying at 30 feet and there was a plane flying underneath them.[30]

On 29 March, several large packing cases arrived in Gibson's office. Handing him a screwdriver, Whitworth told him that inside were models of the targets. He emphasised that no one else in the squadron was to know what they were until the day before the raids took place (though the fact that some of the squadron were already undertaking practice attacks against dams must have given them some strong clues). Carefully taking them out of the boxes, Gibson saw at once that they were models, precisely prepared in every detail as it turned out, of three dams.[31] His first reaction was to thank God that it was not the *Tirpitz* after all.

On 30 March, Gibson visited Wallis again; however, Wallis was not overconfident about the possibilities of success against the Sorpe dam given its different construction from the gravity dams.[32] Wallis's views of the possibilities of success tended to oscillate somewhat, but any reservations he felt about the chances of breaching it would in the event be fully justified.

Full training was now about to begin. Some, like McCarthy and Townsend, took advantage of a last opportunity to take some precious leave to recharge their batteries for the challenge that now lay ahead. There would be no further opportunities to do so for the next seven weeks.

As training began in earnest, Gibson ordered that at first there should be no flying below 150 feet. The squadron should aim to soon be flying into the early evening to help acclimatise to low flying at night. However, there should be no sessions beyond three hours in duration as the men would be tired enough without longer missions to worry about at this stage.

As low-flying practice started, problems emerged. The planes were flying so low that some of them were returning to base with bits of trees in their undercarriages. Many (though not all) of the pilots loved the thrill of low flying, which was normally frowned upon, and were taking their new-found freedom to extremes. Some ground rules were developed; in particular the planes should avoid towns or airfields; it was also said, tongue in cheek, that pilots should try to avoid surprising policemen or unsuspecting lovers in the fields.[33]

As yet, the crews knew that they were involved in something unique (and therefore dangerous) but had no idea of their targets or the nature of the weapon they would be using. Not in their wildest dreams could they have imagined that they were about to take part in a number of raids that would make history, a one-off that had never been attempted before and, to date, has never been tried again. Neither did they know how costly the raids would be.

3

Training Intensifies
1 – 30 April 1943

Given the unusual characteristics of the mission that lay ahead, there were particular problems that faced the crews as they entered intensive training. One of them was the difficulty of replicating the exact conditions of the night on which the raid would be flown. The crews needed to get used to flying at low level at night guided only by the full moon. By definition, this was only possible for a few days each month, which was insufficient given the amount of time that was left to prepare. An alternative method of training needed to be found.

As a result, on 3 April 'Dinghy' Young's aircraft was measured up for night-flying training equipment known as 'Two Stage Amber' (officially the material was known as 'Bexine')[1] which was to be fitted at the Empire Centre Flying School in Hullavington. It was Young who had raised the issue of night-flying practice during the briefing in the previous week so it was fitting that he was the one who was given a key responsibility to sort it out. Whilst recent historians have made much of Gibson's prejudices against non-officer crew, this should not obscure the fact that he was perfectly prepared to delegate; and indeed, given the extent of the task facing him, he had no real choice but to do so. It no doubt helped though that Young came from very much the right background as far as Gibson was concerned.

The night-flying equipment consisted of blue Perspex fitted to the windscreen which, when used in conjunction with the crew wearing yellow goggles, gave the illusion of flying in moonlight. Useful though this was, it had some unfortunate side-effects as after the goggles were taken off everything looked red to the men who had been wearing them; they therefore had to wear dark glasses until their eyes readjusted. It also made some of the men feel sleepy, which was certainly not a desirable side-effect when flying so low that a split second could mean the difference between life and death.

In the event, only a few aircraft would be fitted with this special equipment, and at first there was only one plane equipped with it, so the men would have to take it in turns to practise in it.[2] At first a second 'safety pilot' was on board in case the pilot became disorientated but this precaution was soon dispensed with. By 16 April Gibson was able to write that 'the system is most efficient and it is hoped to equip five more aircraft by the end of the next fortnight'. The next day he was writing approvingly to Harris with similar positive thoughts.[3] Other steps were taken to deal with the challenges of flying at night: a note prepared on 11 April recorded that bomb-aimers had been issued with Livingstone goggles to accustom them to map reading at night.[4]

Gibson had a multitude of tasks to attend to, which meant that he could not devote his attentions solely to training; but he himself trialled the equipment, in particular on a longer run later in April when he flew over Yorkshire and up to Scotland, flying along the Great Glen and then down the west coast, via the Isle of Man and then back to base, a long trip of about four hours.

Training was not always intensive though and sometimes there were gaps of several days. Nevertheless, Dave Shannon thought that there was an average of 100 hours of training per crew between the formation of the squadron and the take-off for the raid.[5] Periods of hectic activity were interspersed with lulls as the crews gradually trained their way towards peak efficiency. On occasion, some ground staff would come up with the aircrews to get a better impression of what the air war was like. Fay Gillon was one of these, as was another WAAF, Ann Fowler. Gibson was particularly fond of her and it was not unknown for him to try and become rather too friendly with her. This could have been especially problematic, as she was in a relationship with Dave Shannon, whom she would marry later that year.

Ann Fowler was the unwitting source of light relief for the crew on one of these occasions. She was in the cockpit when the artificial lighting arrangements were put in place to simulate night flying. With her make-up on, her face looked like a clown's mask in the artificial light. Gibson called in the other members of the crew to have a good look at the hilarious sight, which created a few moments of pleasant distraction which everyone, apart from probably the young WAAF, greatly enjoyed.[6]

Joe McCarthy's bomb-aimer, Sergeant George Johnson, managed to take a few days off early on for the very good reason that he was getting married. In case there was any problem with this as far as Gibson was concerned, McCarthy – whom Gibson seemed to like very much – put in a strong word on his behalf. Johnson later recalled that, when he tried to put back the date because of a special trip that he was going on, his fiancée had told him bluntly that 'if you don't turn up on 3 April don't bother again'. Johnson was in the church in Torquay as arranged on the Saturday and was back in Scampton again by the Monday.[7]

During the initial intensive training period, half or more of the squadron was frequently in the air every day. The training missions lasted from two to five hours. Bomb-dropping was frequently practised as accuracy was so necessary if the raids were to be a success. The conditions would be right in the second week of April to practise in moonlight, leaving just a month until the raids. Every extra hour of training would be precious. Gibson, however, would have a very busy schedule and he could not always be involved in training given his need to be elsewhere to take part in planning. He therefore was forced to rely on some of his other senior officers to take responsibility for training on various aspects of the mission.

The low-flying training continued apace. It was not without its problems. Birds were hit, striking windscreens and getting stuck in radiators. When the planes flew over the sea, they were sometimes fired on by supposedly friendly ships who thought that they were under attack. It was perhaps remarkable that no crews were lost in training given its specific challenges. The training was intense and long-distance but it was needed to deal with the great challenge that lay ahead.

There were a number of important details still to be worked out though. A crucial requirement was to develop some way of helping the bomb-aimers know exactly where they should drop their bomb. Precision was everything. Dropped too early, a bomb had a tendency to veer to the left and explode harmlessly off to the side. Dropped too late, the bomb might bounce right over the dam wall. It was a problem that would become particularly apparent on the night of the raids, despite the great efforts that were made to cope with the challenges.

Gibson was sitting in his office one day when Wing-Commander Charles Dann, from the Aeroplane and Armament Experimental Establishment (A&AEE) at Boscombe Down in Wiltshire, walked in. Dann explained that he had come to help develop a sighting device that would tell the crews when they were in the right position to drop their bombs. Gibson was at first apoplectic, demanding to know how he knew what the squadron was up to. But when Dann explained that he had been fully briefed and had come to help, Gibson calmed down.

The visitor explained that a device could be developed that worked by lining up the two towers at either end of the Möhne dam and working out the optimum dropping distance from this – it was a case of simple trigonometry. The device had an eyepiece and two pieces of wood splaying out in a 'V' shape. Each arm had a pin pointing upwards on the end: once the bomb-aimer saw that these lined up with each of the towers on the dam then it was time to release their load.

The bomb needed to be released at exactly the right point, hence the need for the trigonometric calculations. If the bomb were released in exactly the right place, it would bounce into the wall and sink down the side of it. Each explosive device was fitted with three hydrostatic fuses that would create an explosion when the bomb sank to 30 feet, at which depth Wallis had calculated that it would do maximum damage. This in effect made the 'bomb' a form of depth charge.

Gibson was impressed with the simplicity of Dann's idea, although in the event not all of his men would use it as some found it rather cumbersome because the bomb-aimer had to hold it in his left hand whilst in his right he held the release mechanism to let the bomb go; this was difficult to coordinate, especially when the plane was lurching around as the pilot tried to find and hold exactly the right height. Some bomb-aimers instead knocked up a device using a piece of string and marks chinagraphed onto the Perspex of the bubble at the front of the Lancaster. But Gibson was happy with the experiment when they tried it out by flying over the Derwent dam and he thought that the device worked perfectly. As far as he was concerned, another problem had been solved.

The more positive side of Gibson's character was proving important. He was very much at the cutting edge of tactics and technology development, which made him feel at home with the nature of the mission. But his fighting spirit was also crucial given the levels of danger involved in the raids. This had marked him out to Harris from earlier on in his career. As early as 1940, Harris had called him a 'fire eater' and his aggressive, almost fearless leadership marked him out as an ideal man for this task.

On his deployment to 5 Group in 1942, Harris further remarked that Gibson was 'absolutely first class' – and this was a man who did not give compliments easily. So, whilst it was also convenient that Gibson was free when 617 Squadron was formed (his stint with 106 Squadron was coming to an end when the plans for the raids were being finalised), there was also little doubt that he was superbly equipped for the job. His openness to new technology made him a perfect candidate as his quickness in accepting this new bombing aid from Dann demonstrated.[8]

It should also be noted that Gibson had a sense of fun, even with those who were not in his natural circle. Ken Brown, one of the more junior pilots, was nervous and intimidated by Gibson and wondered if he would ever be up to the required standard (a completely misplaced example of self-doubt, as it happened, as he would prove himself one of the best pilots to take part in the raids). He would, however, be at the butt end of one of Gibson's pranks.

Brown liked to go and take a swim in the public baths at Lincoln, just 5 miles away from the base at Scampton. On one occasion he was standing on the side of the pool, contemplating whether or not to dive in. All of a sudden, he felt a push and the next he knew he was in the water, still wearing his bathrobe. Looking up he saw a laughing Gibson, delighted at the practical joke he had played.[9] It was simple humour, school-boyish even, but at least it shows that there was a lighter side to the usually disciplinarian Wing Commander.

There remained, however, a number of serious issues to resolve and there was now less than two months to go before the raid had to be launched. Any delay could be terminal. The dams were at their maximum capacity at the end of May, after which the water level would drop as supplies were used during the summer months. Therefore, if the timeslot of the full moon at the end of May were not taken advantage of, then a similar opportunity would not be available until May 1944.

A particular problem was that the altimeter equipment available to the crews at that time did not allow them to accurately gauge the altitude they were flying at when they were at low level. This was also crucial. If the bomb were dropped from too high an altitude then trials had demonstrated that it would just shatter on impact with the water. Flying too low could also affect the trajectory of the weapons as well as of course endangering the lives of the crews because they might hit the surface of the water. In training, some men were flying so low that they were skimming the surface whilst others were flying too high. If a solution was not found, then the raids could be a fiasco.

In the end, the solution was found. It was to fit two lights, one near the nose in the redundant camera position below the bomb-aimer and one at the rear of the plane in the ventral gun fairing. They were positioned in such a way that when they touched, forming a 'figure of eight' on the surface of the water, the plane would be at the right height from which the bomb should be dropped. In the event that the plane was too high and had to drop to achieve the right height, the front light would appear to remain still whilst the rear light moved as the plane dropped, whereas the reverse would be the case in the unlikely event that the aircraft had to climb to reach the correct altitude.

The spotlight solution was suggested by a civilian scientist from Farnborough named Benjamin Lockspeiser. Lockspeiser was Director of MAP's Scientific Research and, according to Gibson, got the idea from a method used in the First World War. Lockspeiser himself said that the idea came from a Coastal Command experiment in 1941 that was devised with bombers depth-charging U-boats in mind, a probable resurrection of the method used in the earlier conflict.

On the occasion of the 1941 experiment, it was not considered a success because choppy waters distorted the lights which converged beneath the surface of the water, which could be disastrous if aircrew were judging their height by them; but Lockspeiser felt that with calm waters, as could generally be expected with a reservoir, the idea would work and so it proved. Not everyone was convinced at first. Harris said that he had 'tried that once with a flying boat and it didn't work because the spotlight went through the water'.[10]

Harris was typically forthright in his views concerning the spotlights generally. In a memo he wrote that 'I will not have aircraft flying about with spotlights on in a defended area. Get some of these lunatics controlled and if possible locked up.' Working himself up into a lather, he continued in a similar vein: 'beams of light will not work on water in glassy conditions. Any fool knows that.'[11]

But, in the event, the lights would work very well. On 4 April, Squadron Leader Henry Maudslay became the first to have lights fitted to his plane. Maudslay had flown to Farnborough to have them fitted, returning to Scampton on the 8th. A few days later he had trialled them over the sea and then along the runway at Scampton in the dark, proving beyond doubt that Lockspeiser's suggestion was a workable one.

Direction-finding was also a major issue to be dealt with. The planes would be flying over enemy territory and would need to do their best to find their way by picking out landmarks from the ground as they passed them. This was no easy task when a plane was flying by moonlight at low level and often passed such landmarks before they could be identified.

Technology was of very limited help, though there was a device known as Gee available. This worked with the help of one 'master' station and two 'slave' stations which each emitted precisely timed pulses. These were each picked up by on-board equipment in the cockpit of the aircraft; by means of plotting these pulses on a chart the gap between the stations and the plane could be calculated. This enabled the current position of the plane to be derived.

Whilst useful, there were problems with Gee. First of all, the further the aircraft travelled, the less accurate Gee became. There was a variation of a mile by the time that the planes were over Germany which was towards the end of Gee's effective range. But this was not the biggest issue, which was that the Germans knew of the existence of Gee and could easily confuse it by emitting counter-signals that were especially powerful over Germany. In the event, this defensive mechanism would be particularly effective on the night of the raids.

Flight Lieutenant Dave Shannon remarked that the crews had to master 'what literally became map-reading' because the navigational aids available to the pilots were pretty basic. However, bomb-aimer Leonard Sumpter said that 'when it was pitch dark it wasn't any good trying to map-read from low level, as you just couldn't see anything. You could see rivers and major landmarks, but you'd got to see four or five miles ahead all the time.'[12]

The issue of navigation remained one of the biggest obstacles to the success of the raids. It was never completely resolved. In one case, the wrong dam was attacked. In others, planes were shot down either because they were forced to gain height in order to check their position, which made them easier targets, or because they flew off course over heavily defended positions.

It was a problem that 5 Group was very well aware of in advance of the raids. 5 Group's newsletter for the month of May 1943 had reminded all Bomber Command navigators that they 'must bear in mind constantly the seriousness of allowing their aircraft to stray from the Command routeings. These routes are very carefully chosen and considered from every aspect'.[13] It was an injunction that was particularly pertinent with respect to the dam raids.

Post-raid analysis confirmed the difficulties of navigation. Cochrane's official report concluded that

> in this operation navigation was more difficult than high level navigation for the reason that the whole sortie was flown at low level and because the turning points chosen were minor topographical features only. This made pinpointing doubly difficult but map reading across the lower reaches of the Rhine and Meuse was made easier by the numerous water marks and a moon between the first quarter and full at an altitude of about 30°.[14]

However good navigation was, an error that would at other times be a minor inconvenience could be disastrous. And however accurate the navigation was, avoiding obstacles at low level like church steeples and power cables would remain a matter of luck as much as judgement. Several crews would pay the ultimate price for being unable to avoid such obstacles on the night of the raids.

Security remained very tight. If the Germans knew what was being planned then it would be easy to take counter-measures to protect the dams – all the tremendous effort employed in preparing for the raids would therefore be a complete waste. The aircrews had to be watched, not because they would deliberately pass on information but because, as wartime posters warned, 'careless talk costs lives'. 'Spies' were posted and reported to authority what the crews had said while out on the town.

Other measures were taken too. Telephone wires were tapped and letters were censored. On one occasion when a crew member phoned a girlfriend and was indiscreet, he was hauled before the squadron and told off in front of them all. Gibson was quick to use humiliation as a weapon to reinforce security. On this occasion it should not be seen as the actions of an irascible commander but as perfectly legitimate tactics to reinforce a crucial message. Questions of personal pride did not come into it when the lives of his aircrews were concerned.

Despite these developments and the fact that real steps were being taken to make the raids a possibility, there was still significant debate over the possible effects of the raids even if the dams were breached. These were well summed up in a secret memo from the Ministry of Economic Warfare on 5 April.[15] This concluded that, with regard to the Möhne dam, 'there is every prospect that both the physical and moral effects of the flood which would be produced are likely to be sufficiently great to justify the operation in themselves, even if there were no other significant effects'.

However, there would not necessarily be any large or immediate effect on the supply of industrial and household water in the Ruhr area: 'It is not possible to state that a critical shortage of water supplies in the Ruhr would be a certain and inevitable result of the destruction of the Möhne dam.'

The memo stated that the destruction of the Sorpe dam would be complementary to that of the Möhne and would reinforce its effects. It was believed that it would greatly enhance the prospects of a water supply shortage and should therefore be pursued as an operational objective if operationally there was 'a reasonable prospect of success'. O. L. Lawrence of the Ministry of Economic Warfare noted that if both the Möhne and Sorpe dams were breached, 'it would be worth much more than twice the destruction of one'.[16]

The destruction of the Eder dam would on the other hand have no supplementary effect on the shortages produced by successful attacks on the two primary targets. There would be no significant inundation of any major urban area, though there could well be some destruction of agricultural land. Some power stations would be flooded but the results would be no more than 'a useful measure of interference'.

If the Möhne and Sorpe dams were to be breached then the resultant floods would have a major impact on morale, which would 'become prey to every variety of alarmist rumour regarding the possibility of a shortage of drinking water, the risk of disease and the inability of the fire services to deal with incendiary attacks'. With a final note that was almost Orwellian in its sentiments, it was suggested that 'exceptional opportunities would be presented for successful measures of political warfare'. The destruction of the Eder would, the MEW concluded, have a much smaller impact on morale than would the breaching of the Ruhr dams.

It was further noted that considerable flooding would be caused by the destruction of the Möhne dam. There would be a substantial loss of electrical output and water shortages could have a significant impact on industrial activities, for example by impacting on foundries, coal mines, coke ovens, blast furnaces and chemical plants. Railways and bridges could be badly affected. Breaching the Eder dam though would have much less impact and the economic effects were unlikely to be substantial. The Air Staff had noted on 28 March that 'from the economic standpoint ... this dam cannot be considered as a first-class objective'.

This is an important piece of analysis which outlines well the rationale for the raids. Maximum impact would result if both the Möhne and Sorpe dams were breached. On the other hand, the destruction of the Eder dam would be of little importance economically. In addition, in keeping with the spirit of the times, the effect on morale was as important as economic impact. A successful raid would help break the spirit of the German people. This was the official benchmark against which the ultimate success of the mission should be judged.

However, there remained the problem that although it was much more desirable to breach the Sorpe dam than the one at the Eder, it was also technically much more difficult. It was, to be fair, a difficult dichotomy, but the organisation of the raids when they took place suggests that an unsuitable compromise was reached. In trying to get the best of all worlds, the planners would in fact get the best of none of them.

The fact is often overlooked – perhaps because of their uniqueness and great dramatic impact – that the raids were part of a much greater strategic campaign waged against the German industrial machine. In Harris's vision of strategic bombing, the Ruhr was to be subjected to months of raids from British aircraft, of which the dam raids formed only a part.

Harris would defend the use of strategic bombing for the rest of his life. Despite its devastating effects, he insisted that it was not employed as a 'terror tactic' but as a way of destroying the production capacity of the enemy. He would later state categorically that 'attacks on cities like any other act of war are intolerable unless they are strategically justified'. He would famously write in the same letter that 'I do not personally regard the whole of the remaining cities of Germany as worth the bones of one British Grenadier'.[17] The motivations of Harris may not have been to induce terror, but that was certainly a significant by-product of the raids he directed.

Harris would brook no sentiment on the subject of enemy casualties. A letter to him on 1 May 1942, written by Assistant Chief of Air Staff Air Marshal Richard Peck, related how he had 'been told that some of our bomber aircrews returned from the Lubeck raid somewhat unhappy and depressed. They had seen a whole city afire; they realised the terrible significance of the inferno to civilians, women and children: they felt that what they had done was sheer murder with no military objective to extenuate it.'

Harris responded with typical forthrightness. He told Peck that 'our aircrews are not only unaffected by the prospect, but take a proper delight in burning and bombing the Boche rats out of their holes.' Harris considered that the complaints initially emanated from 'the propaganda of the Boche' and that most people who contacted him did so to congratulate him on giving the Germans a taste of their own medicine.[18]

What some have called the 'Battle of the Ruhr' began on 5 March 1943 when 369 aircraft set out to bomb Essen. The raids continued until 25 July, during which period Essen was attacked six times, Duisburg five and Cologne (strictly not in the Ruhr region but in its catchment zone) four. A number of other German towns were targeted, including Dortmund, Bochum and Dusseldorf. By the end of this period, strengthened German defences would become formidable: 550 night fighters, 1,000 heavy flak guns and 1,500 lighter flak weapons. So tough a nut to crack were these defences that the bomber pilots sarcastically called the Ruhr region 'happy valley' or 'the valley of no return'.

The defences around the Ruhr were therefore considerable and the scale of the challenge facing the new squadron great. But the die was cast and preparations continued to accelerate. At Scampton, pilots continued to arrive. Pilot Officer Lewis Burpee was re-posted to 617 Squadron on 5 April and Pilot Officer Warner Ottley a day later. By 8

April, the first Type 464 Provisioning Lancaster was delivered to the Royal Aircraft Establishment at Farnborough. Two others followed soon after, one delivered to Manston and the other to Boscombe Down. However, none had yet been delivered to 617 Squadron. The initial plan had been to deliver all the converted planes to Farnborough for acceptance testing, but shortage of time would become a factor and the remainder of the planes would be send straight to Scampton.

This modified version of the Lancaster had had the bomb doors removed. In their place two 'V'-shaped callipers had been affixed to the underside of the fuselage between which the weapon would be fitted. Bearings would hold this in place. Between these callipers the device could be spun backwards – crucial to the method of delivery which required it to skim across the surface of the water. The bomb would be spun at a speed of 500 rpm for 10 minutes prior to the attack. Given the massive size of the bomb, this would place a great strain on the superstructure of the Lancaster and caused some sceptics, such as Harris, to think that the plane would be very unstable as a result.

Whilst men were still arriving to join 617 Squadron, some were already leaving. Included amongst them on 9 April was the crew of Flight Sergeant Lovell. It was noted that 'the crew did not come up to the standards necessary for this squadron'[19] though the fact that Lovell had spent his entire time with 617 Squadron in the sick bay cannot have helped.[20] There was no room for sentiment or perceived weak links in the unit and the bar was set very high. Lovell and his men were replaced by Flight Sergeant Divall and his crew.

Later in the month, Gibson wished to remove the navigator of Flight Sergeant Lancaster's crew.[21] Their bombing results had been good but their navigation was suspect. Lancaster was given the option of replacing the navigator or the whole crew would have to leave. Lancaster chose the latter option. This was an insight into how important team morale was for a crew. An otherwise successful unit was withdrawn because of one perceived weaker link.

With only just over a month to go, the weapon to be used had not yet been definitively proven. On 13 April further tests on the weapon took place, this time at Reculver Bay in Kent. Reculver was a perfect spot for the testing: there were no private houses overlooking the sea so the required levels of secrecy could be maintained.

A Wellington and a Lancaster dropped three inert Upkeeps with Gibson and Hay in attendance as very interested observers. With all three bombs, the wooden casing shattered on impact though the missile did bounce for a considerable distance. The dangers of low flying were emphasised when on the third drop by Squadron Leader M. V. Longbottom, who was flying a Lancaster, one piece of debris shot up and seriously damaged the plane, making for an awkward landing at Manston.[22]

With so little time left, this was hardly a reassuring day. The dangers of low-level flying had been graphically reinforced and there was still no certainty that a viable weapon would be ready in time. Wallis must indeed have had incredible reserves of confidence if he still stayed resilient in the midst of all these negative signals.

In fact, 13 April could have been an absolute disaster for the mission, and other events proved that even apparently mundane flying could be dangerous. After watching the disappointing trials in Kent, Gibson and Hay borrowed a single-engined Magister aircraft for the return trip. A few minutes into their journey the engine on their plane cut out and they were forced to look for a place to make an emergency landing. However, as they were flying over Kent the fields were full of obstacles to prevent enemy landings. After managing to identify a small spot of land which appeared suitable, Gibson was able to make an emergency landing. It would have been tragically ironic if Gibson and one of his key crew members had been lost in a routine flight before the main event took place.

The ongoing position of 617 Squadron continued to be defined by Bomber Command HQ even as training continued. On 17 April, a 'Secret' memo from Bomber Command noted that, once the special operation in which the squadron was involved was completed, it would not return to normal operational duties but would remain a 'Special Duty Squadron' under the control of 5 Group. It was expected that the squadron would not be required to take part in sustained operations but would take part in raids that required special training or the use of specialised equipment.[23]

In a surreal aside, the memo noted that 'as the work is not expected to be arduous full use should be made of crews who have completed two operational tours and who apply to take part in further operations'. If the dam raids were typical of what the squadron would be involved in, then one wonders exactly which dictionary definition of 'arduous' Bomber Command HQ was using.

There were further tests on 18 April, the results of which were also far from encouraging. Mutt Summers was doing the flying this time. Two spheres sank and the third shattered. The mood of many around this time, according to the minutes of a meeting held on or around 15 April, was already 'pessimistic'[24] and this latest setback cannot have enhanced Wallis's credibility. He was forced to concede defeat and admitted that the wooden casing around the weapon would have to be abandoned.

However, the cylinder which was surrounded by the casing appeared to be capable of bouncing on its own, so it was hoped – correctly as it transpired – that the weapon would work without it (this had the fortuitous side-effect that the weight of the bomb load would be reduced by 2,500 lb as a result). The casing was now soon removed from all the other weapons which Wallis, under huge pressure, was developing alongside his many other everyday tasks. There were now just four weeks to go before the mission and major design changes were still being made to the weapon.

Low flying also continued to pose dangers. On 24 April, Maudslay's aircraft suffered a tail collapse. Elsewhere, tests were also continuing at Chesil Beach; after one of these Captain H. A. Brown, Avro's Chief Test Pilot, returned to Boscombe Down with pebbles the size of a fist embedded in the fuselage.[25] In the midst of all these near-misses, it seemed a miracle that no one had yet been killed.

For the aircrews, the challenges were about to get even greater. The continuing shattering of weapons on impact forced Wallis to reconsider the height from which they should be dropped. On 24 April, Wallis met Gibson and Longbottom at Burhill and told them that the crews would have to drop the weapon from 60 feet whilst they were flying at 232 mph. This obviously increased the risk to the pilots even more, though the very next day there was the first recorded drop of weapons from this altitude by Astell.

On 26 April the crews were briefed to drop the weapon at 60 feet at an air speed of 220 mph. They should be dropped 450 yards from the target so that they did not hit the dam walls with so much velocity that they shattered on impact: to create maximum damage it was confirmed they needed to roll down the walls until they were 30 feet below the waterline whereupon the hydrostatic pistols would trigger the huge explosion and subsequent shockwave required. All this would require split-second timing and precision in the dropping of the bombs.

The modified Lancasters had now started to be delivered to Scampton and, on 27 April, Mick Martin was the first to try one out – by the 29th twelve of them had been delivered. Some of the Air Transport Auxiliary crew who delivered the modified aircraft were amazed at the sight of these monsters with their gaping underbelly where the bomb doors had been removed. Some mechanics on the ground remarked that it looked as if the planes had had 'abortions', a name that stuck. There were other names too; observing the weapon bulging out from underneath the aircraft, some wag described a fully laden 464 Provisioning Lancaster as being like a 'pregnant duck'.

There were some problems with the new planes when they arrived, though they did not prove insurmountable. Cochrane's weekly update on training for the period 23 to 29 April noted that the situation as regards the aircraft received was 'complicated'. He went to say that although the aircraft were serviceable when received 'there are a lot of local modifications to be carried out, as a result of which these aircraft have not been flown to any great extent'.[26]

Adaptations were quickly made to improve the effectiveness of the planes – nothing clever or sophisticated but simple modifications borne out of accumulated experience from flying on dozens of missions. For example, the pilots pencilled a red mark on the flight controls so that they could be sure that they were at the right speed to release the bomb. At these low levels, there was also a huge responsibility on the navigator to ensure that the plane was at the right level as he was the only person capable of looking out of the plane and seeing when the two spotlights were touching each other, as would be the case when the correct altitude had been reached.

Most of the crew still had not seen one of the weapons though. Now that the spherical casing had been dropped, the Upkeep weapon was a cylinder described as looking like the front end of a steamroller or alternatively as similar to a huge oil drum some 50 inches in diameter and made of steel three eighths of an inch in thickness. Of its weight of 9,250 lb, 6,600 lb was made up of high explosive.

In addition to the three hydrostatic pistols that had been installed, there was a delayed-action fuse which would self-destruct the device 90 seconds after it left the aircraft if it had not already exploded, with the aim of preventing it being captured intact by the enemy. This was a perfectly sensible suggestion but it relied on the fuse being set when it left the plane. In practice, it proved to be a superfluous precaution because a complete weapon would be in German hands even before the last plane returned to base after the raids, though on a number of other occasions the bomb would indeed self-destruct after a plane crashed.

On 28 April crucial tests were carried out at Reculver with the modified devices, this time with the spherical casing completely abandoned. This was a breakthrough day. These tests confirmed that the bare steel cylinder could bounce along the surface in a straight line for up to 670 yards, though there was some veering of the device to the left towards the end of its run. Gibson was there to witness these efforts.[27] Another hurdle, one of the most important, had now been cleared. The technology behind the weapon had now been proven.[28]

Momentum was now gathering. The weapon appeared to be viable and the crews were training hard and coping with the great challenges that they faced. The modified planes were starting to arrive and the pilots and crews were starting to get used to them. However, the risks were still great and as yet no final orders had been given to direct that the raids should take place. This would have to happen in the next month, otherwise there was a very real prospect that the raids would not take place at all.

A successful raid could have benefits far outweighing just the material damage suffered. There was a strong political imperative for the attacks as far as Bomber Command was concerned. Harris in particular had many critics both at home and abroad. He perhaps took it as a compliment that one of them was Josef Goebbels.

Less exulted Germans also spoke disparagingly of Harris, for example newspapers like the *Westdeutscher Beobachter*, which said of him,

> how eagerly he launches his bombs against German women and children to an accompaniment of most unmilitary speeches and articles in which he expresses his grim satisfaction in the doing of it. He is the right man to fight against those who have no defence ... they have small and miserable minds who plan and carry out such undertakings ... Harris may be a savage, he may be the best man for his job, but in him one sees the means to which England, so old and once so proud, is reduced in this fight for existence.[29]

It was no coincidence that this particular quote was made within a week of the dam raids.

Less easy to stomach was the criticism of some of his own side, particularly the acerbic Labour MP Richard Stokes, a critic to the end who would be especially vitriolic in the aftermath of the controversial raids on Dresden in 1945. In 1941, Stokes had asked in Parliament whether there should be an agreement with the German government for the cessation of night-raiding and the bombing of cities. When the answer from Clement Attlee (then the Lord Privy Seal and Deputy Prime Minister in the coalition with Churchill) came in the negative, Stokes quoted a military critic who called the policy 'contagious lunacy'.[30]

It was not just the war against Germany to be won; Harris also had to win a war for the hearts and minds of the British people and their allies, who needed to be convinced that the price being paid by Bomber Command was worth it. The cost had been heavy and the losses hard to bear and, in war, everything depended on ensuring that the enemy's losses were proportionately greater. Looked at logically this may indeed have been 'contagious lunacy' but such is the impact that the inverted morality of warfare can have on otherwise rational minds.

All this 'big picture' thinking would have not found a sympathetic audience amongst many members of 617 Squadron. Amongst the men at Scampton, tension was building as the clock ticked down. There were less than four weeks left to get everything ready, but at least now they were in for a real shot at pulling it off. Training was advanced, planes had been delivered, a workable weapon had now been developed and tested. The design phase was almost over. It would soon be time for delivery.

4

Operation Chastise Approved
1 – 15 May 1943

Despite encouraging developments, there was still no certainty that the raids would be finally sanctioned or that they would be practically deliverable. The accurate dropping of the bombs would require first-rate flying skills and would, even with top-notch pilots, be very dangerous. Wallis was aware that he was asking a lot of the pilots and crews to fly at such low altitudes but was pleased to hear on 1 May from Gibson who, over the telephone, said that he was confident that the aircrews could fly at the altitude required for a successful bombing. This was another key breakthrough as, if the bombs could not be dropped from as low as 60 feet, they could at worse break up on impact or, if this did not happen, fail to bounce as needed for the subsequent explosion to break the dams.

Secrecy was essential and it was therefore a shock when on 2 May Gibson discovered that Pilot Officer Watson, 617 Squadron's Armaments Officer, had been shown a file containing possible objectives, including a map of the Ruhr showing the potential targets of the raids (a Coastal Command junior officer had also been privy to this information). This followed on from suggestions passed on to Gibson from Fay Gillon, after returning from a meeting in London, that details of the operation were common knowledge at the Air Ministry. Gibson passed on a largely handwritten note on the subject in which he professed himself 'astonished' at what Watson knew[1] and sent it on to Cochrane, who was furious at the implications for security and despatched a withering note to Bomber Command.

Cochrane was particularly annoyed at the actions of Wing Commander Garner of MAEE (the Marine Aircraft Experimental Establishment), who had shown copies of this 'most secret' file to the junior officers involved. Cochrane did not pull any punches, stating that 'this information is of a most secret nature and it is criminal that he should have discussed it with Junior Officers'. In his view, the file should be taken away from Garner at once.[2]

During May, Gibson would be more involved in training than in April with frequent but typically short exercises being flown by him. This was much needed. By 29 April Gibson and his crew had only 19½ hours of daytime and 4¼ hours of night-time training under their belts. This was significantly less than anyone else (especially for the night-time element). By way of contrast, the highest totals had been clocked up by Byers for daytime training (50¼ hours) and by Townsend for night-time (16¼ hours). Everyone else except Burpee (9½ hours) had over 10 hours night-time training under their belt by the end of April.[3]

There were clear signs that the strain was beginning to tell on Gibson. He developed a troublesome carbuncle on his face. This was painful and would be so at a particularly crucial part of the raids as he would have to clip his oxygen mask on when the final attacks were under way as it contained his microphone through which he needed to coordinate the assault. A consultation with the Senior Medical Adviser at Scampton, Dr Weddle, led to the latter suggesting that the best cure for Gibson was rest. Given the intensity of what lay ahead (of which of course the uninformed doctor knew nothing) this caused Gibson some inner mirth.

There was ongoing danger arising from the dangerous training missions which continued apace. Some of the crews had lucky escapes, such as when Dave Shannon struck a pole whilst taxiing on 3 May. Close shaves continued but the crews were making real progress in preparing for the raids. Nearly all of them though still had no idea of the weapons they would be using and none of them apart from Gibson knew the details of the raids that they would be taking part in.

However, some high-powered visitors were making their way to Scampton and aircrew members with more developed political antennae must have started to realise that something out of the ordinary was afoot. On 5 May, Lord Trenchard, the founding father of the RAF, visited the base. His predictions about the role of air power way back in 1919 had certainly come to pass. The day after, Air Marshall Sir Arthur Harris visited the station and addressed the aircrew. Visits from such high-powered members of the RAF hierarchy (Harris in particular did not visit airbases very often) suggested that an exceptional mission could not be far off.

Harris's visit at least showed some public support for the plans that were being developed. In some ways, this was surprising as the raids did not fit in with the preferred tactics of Harris as far as his overall approach to the bombing campaign was concerned. The raids would not be the first to launch a pinpoint attack on a specific target. Such raids had been tried before, for example an attack on the MAN diesel engine factory at Augsburg on 17 April 1942 which had ended in a costly failure with seven out of the twelve participating planes lost. Harris derogatorily called such missions 'panacea' raids, suggesting that they were meant as a cure for the heavy losses of war by knocking the enemy out of the conflict with targeted heavy attacks against specific targets. It went very much against the precepts of his area bombing strategy. Nevertheless, he swallowed his pride and put on a very public display of support for the new squadron whatever his inner misgivings.

As the time for the raids grew potentially ever closer – subject to final clearance for them to take place at all – the training became more specific. On 6–7 May a full exercise was undertaken over the Eyebrook, Abberton and Howden reservoirs as well as the Derwent dam, Wainfleet ranges and the Wash. These were planned to simulate the raid conditions as closely as possible.

At the same time as these raids took place, the British Prime Minister, Winston Churchill, boarded the pride of the British ocean-liner fleet, the *Queen Mary*, as she set sail for the USA. Here there was to be a major conference, codenamed Trident, which he was to attend to discuss the conduct of the war with President Roosevelt. It meant that he was out of the country just as the major decisions on the raids needed to be made. But although this would handicap the speed of decision-making, it would also, when the time came, allow Churchill to score a major propaganda coup once the raids had been successful.

Full details of the proposed raids had been given to the RAF delegation in Washington during April in a 'Most Secret Telegram'. This gave a detailed description of what the new weapon was like:

We have been developing a spherical bomb which will be dropped from low-flying aircraft and act in the nature of a surface torpedo. The bomb is suspended in the bomb-bay and given a backward spin of about 500 revs per minute before dropping. The initial spin lengthens initial flight before impact on water, increases the angle of incidence of ricochet and serves to counter the action of the water drag and the tendency of the sphere to roll under water. Investigation so far shows that the spherical bomb will not be checked by booms carrying protective torpedo netting.[4]

Details of the bombs' structure followed. (The information covered both the Upkeep weapon that was to be used in the dam raids in what was to be known as Operation Chastise and the anti-ship weapon, known as Highball, that was to be used in what would be known as Operation Servant.) The message had ended with an admonition that the delegation should 'personally inform Generals Marshall and Arnold and Admiral King and impress on them at the same time the need for absolute secrecy'.

The engine used to spin the weapon was in fact a standard model used in submarines. This was something that gave Harris, who did not enjoy a comfortable relationship with the Navy, an inordinate amount of pleasure as he could claim that the equipment had been 'pinched' on behalf of the RAF.[5]

An important development as far as the planes were concerned was the installation of high-quality VHF radio equipment, which began on 7 May. This process continued on the 8th and was completed on all aircraft by the 9th.[6] Trials with other radio equipment had been hopeless. The standard equipment available to the squadron was the TR 1196 HF R/T set. This was very susceptible to bad interference, a problem that worsened at night. Messages often became indecipherable and were particularly bad over longer distances. Persisting with this equipment could have had a disastrous impact on the raid given the role Gibson would play in coordinating the actions of all the planes involved in the attacks on the Möhne and Eder dams.

The situation was exacerbated as the raids would be innovative in more ways than one. A new tactic was to be used, for which Gibson would take the role of what was known as the 'master bomber'. This meant that he would coordinate the raid after dropping his payload first of all and then choreograph other bombers in their attack on the

Möhne dam. This gave an overall sense of direction for the raid that had been previously lacking in others (up until now each bomber was essentially on its own once it took off) and this would be one of the more successful innovations used on the night. This role though could obviously not be performed without good communications so alternatives would have to be found to the standard equipment available.

A good deal of thought had been given to communications during the raids. When they eventually took place, radio silence was to be maintained as far as possible and wireless telegraphy (W/T) would be used to communicate with 5 Group HQ using Morse code. However, voice control would be needed in the vicinity of the dams, hence the need for the VHF equipment. Radio silence would only be broken in extreme circumstances before this; but once the planes were in situ and ready to attack, the equipment would be switched on and Gibson would talk the other crews through the attack after he had been the first man in.

The equipment finally chosen, TR 1143 VHF, was of a type normally used by fighter aircraft and this in itself was innovative in a bombing raid. Now Young and Maudslay were given the task of trialling the VHF equipment and found it a massive improvement on what had been available before. In the event, it was found that there was an effective communication range of nearly 50 miles, more than adequate for what was needed for the raid. Reserve equipment was also probably installed in some of the planes in case of malfunction. As a last resort, Very lights would be fired as a simple alternative form of signal – if one were fired it would mean 'wait your turn to attack as best you can, when target is breached proceed to next target'.[7] Flight Lieutenant Bone was called in from Bomber Command HQ to install the VHF equipment in all the planes.

SASO Satterly sent draft orders for the raids to Whitworth at Scampton on 10 May. These were discussed with Gibson but otherwise absolute secrecy was still maintained within the squadron. It was agreed that twenty planes would take part in the raids and the detailed plan of attack was mapped out, including how many planes would take part in each wave of the attack. All that remained was to assign specific pilots to each wave and of course to get the green light to go ahead.

On 11 May there was the first test involving the squadron using a real Upkeep weapon though the devices dropped were inert. It was the first time that most of the crews had seen the bomb. Many of them were flabbergasted when they saw the devices and could not believe that they could be successfully delivered.[8] These first tests were led by Gibson at Reculver, with two screens erected on the shore to simulate the twin towers of the Möhne dam. The following day Shannon, Knight and Munro led their crews on the same exercise.

For some of the pilots, the flight to Kent took them very close to home. One of them, Flight Lieutenant David Maltby, had a coded message for his wife; every time that he flew over his home in Kent he would waggle his wings to let her know that it was him. A photograph by his wife Nina, probably taken on 12 May, still exists in the Spitfire Memorial Museum at Manston and shows his plane flying overhead.[9]

Thoughts of home and loved ones would play heavily on everybody involved in the raids as the time to set out on their dangerous and potentially life-threatening mission drew inexorably near. The training was finely honing the skills of the crews as the moment for using them for real was close at hand. Not only were pilots able to fly their planes at 60 feet, but the average margin of error for a bomb drop was now down to 117 feet.[10]

However exciting it must have been to realise that the moment that they had all been training for was drawing near – though most of them still had no idea when they would be flying or even the general direction of where they would be headed – there were about to be several demonstrations of the dangers involved in dropping such a large weapon at such a low altitude.

On 13 May, Maudslay dropped his bomb in practice; he was possibly too low but in any event the splash as it hit the water damaged his aircraft so badly that it could not be used in the raid. This left only nineteen planes available for the twenty crews that were supposed to be going on the mission. In reality, dropping the weapon at 60 feet was incredibly dangerous; when the bombs were dropped for real, there would be repeated accounts of a plume of water 1,000 feet high shooting up into the sky. The effect of this on an aircraft (even one as robust as a Lancaster) should it be hit by the large plume of water is not hard to imagine.

Maudslay's plane was not the only casualty in practice. Munro also dropped his weapon from a little below the correct height. The large plume of water that spouted up drenched the fuselage. The rear turret was damaged so badly that the rear gunner, Flight Sergeant Weeks, was jammed in his position and could only be released when the plane arrived safely back at base. This confirmed, amongst other things, just how dangerous it was to be in the rear turret, probably the most exposed position in the entire plane. The aircraft also vibrated very, very badly, which was hardly surprising when the aerodynamics of it were so badly compromised by the bomb bulging out from underneath, especially when it started to spin at 500 rpm. Despite the potentially serious nature of the damage, sterling work by the ground crews returned the plane to working order in time for the raids.

On 13 May, a live Upkeep was dropped from a height of 75 feet five miles off Broadstairs. It bounced seven times for more than 700 yards then sank and blew up as planned – a very reassuring outcome and strong evidence that the weapon was indeed viable. This weapon was dropped by the test pilot Longbottom; Gibson was nearby in a second Lancaster watching on. With only a fortnight to go before the optimum time for a raid in 1943 had passed, this was a very welcome demonstration of the bomb's effectiveness.

By now, fifty-six bombs had been delivered to Scampton, many more than the twenty theoretically required for the raid. They came in by road transport, covered by tarpaulins. When the pilots were given dummies to practise with, it was the vibration that was the greatest challenge as it made it difficult to hold the plane steady, which was a major problem when precision was of the essence. The dummies were filled with concrete to simulate the weight of an armed weapon.

Sergeant Ray Grayston, the Flight Engineer on Les Knight's plane, was amazed at the thought that the bomb, 'this bloody great lump of metal', could work at all. It had a significant impact on the slipstream, a problem that was exacerbated when the on-board spinning process was commenced. The instruments were virtually unreadable whilst the bomb was spinning.

Flight Sergeant Leonard Sumpter, in Dave Shannon's aircraft, recalled that in practice they lined the bombs up on the church towers of Reculver. He dropped the bomb about 40 yards short of where he should have done so that it didn't make the distance. Gibson called Sumpter in the next morning and gave him a telling off, suggesting that he was not paying attention. Another plane dropped its payload late and it bounced up onto the promenade, causing a couple of photographers to dive for cover. Most planes only had the chance of two practice runs before the raid itself and there was more than an element of hoping that everything would come together and that it would be 'alright on the night'.

There was understandable continued concern at the prospect of this massive weapon gyrating at a rate of 500 rpm. To guard against the possibility that this would destabilise the plane, each bomb had to be individually balanced between two discs, often requiring that the equipment be modified; a number of trips backwards and forwards to the machine shop were often necessary before the weapons were ready to be used on a mission. This was very much a process of trial and error where fractions could equate to the difference between success and failure.

The training at Reculver was also something of an audition for the raid itself. The top nine crews would be picked out to inform the choice of pilots for the main raid. One of the pilots who was not in the top crews selected tried to pressurise Gibson to change his plans but, even though the Wing Commander was a friend, he refused to bow to the pressure.[11]

It now appeared that the Upkeep was ready and that the crews and aircraft were ready too. However, there was still no guarantee that the raid would go ahead and there was now little more than a week's window before the moon had passed full and the dam levels started to subside. Time was now of the essence. It was not all good news: an update meeting on the other weapon, Highball, reported disappointing progress: the bombs were shattering on impact and this could have major consequences for the raids.

But it was approaching the time when it was now or never and the decision to go or not needed to come from the very highest level. The message requesting clearance for the raids was sent by the Air Ministry to Washington on 13 May; it made a strong case for making an immediate decision to launch the raids:

i. Subject to final confirmation by reconnaissance flown today, water levels believed satisfactory for attack this moon period. Chances of success will be seriously reduced by even slight falls below optimum level of 5 feet below spill. Heavy withdrawals possible in coming weeks and postponement to June would gravely prejudice success.

ii. 23 operational Lancasters 'frozen' for this special operation which will include the three objectives 'X', 'Y' and 'Z'. Further operations of this character considered impractical in view of enemy counter-measures. Postponement till June means loss of normal bombing effort from these aircraft for further month.

iii. Subject to one further test today, weapon now satisfactory and crews have reached peak of training and are keyed up for this very hazardous operations. Delay undesirable on these accounts.[12]

All these factors argued in favour of a prompt attack, though the first of them perhaps even more than the others. On 14 May the final decision to go ahead with the raids was made. The decision was ultimately taken in Washington, which was then being visited by the Joint Chiefs of Staff alongside Churchill. It was not a fait accompli: the Navy were arguing strongly that the use of Upkeep before Highball was ready would compromise the latter's effectiveness. The great virtue of the weapons was that they were a surprise. Using Upkeep before Highball was ready could forewarn the Germans of future danger from the latter and they could then easily take appropriate counter-measures. It was the RAF that won the argument and approval was given. The stage was now set for the raids to take place.

That same night a final, full dress rehearsal was held. However, Maltby did not take part; he was having his plane repaired at Woodford in Cheshire. A number of passengers were taken along, including Intelligence Officer Fay Gillon. Gibson, who was accompanied by 'Charles' Whitworth for the flight, felt that the dress rehearsal had been a total success.

Fay Gillon, who flew with Mick Martin that night, was much impressed by the dry run (though of course she did not know specifically what it was a dry run for). She sat in the flight engineer's seat and watched intently as they flew over the sea and then back over the land with the moon gently rising as the night passed. She looked on as planes swooped in for ground-attack training runs. She felt the plane drop to 60 feet and then soar up into the sky as the bomb was dropped. Then it was back to base, a safe landing and a taxi in to dispersal. The engines were turned off one by one and the crew disbanded. Then it was back to the mess for a pint, and eggs and bacon for supper. Unknowingly, 'Famous' Gillon (as she was known) had played a small part in history.[13]

The dress rehearsal lasted for four hours and was important for the obvious reason that it was the last chance to get everything right before they were flying 'for real'. Gibson had now decided on the order of attack. He and his men would lead the raid against the Möhne and Eder dams with eight other crews that he deemed to be the best: they would practise first of all against the Eyebrook reservoir to simulate the Möhne attack, then the Abberton reservoir as a surrogate for the Eder dam.

The second wave would be led by Joe McCarthy and would be targeting the Sorpe dam; they would practise against the Derwent dam. The remaining planes would form a mobile reserve to be used against dams as needed: to attack the Möhne dam if it had not been breached first of all, then the Eder. In the event, it was left somewhat flexible whether or not they would be used to attack the Sorpe dam. This reserve had its final rehearsal at the Wainfleet range.

Although final confirmation of the raids was still awaited, that a dangerous mission was now believed to be imminent was obvious when Flight Lieutenant Bill Astell wrote what would prove to be his last letter home on 14 May as he enclosed a copy of his will in it,[14] a sure sign that 'something big' was brewing. His will was witnessed by fellow pilots Henry Maudslay and Norm Barlow. It was a sad irony that none of them would survive the mission that lay before them.

And so Saturday 15 May dawned. It would take 24 hours for official orders to reach the UK from the other side of the Atlantic and for them be circulated. From now on a cumbersome and hectic process of disseminating orders for the raid was put in train. There was a chain of command for the orders to pass through, which would inevitably make this a drawn-out process – from the Assistant Chief of Air Staff (Operations) in London, Air Vice-Marshal Norman Bottomley, who had to tell Bomber Command at High Wycombe, and then to Cochrane and Satterly at 5 Group HQ in Grantham. The order was handwritten and Satterly put it in his safe so that it could be typed up later.

At 0900 on the 15th the order to proceed with Operation Chastise was received. Its simplicity could not disguise its importance:

Immediate attacks on targets 'X', 'Y', 'Z' approved. Execute at first suitable opportunity.[15]

'X', 'Y' and 'Z' were the Möhne, Eder and Sorpe dams respectively. A degree of flexibility was built into the timing of the raids so that the vagaries of the weather could be taken into account. But with the moon approaching full there was no doubt that, subject to any meteorological intervention, the raid was imminent.

Details of reconnaissance were forwarded from Bomber Command HQ to 5 Group HQ. The information obtained on a flight the day before had not been as comprehensive as desired. It was noted by Squadron Leader Fawssett, the Chief Intelligence Officer, that

> a sortie flown yesterday on 'X' did not show the dam, but it has been calculated that the water level of the lake has risen 8 feet since the last sortie on 19th Feb. 1943 and it is now 2 feet from the top of the dam. A further sortie is being flown today and if this indicates any change in level you will be telephoned.[16]

There was a final pre-raid reconnaissance flight over Germany that day flown by Flying Officer Gerry Fray in a specially adapted Spitfire from RAF Benson. Such missions had been going on over a number of months with a view to accumulating as much intelligence on targets as possible (though Fawssett's note that there had not been a sortie to the Möhne dam for three months is surprising). Great care was taken on these reconnaissance flights to follow circuitous routes to confuse the Germans and hide the object of the planes' interest; on this mission, for example, as well as flying over the Möhne, Fray also passed over Bochum, Duisburg, Oberhausen and Antwerp.[17] RAF command were particularly interested in whether or not the Germans appeared to be taking extra precautions as this would suggest that they had received intelligence that raids were imminent. The ability this would give them to take counter-measures could stop the raids dead in their tracks.

Orders to undertake reconnaissance flights had first gone out to 541 Squadron at RAF Benson in Oxfordshire on 25 January 1943 with instructions to obtain information on the Möhne dam. The first sortie to do so had taken place on 7 February and had been followed by eight others soon after. The weather had not been helpful at first and not until the seventh mission were any useful photographs brought back. Further reconnaissance was ordered on 5 April, this time over the Eder and Sorpe dams. The same pilots typically flew these missions so that they could get acquainted with the countryside and its landmarks. Now their photographs would be crucial in mapping out the finer details of the raids.

There was little flying from Scampton that Saturday, 15 May, with the only recorded flight made at 1405 by Byers.[18] It was almost as if, even though no official orders had been received as yet, the men knew that something was in the air and were steeling themselves for the challenge. Cochrane in the meantime made his way over to Scampton in a staff car so that he could verbally brief Whitworth and Gibson that the raid was probably now only one day away. At 1600, Cochrane left Scampton to return to 5 Group HQ at Grantham, an imposing building set amongst trees that was named St Vincents. Gibson went with him.

If there was little flying taking place for 617 Squadron that day, this was not the case for the test pilots who were still trying out the new weapon. On the 15th, a bomb was dropped off the coast at Broadstairs. Significantly this one was not spun before release, which was presumably to trial the effect on the weapon prior to it being dropped in such a fashion at the Sorpe dam, for which a different mode of attack would be required.

By 1800 that evening, Gibson was back at Scampton. Wallis had also arrived with Major Hew Kilner, Managing Director of Vickers, in a white Red Cross Wellington flown by Mutt Summers. They made their way to the house of Air Commodore Whitworth, the base commander. Here Wallis spent some time with Gibson and some of his senior men: Young, Maudslay, Hopgood and Hay. Hopgood was able to offer good advice about an uncharted anti-aircraft threat at Huls, where there was a large rubber factory that was well defended. As a result of this, they changed the route to avoid the danger.

There was much to be organised and not a lot of time to do it. There were a number of roles assigned to those on board: the pilot, the flight engineer, the navigator, the bomb-aimer, the wireless operator and both a front and rear gunner. A senior man from each function was assigned to be the leader of each particular group within the squadron; his role would be to brief all the other members of the group on what had been decided and also to raise any questions they might have at a higher level. There was a leader for the bomb-aimers, the navigators, the signallers and the gunners.

The Australian Bob Hay, for example, was the squadron's bombing leader.

The revisions to the Lancaster that were necessary for the raid necessitated a rethink of the duties normally undertaken by members of the crew. The bomb-aimer, for example, had to take on different tasks. He would normally man the front guns until approaching the target when he would take on the bomb-aiming responsibilities. However, as the Lancasters would be flying in at low level with anti-aircraft defences anticipated, suppressing fire would be needed from the front-gunner to keep the enemy occupied whilst the aimer looked after the crucial task of dropping the bomb in exactly the right spot.

So for this raid, the mid-turret gunner, who would normally be present in an unmodified Lancaster, would be moved to the front as his previous role was redundant because the mid-turret had been removed on the modified aircraft. This required another modification to the planes – something of a Heath Robinson approach by which stirrups were installed that the gunner could put his feet in to raise them up and stop him from bumping the bomb-aimer who was immediately below him when the latter was concentrating on ensuring that exactly the right spot for dropping the device had been reached.

The bomb-aimer also took on another crucial role. As the whole mission would be flown at low level, he was requisitioned as an extra pair of eyes to ensure that the aircraft was not flying too low. He was perfectly placed for this, being in the nose of the plane and being available to do it until the very last moments of the mission before the bomb was about to be dropped. There had in fact been a modification to the Lancasters to facilitate this: the Perspex bubble at the front had been enlarged to enhance visibility.[19]

But despite the efforts to maintain secrecy, the tension was palpable. Most of the men sensed that something was afoot and the officers' mess that night was a very 'dry' affair, with orangeade the most popular drink. The only evidence of serious drinking came from Gibson's pet black Labrador, Nigger, who was treated to his pint. Some of the officers were standing in groups by the fire; others were reading in the armchairs or sitting on chairs, tables or the stone-cold radiators. The mess was unusually full.[20]

However, later that evening Gibson received some terrible personal news. After the four-hour meeting at Whitworth's house ended, the base commander approached Gibson looking very uncomfortable. It transpired that Gibson's beloved pet had been run over and killed outside the base gates. Contrary to one myth that has grown up around the raids (fuelled by the 1950s movie), this was not a 'hit and run' accident in which the driver simply drove off without informing anyone of what had happened. Instead, he stopped and the lifeless dog was carried into the guardroom, where Nigger was formally identified by 'Chiefy' Powell.

The dog was an unofficial mascot for the squadron, who had freely plied him with generous amounts of beer. Everyone knew Nigger and a key code word, which was to be relayed if the Möhne dam were to be breached, was to be his name. The loss of Nigger could be a major blow to morale, an ominous portent to those of a superstitious bent – though not everybody liked the dog, who had a temperamental nature.

It was though the worst possible start to the build-up to the raid in many ways – a small, almost petty incident, in the scheme of things perhaps, but given the way that nerves were stretched on such an occasion the death of such a familiar character did not bode well, especially when elements of superstition inevitably crept in for men who were faced with the possibility of their own imminent demise. Gibson was clearly upset at these sad tidings, and his emotions would not have been helped when he argued with a flight sergeant who refused to make a coffin for Nigger.[21]

Nigger would be buried with much dignity while Gibson was flying over the dams of the Ruhr; at least this was the accepted version of the story. However, stories developed that the site which is now Nigger's grave at Scampton is not his burial place at all. Other tales, which may of course be merely 'urban myths', suggest that the grave of the dog, far from popular with everybody, was treated with something far removed from reverence.

Nevertheless, the news of the death of his beloved pet came as a shattering blow to Gibson, who returned very depressed to his room, where he contemplated the scratch marks on the door made by the reliable friend who was no more whilst his aircrews made their way off to sleep, some armed with sleeping pills to ensure a good night's sleep when nerves were taut. The objective of the raids was still a closely guarded secret, although Hopgood, Young and Maudslay were now in on it; but no one else who would be involved in the flying next day was yet aware of where they were headed.

As the men prepared to turn in for the night, some of them for the very last time in their lives, it seems that most of them sensed that tomorrow would be something special. Not that this would change the normal pattern of fraternisation at Scampton. There was little mixing between the two messes on the base, one of them for officers and the other for NCOs, and many of the crews did not mix with each other either. There was camaraderie but it tended to be within crews rather than across them.

This situation was corroborated by several sources. Navigator Harold Hobday, in Les Knight's crew, confirmed the segregation between messes and the lack of mixing outside of hours even though the crews were close in their working time. Bomb-aimer Leonard Sumpter recalled that the crews rarely mixed with each other; the intensity of the training meant that one tended to mix with one's own crew most of the time.

In many ways that was appropriate. Very soon, the men would have no one to rely on but themselves and their crewmates, a close-knit group in which the actions of each individual cog in the wheel would be crucial. As they made their way back to their sleeping quarters, they did not yet know anything for certain. They did not know that they were about to make history, that tomorrow they would be using weapons never used before in anger against targets that none of them suspected except for those few who were in on the secret. It was perhaps as well, for if any knew of the adrenaline rush and the sheer, blind terror that would face them on the morrow, then sleep, in all probability, would have remained a stranger.

5

Last Minute Preparations at Scampton
Sunday 16 May 1943, up to 21.00 hours

With confirmation from Washington now in, the scene was set for the historic raids to take place. An important piece of last-minute information to arrive was reconnaissance from the dams that would be the targets. This confirmed that the water in the reservoirs was within a few feet of the top and only the Möhne appeared to be lightly defended. This was reassuring from several perspectives, as it suggested that there had been no leaks of information that had alerted the Germans to the imminent attack, and that the attackers would only have token resistance to deal with – and at only one dam. However, in the event, the resistance would be far fiercer at the Möhne dam than suspected and the very terrain over which the planes would have to approach the target would act as a defence mechanism for the dams.

For one man in particular, Flight Engineer John Pulford, who was flying with Gibson, this was a particularly poignant time. His father had just died and he had been given compassionate leave to attend the funeral. Just in case, he was accompanied by military policemen who were there to ensure that he did not let any sensitive information slip (Gibson did not like Pulford particularly and thought him 'dull' and this may have added to his sensitivity about the issue). What was already a traumatic personal experience was made considerably worse by the close watch that he was kept under, but no chances could be taken.

The orders for the raid, still classified 'top secret' to all but a privileged few, were to be found in No. 5 Group Operation Order No. B.976.[1] They noted that 'destruction of Target X [the Möhne dam] alone would bring about a serious shortage of water for drinking purposes and industrial supplies'. Target Z, the Sorpe dam, was to be the next priority – that being the case, it is not clear why the Eder was a secondary target for Gibson's flight rather than this. It was said that the destruction of Target Y, the Eder dam, would 'seriously hamper transport in the Mittelland canal and in the Weser, and would probably lead to almost complete cessation of the great volume of traffic now using these waterways'. However, that would prove to be a much smaller result than would be the case if the Sorpe were successfully attacked.

Due to the fact that the dams would be at their maximum capacity at this time, which would result in the greatest potential for damage should their walls be breached, the raids should be launched on the first suitable date after 15 May 1943. This turned out to be Sunday 16 May. Twenty Lancasters should take part. (Although in the event, due to illness amongst some of the crews, only nineteen would actually fly. These illnesses were actually somewhat fortuitous as there were only nineteen suitably adapted bombers fit to fly on the raid.)

It was deemed likely that three effective attacks might be needed to breach the Möhne dam but in any event the attacks should continue until this had been done. The wave of aircraft attacking this dam should then, once this objective had been achieved, move on to the Eder dam. If this too should be breached by the aircraft designated as part of this first wave, then they should move on to the Sorpe dam.

The second wave, which was to cross the coast of the Continent at the same time as the first (but further north), was to attack the Sorpe whilst the third wave, which was to follow the same route as the first (but would leave later), was to effectively be an airborne reserve that could be recalled should all objectives have been achieved by the first two waves.

There would be a two-and-a-half-hour gap between the first wave and the third. In the event, the uses to which the reserve was put was one of the least successful elements of the mission as it was deployed so piecemeal that it could not make a real impact and was inadequately briefed on some of the targets it was given. It also suffered significant losses from enemy defences that were much more aware of what was going on over Germany by the time that their wave set out.

The aircraft were not to fly above 1,500 feet when they were in English airspace. On crossing the English coastline they were to descend to a height of 60 feet throughout the rest of their journey to their targets and for most of their trip back again. On reaching a point 10 miles away from the targets, the leader of each wave was to ascend to a height of 1,000 feet. At this point, VHF radio contact should be made by each pilot with the leader. For the first wave the bomb, described as 'the special store', should be set to spin from 10 minutes before the time that any attack was launched. However, for the attack on the Sorpe dam the bomb was not to be spun at all as it was not required to skim across the surface but would be dropped at right angles to the target.

The leader of the first wave, who was of course to be Gibson, was to launch the first attack on the Möhne dam and then direct all others there and then on to the Eder once he was satisfied that the raid on the first target had been a success. Even if the Möhne dam were damaged, Gibson could carry on attacking it to widen the breach made provided that there were at least three aircraft left to proceed to the Eder dam (again, something of an anomaly given its relative unimportance).

For all attacks there should be a gap of at least 3 minutes between each bomb drop – this would give time for both any damage to be assessed and also for any turbulence in the water to die down to make the path of the next bomb unleashed truer. The pilot of each plane was to be responsible for the line of attack, the navigator for its height, the bomb-aimer for the range and the flight engineer for the speed. On Targets X and Y a Very pistol was to be fired from the aircraft when they were immediately over the target dam. For Target Z the Very pistol cartridge was to be fired as each bomb was dropped. All watches should be synchronised to BBC time before take-off.[2]

A change was also to be made to the guns to be used in the planes. Normally there would be tracer included at a rate of every two or three bullets but now all of them were to be Mk VI night tracer rounds. The thinking behind this was that it would 'look more fearsome to the Germans'[3] and anything that could be done to put off the flak gunners at the Möhne was to be welcomed. The white light might also confuse the Germans into thinking that cannon shells were being fired.

The day began early for Gibson who had spent an uncomfortable night. As well as the anxiety he felt about the now imminent mission and the distress at the tragic loss of Nigger, Gibson's feet were also playing up. He was up and about at 0530 and made his way to the surgery. Dr Upton, who treated him, was unable to do much for him as he was made aware that Gibson would be flying later that day, which meant that pain-killers were out of the question. Gibson would just have to grin and bear it.

During the course of Sunday 16 May, it would become increasingly obvious around the base that a major raid was likely to be launched within hours. At just after 0900 Gibson hinted to Humphries in his office that there was to be a major action that day. However, Humphries was not to let anyone else know even this until further orders were given. Gibson told him that he would apprise him of details of mealtimes and a night-flying programme later that day, then disappeared carrying a bulky red file marked 'Most Secret'. The game was most definitely afoot.

Even now attention was being devoted to how the news of the raids should be regulated so that ultimate secrecy could be maintained not only before the mission but also after it. Press access to Group staff or aircrew was to be strictly regulated. All press communiqués were to be 'strictly controlled and supervised' by the Air Ministry. Only very limited information was to be released which would tell very little to anybody; tying in with a plan developed at a meeting at King Charles Street on 25 March 1943, it was to be emphasised in any communiqué issued after the raids that 'in the event, the crews displayed the greatest skill in executing the operation as planned'.[4]

Later on, Humphries received from Gibson firm details of the times that the night-flying programme for the day was to begin and end. There was much for Humphries now to prepare. Buses needed to be organised to take the aircrews out to their planes and meals needed to be synchronised with the flight times. Flying rations needed to be made available, including coffee and refreshments that the crews could carry with them. It was also Humphries's job to accept cash, wills and letters for next of kin from anyone who was due to fly.

Humphries's major problem was a surprisingly mundane one. He asked the WAAF sergeant in charge of the mess kitchen for a special meal but she stubbornly refused to comply, saying that she had no specific orders to do so. Humphries was left with virtually no option but to tell her that this was not a normal training flight today but that the men were going into action. Informed of this, her attitude changed at once and she confirmed that the meals requested would indeed be prepared.

Despite the building sense of excitement, even now secrecy was rigorously maintained by those in the know. It was perhaps a surprise that the element of secrecy was so well maintained during the build-up to the raids. Scampton was shared with another unit, 57 Squadron, but there was barely a hint of anything unusual afoot coming from 617 Squadron at any point.[5] The members of the newly formed unit had performed their part in maintaining secrecy very well indeed. The greater concerns, as has been seen, came from sources outside the squadron.

The ground crews would also be frantically busy with last-minute preparations to attend to. This was the period at which they really came into their own. One oversight on their part could have disastrous consequences. One of their main tasks was to test the compasses with and without the weapon in place as the huge mass of metal had a major effect on their accuracy. Deviations were then noted and placed in the plane for future reference. Without this information a pilot could be miles off course and completely lost – this would be a problem especially for Joe McCarthy later that day.

Then of course the bombs needed to be fitted and balanced; no easy task with a weight of nearly 10,000 lb involved. The planes would also carry six 4-lb 'stick' incendiary devices and these would also prove to be of use to some of the crews during the raid. In addition, the planes needed to be fuelled up: 1,740 gallons each for the long journey to their targets and back (though the distance involved was well within the Lancasters' range of 850 miles). This was a moment of intensive activity, with so much to be done and a strict deadline within which to complete their tasks. There would be no rest until the planes were safely up and away and even then only a few hours of snatched sleep would be possible before the planes returned again.

It could also be a dangerous period. There was a moment of panic whilst the bombs were being loaded. The one being fitted to Martin's plane dropped out onto the tarmac. Bomb-aimer Bob Hay yelled that it might have fused itself and could explode within a minute. Everyone frantically exited the Lancaster as quickly as they could. Martin rushed off to pick up the Armaments Officer, 'Doc' Watson, who, with breathtaking calmness, inspected the weapon and told everybody not to panic as the bomb had not fused after all.

This was no idle panic though as memories of a recent serious incident at Scampton were still fresh. On 15 March 1943, a bomb was accidentally released from a 57 Squadron Lancaster. The weapon subsequently detonated and destroyed this plane and four visiting 50 Squadron aircraft parked nearby. This would have a catastrophic impact on the raid should any similar incident occur given the fact that all the planes had been specially modified. With no spares at hand, the raids might not have happened at all.

The secret of the raids would gradually and selectively be disclosed during the course of the day. It was late morning when the first briefings were held; there would be several over the course of the day. There would be a progressive rolling out of information as the day went on. At midday, the SASO, Group Captain Satterly, passed on the orders to Wing Commander Dunn, 5 Group's Chief Signals Officer, so that signals could be put in place for the raid. Satterly was responsible for the detailed plans for the raid but is often overlooked in histories of the raid. The plan would not be perfect but it would achieve a number of its objectives, so some credit should go to Satterly for that.

At these first briefings, Gibson and Wallis briefed the pilots and navigators whilst Wing Commander Dunn, 5 Group's Chief Signals Officer, briefed the wireless operators. The plans of attack were explained. Gibson would be in first from the first wave of nine planes to the Möhne and, if that was successfully breached, then on to the Eder. New Yorker Joe McCarthy would lead a wave of five planes to the Sorpe. Flight Sergeant Townsend would be in charge of six planes as a flexible reserve (there would only be five in the event due to illness and a lack of planes). After lunch at 1400, the bomb-aimers and gunners joined the navigators and pilots. More and more people were now starting to learn of the raids and their targets, though there were still stringent measures being taken to ensure that the news did not leak outside the base.

Initial briefings on radio control and the route to be taken – some 400 miles of it – were held. Those who had this briefing were still sworn to secrecy as far as the other crew members were concerned.[6] At these initial meetings, contour scale models of the Möhne and Sorpe dams were unveiled. There was though no model of the Eder to study; it would not arrive until after the raids were all over. Bomb-aimer Leonard Sumpter later remarked that 'the first time I saw the Eder was when I got there'.[7]

It was a boiling hot day, unusually so for the time of year, and there was frantic activity with ground crews buzzing around now getting everything ready for the mission. Slow-moving tractors trundled around the airfield laden with bombs to be loaded onto the planes. Summers and Wallis walked around the planes ensuring as far as they were able that everything was right. The crews spent three hours of the afternoon studying maps of where they were headed. The last-minute briefings had helped to preserve the element of surprise.

But the downside of this was that the crews had little time to become familiar with the route and the targets. In retrospect this would create significant problems. A number of crews flew off course and some of them would pay the ultimate price for this error. Others would find it difficult to locate the right targets; for the reserve wave in particular, effectiveness would be significantly compromised by the lack of clear instructions for where they should head. This would compromise the achievement of some of the raid's objectives.

There were also some last-minute problems to be dealt with. Wallis noticed that the wrong oil was being used for some of the equipment and alternative supplies had to be found with some difficulty. There was also a shortage of spare planes. With one plane out of commission there were no spares and it was important to rectify this just in case of a last-minute hitch. In addition to the 464 Lancasters delivered to Scampton, three other planes had been developed and delivered elsewhere for use in ongoing testing.

One of them was at Boscombe Down in Wiltshire. Commander H. C. Bergel was delegated to fly it up to Scampton as a reserve (this would turn out to be a particularly useful move as it happened). He arrived, accompanied by Third Officer Salter of the Air Transport Auxiliary, with what would be designated plane AJ-T at 1530. There was no time to mount the TR1143 radio or the spotlights to the aircraft. This could have been disastrous if the plane needed to be used in an attack on the dams at the Möhne or Eder, though as it happened this would not be the case, which was just as well. Another plane was also flown in but this was so last-minute that it arrived too late to be of any use. After the raids, it would be given the code AJ-C, replacing a plane piloted by Pilot Officer Warner Ottley which would no longer exist by the time that the raids were over.

These last-minute arrivals were something of an oversight in the plan. It would have been much more sensible to deliver them before this late hour, especially as two planes had been damaged in the recent training flights. The design of the aircraft also came as a surprise to those pilots who were required to fly them up to Scampton (who were not their test pilots). When flying his plane, Bergel wondered why the bomb-bay was so different and had no idea what some of the equipment on the instrument panel referred to. He was even more surprised when he arrived at Scampton to see other aircraft in the same condition, one with a slowly rotating object in its belly.

Bergel's curiosity was roused but he was warned off before he could ask too many questions – the suggestion that those involved with the project had been confined to base for the last eleven weeks did the trick as it implied that the same thing might happen to him if he became too inquisitive.[8] Bergel boarded a waiting Anson and flew back to his home base, unaware at the time of the small part he was playing in creating history.[9]

At 1610 a 'secret cypher message' was sent from 5 Group HQ to the Officer Commanding at Scampton (Whitworth). Its message was simplicity itself but gave the green light for one of the most amazing air raids ever launched. It simply said, 'Executive operation Chastise 16/5/43 zero hours'. The raids were on.

All crews of 617 Squadron were directed to assemble for a report in the briefing room at 1800. Over 130 young men crowded in, waiting to hear the final details of what they had been training for so hard for the past couple of months. Wallis would play a key role in the discussions, explaining key facts and figures about the dams and how difficult they would be to crack.

This was a general briefing for all crew members. There were 132 of these in the room along with Gibson, senior officers and Wallis sitting on a dais at the front of the room. There was also a civilian, Herbert Jeffree, who was a scientist who worked with Wallis and, in a potentially serious breach of security, had bluffed his way into the room; despite the tight controls over the operation, there was a gatecrasher at the briefing. The room was packed with the luminaries lined up at the front of the briefing room where there was a large map of Germany on the wall, covered over for the time being with a black curtain. It was time to begin the briefing.

Gibson opened proceedings and told the crews that the target was to be the great dams of Germany. He then introduced Wallis, who relayed more about the problems he had had with developing the weapons and put on a brave face but privately he was worried. Reality was starting to hit home as he earlier told Gibson, 'You know, I hardly look upon this as an operational mission. My job has just been to develop something which will break down a dam wall. I look upon this raid as my last great experiment to see if it can be done on the actual thing.' He also said to Gibson, 'I hope they all come back.' The scientist was starting to understand the potential human cost involved.

However, Wallis was still a scientist at heart. He concluded his remarks to his assembled audience with the following comments: 'You gentlemen are really carrying out the third of three experiments. We have tried it out on model dams, also a dam one-fifth of the size of the Möhne dam. I cannot guarantee it will come off but I hope it will.' When he sat down, he muttered that 'they must have thought it was Father Christmas talking to them'.[10] Wallis's reactions after he heard of the heavy losses later suffered in the raids give all the evidence of a man completely in shock at their scale. Judging by his comments before the mission, the high number of casualties was something that he was not expecting except for the odd pessimistic moment when the true dangers of the raids broke in.

Wallis in his briefing advised that the planes should fly at a speed of 220 mph and at a height of 60 feet. The bomb should be dropped 410 yards from the dam wall and should then bounce three times before hitting it, rolling down to a depth of 30 feet and then exploding. Reconnaissance had been taking place for two months to monitor the rising of the water levels and the weather forecast was good for that evening. It was the right time to go.

Wallis was very enthusiastic in his presentation and drew models on the blackboard rather than using slides. He came across as a kindly man, very clever and something of a father figure. He also inspired confidence despite the novel nature of the mission.[11] But Sergeant Jim Clay, a bomb-aimer with Les Munro, thought that 'it seemed incongruous that this kindly and quietly spoken man, Barnes Wallis, should be involved with devastation'.

Cochrane was another of those who spoke to the men and told the crews that the raids might do a lot of damage but 'it may be a secret until after the war. So don't think you are going to get your pictures in the papers.' In the event, he could not have been more wrong. But at this point in proceedings the crews were reminded that they must keep every detail of the raid secret, even when they returned to England. There were other uses for the weapon, they were told, with the naval weapon codenamed Highball in mind.

Cochrane's speech was followed by more words from Gibson, who repeated the details of the roles of the three waves to all the crew. Ever a stickler for detail, he took no chance that anybody in the room was unsure of their role in the historic mission that lay before them. There was a discussion following this during which the interloper Jeffree, showing considerable brass neck, pointed out that it might be dangerous to return to base with an undropped bomb that was still fused. Gibson told the crews that no one was to bring an unused bomb back, an injunction that not everyone would comply with.

Given the fact that they were relatively lightly defended, there was widespread relief that the dams were the target. There had been some speculation about what the target might be; the most popular choice was the U-boat pens on the Atlantic coast which were heavily defended. Others thought, as in Gibson's original reaction, that it was the *Tirpitz*. But most were fatalistic about coming back anyway, though some did not take any special precautions – Navigator Arthur Hobday, for example, did not take the precaution of making a will, perhaps thinking that he would be tempting fate by doing so.[12]

Although some of those present had already had one earlier briefing on the raid – or perhaps because of the fact, as they knew, that it would call for precision flying of the highest order – the atmosphere in the briefing room was very tense. Sergeant Frederick Sutherland thought it was like going into an exam room.[13] He did not like what he heard, telling himself that 'this was going to be really touch and go'.[14] However, some tried to reassure themselves by focusing on certain aspects of the briefing; Hobday told himself, for example, that navigation would be helped by canals which were quite visible at night. Navigator Dudley Heal said that many of the men went to the bar and had a drink, shaking their heads at attacking the dams at a height of 60 feet. [15] This would suggest that in some quarters normal injunctions against drinking on the eve of a raid went out of the window.

Whilst the briefings were taking place, Humphries returned to his room. He had noticed a lot of strange faces around the place belonging to people that he did not recognise, including that of Wallis. Despite his closeness to Gibson, Humphries still had no idea where the raids were headed. But he knew that whatever was happening was big.

As the crews left the briefing room there was much to be done before their departure and not a lot of time to do it. There were mundane details to be attended to, such as a meal in the mess. Then there were operational matters to consider. Navigators had to make sure that their routes were properly prepared. Notes were marked on the route and power lines were marked with red crayon: the pylons were 100 feet high in the Netherlands but the cables between them sagged dangerously lower, forming a deathly spider's web for any aircraft that was flying too close to them. The crew went back to their rooms for a wash or a bath or a shave – anything that might bring a modicum of normality and relaxation when they were faced with their epic task.

Flight rations also needed to be issued to the crews: some bars of chocolate, tins of orange juice, an orange, chewing gum, Horlicks tablets. Escape equipment also had to be handed out: a wallet with the currency of the countries that the crew were flying over, a compass, morphine with needles. There was also a silk map issued which covered the countries that were en route. There was always a chance, however slim, of an escape should a plane be brought down over enemy territory, and one of the crew would certainly give the Germans a run for their money before the night was out.

Attention to secrecy was still all important. Ruth Ive, a WAAF who was a radio operator, was called into the telephone exchange to make sure that no one was breaching the rule that there should be no external phone calls by eavesdropping on all attempted conversations; she was to disconnect anyone who was trying to break the injunction. However, she herself had no idea that the raid was on.

At 1930 the crews went off to their meal of egg and bacon with an extra egg for anyone who was flying that night. Weak jokes were made about who would have the spare egg of crew members who did not return, a typical piece of black humour that helped to defuse the tension.

There was no time to hang about with the meal; there was just an hour until the crews had to make their way out to their aircraft.

Time took on its own momentum now, although its pace varied from man to man. To some it flew past; to others it dragged interminably. Harry Humphries later remarked that the scenes outside the crew rooms were unforgettable. Some crews had 'don't give a damn' looks on their faces whilst others looked grim and determined.[16]

Even the ground crew felt a sense of emotional involvement. Some of them had been allocated to one aircraft, so they had sometimes formed a strong relationship with the crews, though it varied depending on the personality and approach of the pilot. Other ground crew were responsible for covering a number of aircraft but even then it was possible to have a special affinity for one or more of them – Beck Parsons of the ground crew, for example, thought very highly of Mick Martin. A number of ground crew had gone up with the planes when they were training, which helped to form an even closer bond.

The time for preparation was almost complete and the time for action was drawing close. As the hour for departure approached, Humphries was on hand to make sure that all the busses ordered to take the crews out to their planes had arrived as planned. Small details needed to be carefully choreographed as time was of the essence – the last thing needed was any delay as it might result in the bombers flying back from the raids in broad daylight. As the busses were loaded, pilot Dave Shannon was the last to get on, in return for which a number of sarcastic comments were pointed in his direction. The weather was warm and inviting, a pleasant, balmy evening in other circumstances, but few of the crew members would have much appreciated the tranquillity.

In the distance across the airfield the Lancasters stood silently and ominously, waiting to take off for a destination that was still unknown to most people other than the aircrews. Some of the latter were lying around on the ground, Mae Wests and parachutes scattered carelessly around them. Nineteen planes, 133 pilots and crewmen, not just British but also Canadians, Australians and New Zealanders (and, if one were to be pedantic, an American who had enlisted in the Royal Canadian Air Force). The cosmopolitan nature of the crews was in fact broadly representative of the nature of Bomber Command in 1943; in January of that year, 37 per cent of all the Command's pilots were Australians, New Zealanders or Canadians, a figure that would rise to 45 per cent later in the war.[17]

Gibson arrived in his car. Getting out, he walked around the men chatting to them, putting minds at rest and offering an encouraging word or two to those who needed it. Humphries walked over to speak to him but before he could do so Flight Lieutenant Trevor-Roper, one of Gibson's crew, greeted him with a characteristically rude 'hello short arse'. Humphries did not take kindly to this but rather than further antagonise Trevor-Roper he just blushed.[18] To his subsequent question to Gibson about whether anything was needed, the Wing Commander just asked that plenty of beer should be available for the party that they would be having when they came back. Gibson thought for a second and then added ominously, 'I hope'.

Some of the men carried mascots or good-luck charms. Martin for example always carried a toy koala bear, whilst Gibson had a German Mae West inflatable lifejacket he had had since early in the war. Maltby always took an old, dirty hat with him. Gibson perhaps thought that he was in receipt of a lucky omen; his plane's code was AJ-G, his father's initials – and this was his father's birthday.

By 2030 the crews were out by their aircraft waiting to board. Moods varied; Hopgood's crew for example were mostly engaged in a game of cricket. Others though were more reserved. Hopgood's navigator, Flight Officer K. Earnshaw, predicted that eight aircraft would not come back,[19] a figure that would be exactly right.

It was a sentiment shared by his pilot. Hopgood had confided to Dave Shannon when they shared a cigarette behind the hangar before taking off: 'I think this is going to be a tough one, and I don't think I'm coming back, Dave.'[20] Wireless operator Abraham Garshowitz chalked a message on the bomb of his plane: 'never has so much been expected of so few' – a Churchillian sentiment that probably many of the men shared.[21]

These planes would not be the only British aircraft flying that night. On the same evening there were actions by other British planes that might throw the German defences off their guard, but these were limited as the full moon made it a dangerous night for flying. Eight Mosquitoes were deputed to attack four German cities, and six German Luftwaffe bases in the Netherlands were also to receive unwelcome visits. Fifty-four planes were to drop mines in the German Bight whilst ten others were to drop leaflets in France. These activities might at least help to focus the German defences elsewhere whilst the raids were in progress.[22]

Now the waiting was over and it was time to board the strangely-laden Lancasters. There was a strict order in which men boarded, based on where they were to be sitting in the plane. The bomb-aimer was first, scrambling up a small ladder and through the rear starboard door, from where he climbed forward into the nose. This was not easy; there was a high spar across the middle of the plane which made access from the rear to the forward areas difficult – this could be disastrous if the plane had to be abandoned quickly, especially if a man in front of the spar was injured and immobile.

Placed above the bomb-aimer in the forward part of the plane would be the front gunner, his feet in stirrups to stop him from getting in the way of the bomb-aimer, who was laid face downwards on the floor right at the front of the aircraft. Perched behind his .303 Browning machine guns, the front gunner would have a vital role to play against the flak gunners in the vicinity of the Möhne dam.

Then came the pilot, followed by his flight engineer. The latter would assist the pilot during take-off and landing and would keep an eye on the instruments whilst the aircraft was in flight. Judging from the small number of medals handed out after the raids, the flight engineer was considered a rather unsung hero, there only to help the pilot out, though in an emergency it would be his job to take over the controls if the pilot were killed or seriously injured.

Last of all came the navigator, the wireless operator and finally the rear gunner. Passing the chemical Elsan toilet on board, the rear gunner made his way into the rear turret. This position was precarious and also freezing cold. Worst of all, it was hard to get out of quickly. Just to compound the problem, there was not enough room in the turret to wear a parachute in it so getting out of a burning aircraft quickly would be very difficult for someone in this position.

The inside of the Lancaster left little room to manoeuvre. It was uncomfortable in other ways too. The temperature on board varied according to altitude and how good the engines were; it also depended on where you were sitting in it. The pilot, the engineer, the bomb-aimer and the navigator sat forward whilst the radio operator sat behind them, behind the massive main spar which everyone had to climb over to reach the front of the plane. The navigator sat at a table and could not see outside – only the bomb-aimer, the pilot and the engineer could. The navigator therefore relied on those who could see to feed him with landmarks from the ground that he could use to plot their position.

It was now time for the off, for the planes to climb cumbersomely into the sky, weighed down with their heavy burden and headed for their appointment with destiny. Gibson and his crew, along with the others, climbed the rickety-looking steps into their planes. Flying Officer Bellamy was on hand to snap a number of historic photos as they did so, Gibson thinking that 'these men certainly choose the queerest times'. In any event, he entered into the spirit of the occasion, looking back towards Bellamy and allegedly telling him, 'Make sure you send a copy back to my wife!'[23]

There were only nine photographs in all taken of the moments before and after the raid at Scampton and only four of them were released to the public, meaning that for all the remarkable events that were about to unfold there was very little photographic record of the raids though plenty of their aftermath. A famous photograph of Gibson standing at the top of the rickety ladder into his plane at the head of his crew strikes a slightly artificial pose as it would not normally be the pilot who was first into the plane. Still, a hero needs to adopt a hero's posture and it was understandable photographic licence for this slightly staged arrangement to be employed.

The clock was now ticking towards zero hour and a great moment of truth was at hand. Wallis's bombs had worked well, if not consistently, in trials and the crews had become dab hands at low flying. But they had never yet experienced such low flying whilst being fired at by German guns. Now their trial by fire was about to begin. Some would pass with flying colours. Others would pay the ultimate price for failure.

6

Take-off & Flight Over the North Sea
21.00 – 22.50, Sunday 16 May

The nerves were now really starting to kick in. With the crews now boarded, it was just a question of waiting for the signal to take off, and the waiting could seem endless. Unlike most raids, which just formed part of a seemingly non-stop procession of sorties, men had been training specifically for this one. This was a special mission and they were by definition special aircrews but they all faced a special risk. The very uniqueness of what lay before them only served to set the nerves even more on edge.

Of the three waves scheduled to take part in the raids, the designated first wave, led by Gibson, would, counter-intuitively, take off after the wave which was due to attack the Sorpe, led by Joe McCarthy. This was because the latter group of aircraft was flying by a northerly route and had further to go, even though the Sorpe and Möhne dams were within a few miles of each other.

It was at 2110 that Flight Lieutenant Hutchison in Gibson's plane gave the signal by Very light for the planes to start their engines. This was the instruction for all first and second wave planes to start up and move around the perimeter and begin preparations for take-off.[1] In the planes that were due to begin their journey in the next twenty minutes or so, ignitions were started and starter buttons pressed. Most of the aircraft chugged and spluttered into life but in one of them at once a problem became apparent. Joe McCarthy's plane (code AJ-Q) had a problem with a glycol (coolant) leak with the starboard outer engine which meant that it would not be going anywhere that night. The crew abandoned the plane as fast as they could and sought out a replacement.

This one event could have been disastrous. As the leader of the raid on the Sorpe, McCarthy had a particularly important role, though the logistics of the attack on the dam were different to those of the raid against the Möhne. McCarthy's should have been the first plane to take off but that was not going to happen. It was just as well that Commander Bergel had flown up a replacement that afternoon as there was no other plane available. It was also a stroke of luck that there were nineteen planes available and nineteen crews as two of those who were supposed to be involved were incapacitated.

This was because there was illness affecting two crews which consequently could not fly. Those involved were Pilot Officer Divall and Flight Lieutenant Wilson and their crews (the latter man should have flown on the mission against the Sorpe dam, which meant that this wave was already a plane down without McCarthy dropping out). Divall had a knee injury and Wilson was ill. But if their luck was in on this particular night, this was certainly not to continue in the future; their reprieve was temporary as both would be killed in September 1943 during a catastrophic raid on the Dortmund – Ems Canal. Divall had been due to fly with the reserve wave but it is not at all clear that a plane would have been available for him to fly anyway.

McCarthy came running back towards the hangars from his abandoned plane looking, according to Humphries, 'like a runaway tank'. Desperate to see the action, the thought must have crossed his mind that if another plane was out of action then someone might get there before him to bag the 'spare'. McCarthy originated from Brooklyn, a part of the world whose residents were not renowned for their patience. He was a big man and the sight of him this angry must have been extremely disconcerting. Flight Sergeant 'Chiefy' Powell, an unheralded backroom hero of the raids, did his best to calm him down.

This, however, was not easy, for the spare plane (which would be designated AJ-T) had not been fully prepared for the mission. It had not yet been equipped with a compass card, which was vital given the difficulties in navigating on the raid. McCarthy furiously demanded to know, 'Where are those lazy, idle, incompetent compass adjusters?' According to Humphries, 'Mac' was in something of a mess, his rage having disturbed his equanimity. Humphries suggested that he should calm down and everything should be alright.[2]

This was not a good start. Not only would the wave attacking the Sorpe dam be without its leader when it took off but, if and when McCarthy did manage to get up, it would be difficult for him to be at his best given this unsettling start to his flight. That said, it was clear that McCarthy was spoiling for a fight and it would take quite exceptional adverse circumstances to dampen his martial spirit. But these problems with the leader of the Sorpe wave were an entirely appropriate portent for what was to follow as far as this particular wave was concerned.

At 2128, another signal was given showing that it was now time to take off. In the absence of McCarthy, it was Flight Lieutenant Robert Barlow who was first away. There was a little caravan at the edge of the runway instead of a control tower and from inside this a green Aldis light was to be shown when the moment for take-off had arrived. The planes lined up and the crews aboard waited with a mixture of apprehension and excitement. When at last the light shone forth, they roared down the grass runway, starting at its southern end. It was an extra long run as the weight of the planes was especially heavy. The pilots all knew that there was no pulling out at the last moment – once the planes were committed that was it.

The moment of take-off was therefore one of great tension. The Lancaster was a much heavier bomber than any of the men would have been used to at the start of the war; for example, it was about twice the aircraft, weight-wise, that the Wellington was. Take-off safety speed was 130 mph so the aircrew were always reliant on the four engines holding out whilst under extreme pressure during the build-up to take-off and during take-off itself. This was exacerbated because of the heavy load that the planes were carrying.

The Sorpe wave now led the way into battle minus, at this stage, its leader. The true purpose of the raid on the Sorpe was, according to Gibson in his later account of the raids, a diversionary one. He said that the reason for routeing them far to the north of the wave that was headed for the Möhne was to get them to draw off the night fighters. Then they were to fly down to the Sorpe and the attack there was to take the fighters again away from the planes attacking the Möhne.[3]

Yet this explanation of the diversionary role of the planes attacking the Sorpe is not at all convincing. The official order for the raid[4] gives no such suggestion. The Möhne dam is recognised as the most important target for sure, but the Sorpe was officially the next most important. To devastate the Ruhr valley to the extent desired, both would need to be breached. As supporting evidence that the Sorpe was never intended as a diversion, paragraph 27 of the order is devoted entirely to the issue of diversionary attacks but makes no mention of the attack on the Sorpe dam in this respect and merely refers to the other diversionary raids taking place across the Continent that night.

A more likely explanation is that Gibson later sought to play down the attacks on the Sorpe because they were the least successful part of the raid. This was through no fault of the pilots, some of whom lost their lives in the mission whilst others dropped their bombs after taking great care to follow instructions. The problem was that the weapon they were carrying was simply not up to the task of breaking the Sorpe dam open given its different construction. This would have been an embarrassing admission given the euphoria that attended the successes enjoyed by the raids and therefore it was much more convenient to suggest that the attack on the Sorpe was a diversion all along.

With Barlow in the lead, the wave headed for the Sorpe set off at one-minute intervals. At 2129, Flight Lieutenant Munro of the RNZAF in AJ-W took off, followed at 2130 by Pilot Officer Vernon Byers in AJ-K and then Pilot Officer Geoffrey Rice in AJ-H at 2131. These first four planes flew in a long formation at around 50 feet at a speed of 180 mph about 3 miles apart. They made their way towards the east, across the waters that would take them right into the heart of the enemy's lair.

As they made their way towards the North Sea on a northerly route that would take them over the Netherlands, the scene was now set for Gibson at the head of the first wave to set off for the Möhne. Whitworth, the Scampton base commander, made his way on board the plane to wish Gibson luck; Gibson smiled back with a weak grin. A photographer ran up and asked to take his photo: weird timing again, thought Gibson. Despite his implacable exterior, Gibson later admitted to being very nervous but now it was time to go. There is no reason to doubt that he really was anxious and the calm exterior probably reflected more a leader who did not wish to betray his fears rather than any lack of nerves.

Gibson's wave now prepared to roll off down the grass runways and into the air. At 2139 the green light from the Aldis lamp was given for his flight. Alongside him were 'Hoppy' Hopgood (in AJ-M) and 'Mick' Martin (in AJ-P). Unlike the Sorpe wave, they took off in a loose 'vic' formation (a 'vic' was a triangle of planes with one in the lead and two slightly back to either side). It was very unusual to see Lancasters take off in this formation (it was normally associated with fighters) and it was quite a sight – Rear Gunner McDonald from AJ-F in the reserve formation, who were taking off later, looked on disbelievingly.[5]

As the planes took off, Ruth Ive, who was in a Nissen hut at the end of the airfield, felt it rattle and shake as the planes flew over. She had no idea where they were going and the two sergeants who were with her were not letting on – instead they would wait up all night and teach her how to play poker. Humphries waited up with Fay Gillon – he still did not know what his squadron's destination was. Kenneth Lucas of the ground crew on the other hand made his way to bed – he had been working solid for over 24 hours repairing the tail planes on two of the aircraft and would enjoy a very good night's sleep.[6]

There were two more waves of Gibson's flight to take off; the journey over the North Sea would basically be made in three flights of three planes each, flying in close formation. At 2147, 'Dinghy' Young's aircraft (AJ-A) left Scampton along with David Maltby (AJ-J) and Dave Shannon (in AJ-L). Shannon's plane was particularly striking. It had a picture of Bacchus painted on the side in recognition of the crew's capacity to drink enormous amounts of alcohol. These pilots and their crews were mostly experienced flyers but Vivian Nicholson, Maltby's navigator, was on his first operation. Nicholson came from Sherburn, a pit community in County Durham. His father Arthur had a joinery and undertaking business, far from the prestigious social background of some of the other 617 Squadron crew members.

At 2159 Henry Maudslay's plane (AJ-Z) left Scampton along with Bill Astell (AJ-B) and Les Knight (in AJ-M). Struggling sluggishly over the hedge at the end of the runway, the Lancasters climbed cumbrously into the sky, circled once and then disappeared over the horizon. Destiny lay ahead of them, life or death, fame or failure, triumph or tragedy.

The reserve wave would not depart for several hours yet but there was one more plane left to take off. Joe McCarthy had taken command of the spare plane (AJ-T) and had managed to get it into working order.

It was all very frantic. Flying Officer Dave Rodger, the rear gunner, bashed out the panel in the rear turret window to improve visibility as the plane prepared to taxi.

Removing the central Perspex window in the rear window was almost routine – it made little difference to the temperature, which was freezing with or without it and only dropped by one degree if this was done, but it seriously increased visibility and therefore chances of survival. On the night, every plane that flew would have the window removed in this way.[7]

McCarthy, over half an hour late, was in a tearing hurry to make up for lost time. In his haste to board the plane he accidentally pulled the ripcord on his parachute, rendering it useless, but at the last moment a spare was handed to him. Humphries thought that he was in such a state that he might make a mess of the take-off but fortunately he did not. A compass deviation card had been fitted but McCarthy would experience serious problems with navigation later on in the flight. There was also a problem with the number three engine, which had led the man who had delivered the aircraft, Commander Bergel, to think that it was unserviceable. Regardless of this, McCarthy now put the plane at full throttle in a desperate attempt to catch up with the wave that he was supposed to be leading.

Having witnessed the departure of the first two waves, the reserve crew in the third returned to their games of poker and waited until it was their turn in a couple of hours' time. For them the wait would have been difficult; they were not even sure where they would be headed for, as this depended on the success or otherwise of the first waves; if the primary targets had not been breached then it would be their job to attempt to complete the task; if not they would be sent to one of the reserve targets. At about 2300 they went to see their ground crews and thanked them for the efforts they had put in and then sat and waited.

In the meantime the first and second waves headed for the English coast and then across the no man's land of the North Sea and the dangers of the German defences facing them on the coast of Europe. There was to be strict RT silence until they crossed the enemy coast. Early on in the flight the aircraft were to drop low over the Wash and test out their spotlights, which were of course critical given the need to drop their weapons from exactly the right height. Maltby tested his at 2210.

The Wash indented the coast of East Anglia and on the other side of it they were back over the land. But at 2219 Gibson's flight crossed the English coast for the last time before reaching the North Sea, Southwold being the departure point. Now they headed towards the darkness, bidding farewell to England, unsure if they would ever see it again.

They were to fly over the North Sea at the very low level of 60 feet and were to set their altimeters at this level, though down that low the instruments were inaccurate and it would be all too easy to make a catastrophic error of judgement. One of the pilots would almost fatally misjudge the altitude that his plane was at and, although he would survive, his mission would be over before it had even really begun.

The second and third wings of this 'first' wave continued on behind. At 2238 'Dinghy' Young crossed the English coast. They too headed for occupied Europe, uncertain of the reception they would find. The element of surprise was all-important and they had to hope that flying at such low heights they would be able to avoid the flak guarding the approaches to Fortress Europe by being past it before the gunners had time to react. They were within an hour of finding out or not whether their luck had held and whether indeed the gods of war were with them.

7

Fortress Europe Attempts to Repel Raids
22.51 – 23.59, Sunday 16 May

The crossing of the North Sea was uneventful. The waters slipped away behind the raiders with no interruption from enemy aircraft or other scares. It was a deceptively smooth introduction to the events that were about to unfold. Just over an hour after leaving Scampton, the first planes were approaching continental Europe, hoping that they would be through the first line of defences before they were spotted. As they neared the coast, they fused their bombs though they would not be fully armed until released from the plane and dropped on a target.

Perhaps the pre-flight briefing from RAF Tempsford concerning low-level flying particularly started to resonate as the borders of Fortress Europe loomed large. Special Operations Executive missions to land agents in occupied Europe were flown from here and staff there were therefore experts in working out how aircraft could avoid known flak positions. In advance of the raid, 5 Group had asked RAF Tempsford to comment on several proposed routes whilst trying not to give too much information away about what it was needed for. In an ominous warning, the briefing subsequently prepared had noted that 'from experience it has been found that the time when an aircraft is most likely to be shot at is when crossing the coast'.[1] It was a prediction that would turn out to be distressingly accurate for some of the planes involved in the mission.

Gibson's first wave, as it had a shorter distance to travel, would cross the enemy coast before the wave that was headed for the Sorpe even though it had left later. However, even this early in the flight there were issues with direction-finding.

About five minutes before reaching the coast of Europe, Gibson had received a warning from Torger Taerum that they were approaching enemy-held territory. The spotlights were put on to check their height and they found that they were flying too high at about 100 feet. Flight Sergeant Deering in the front turret got ready to fire back at any flak guns that were insolent enough to try and shoot them down. The tension noticeably tightened a notch or two.

As the coast came into sight, it appeared to Gibson to be 'low and flat and evil' under the spectral light of the moon. They weaved in and out trying to evade the defences they knew were there which had been as fully mapped out as possible in advance. Gibson thought the planes seemed like ships trying to pick their way through a minefield. They roared over the Western Wall, initially catching the defences off guard.[2] However, they had not yet crossed the coast proper, merely an island just off it, and were soon back over the sea once more, though not for long before reaching the mainland.

At 2252 Gibson and the first group crossed the Scheldt Estuary. He was slightly south-west of where he should have been and had crossed Walcheren Island instead of passing between here and the island of Schouewen as he should have done. This was not good as Walcheren was strongly defended. Unsure of where he was, Gibson climbed to 300 feet to orientate himself properly. Once up at this height, Navigator Taerum calculated a revised heading.

As Gibson turned left to get himself back on track, 'Hoppy' Hopgood lost sight of him and they flew on out of sight of each other. The fact that crews were off course even as soon as they reached the Continent hinted at the difficulties that lay ahead for the raiders. The areas they were to pass through to reach the dams were heavily defended and the smallest of errors could lead them into trouble as they flew into heavy flak. A margin of just a mile or so could mean the difference between life and death, as some of the crews would soon find out.

Gibson was fortunate to escape the flak of the coastal defences without harm. His plane had sprung out of the darkness over the coast and caught the gunners off their guard. They flew on, so low that more than once they were forced to suddenly shoot up in the air to avoid trees or high-tension cables. They then came across a canal, which was to be a point of reference for them to follow, and had soon reached a turning point at which they were to divert towards the Rhine. The canals were indeed godsends in terms of finding where they were.

This was helpful but it was an inherent problem of such low flying that it was very difficult to navigate accurately. In the dark the planes were often past a landmark before they even realised they were there. The moonlight helped with more obvious markers such as rivers and canals, but many others were hard to identify as the planes shot past objects that would, in the daylight, have been much easier to pick out.

Gibson would not hit problems with flak until he reached Germany proper, where he later had to take evasive action. With a dozen searchlights illuminating the sky over enemy territory, Gibson and his crew felt very conspicuous but he managed to weave his way in and out of the gunfire without being hit. At these low heights, heavy flak – 88- and 105-mm Anti-Aircraft (AA) guns – would be ineffective as the planes would be past them before they could home in on them. However, 20-mm guns would be a definite threat – these could fire at 120 rounds a minute and were more than capable of hitting low-flying aircraft. The British pilots just had to hope that their sudden arrival without warning would catch the gunners off-guard.

Martin described the threat from the flak rather well: 'from 7,000 feet upwards there was so-called heavy flak, and down to 3,000 feet there were night fighters. From 200 feet up to 4,000 feet there was light flak. Below 200 feet it's hard to hear low-flying aircraft approaching and it's damned difficult for ground gunners – if they did hear – to swing on and lay off the necessary deflection.'[3] Such was the hope and for some of them it would be fulfilled; some but not all.

The route had anyway been carefully planned to avoid flak as much as possible. Tempsford had recommended key points along the track to particularly watch out for. A certain degree of precision was required; for example, the northern route should fly over the middle of the island of Vlieland as there were flak positions at either end. This confirmed that margins of error were extremely small.

Landmarks were carefully chosen on the route too, in an attempt to help the crews stay on track; water features were especially useful for this purpose. The bomb-aimer was to remain face down in the nose for the entire trip to assist with navigation, which cannot have made for a comfortable mission.[4]

If Gibson's wave was to escape unscathed from their crossing of the coast, the same was not true of the planes of the second wave over a hundred miles to the north. At 2255, just a few minutes after Gibson had crossed over miles to the south, Flight Lieutenant Robert Barlow in AJ-E was the first of the northern wave to reach the Continent, passing over the coast of the Netherlands. He was fortunate to catch the AA defences off their guard. His comrades would not be so lucky.

A minute later Les Munro in AJ-W fused his bomb. Another minute passed and then Pilot Officer Geoffrey Rice in AJ-H was aware of an explosion lighting up the sky. It was the sight of the plane of Pilot Officer Vernon Byers being hit by gunfire.

Byers was just off the coast of the Netherlands when his plane was hit by gunfire from the coastal defences guarding the approaches to continental Europe. It was a fatal blow. The bomber crashed into the sea off the island of Vlieland, one of the chain of isles shielding the Netherlands from the North Sea. There were no survivors. Only one body was found, that of Sergeant James McDowell, who was a gunner. He was later buried with dignity in the General Cemetery at Harlington. It was the worst possible start. The Sorpe flight had not even reached the mainland and the first plane had been lost.

Byers was a Canadian and, at thirty-two years of age, one of the oldest men flying that night. He had passed through 1654 Conversion Unit earlier that year, where he had got to know 'Mick' Martin, who was an instructor there. Despite his maturity, Byers was a very recent recruit, having joined the RCAF in 1941. He had then passed through 1654 Conversion Unit, where he had flown with Mick Martin on four occasions. Following that, he had been posted to 467 Squadron on 5 February 1943, where he spent only seven weeks before being moved to 617 Squadron. He had had a relatively short and fatally unlucky stint as a bomber pilot.

The route of this wave headed for the Sorpe was planned to take a path over the island of Vlieland. However, in the dying light it would be difficult to distinguish this from its southerly neighbour, Texel, which was very heavily defended. The wind that night was stronger than forecast and may have driven the planes slightly off course to the south. This had already led to potential danger for Gibson himself as he could have found out over the heavily defended island of Walcheren if his luck had not been in.

Byers had been seen gaining height, a hint that he was unsure of his correct position and was climbing to try and establish it. This led to danger; at very low levels the planes would be over the defences before the gun crews on anti-aircraft duty had spotted them. At any rate, only light guns could be manoeuvred into position quickly enough to get a shell away at the planes going over. But once the aircraft rose higher up, even marginally so, they would be vulnerable.

The Dutch Frisian islands chain was defended by seven batteries of AA guns from Marine-Flakabteilung 246 of the German Navy. RAF Intelligence believed that this area was lightly defended. Where the shell that brought Byers down was fired from remains a matter of debate. The intended route took the wave just north of Vlieland, well out of reach of the guns around the Dutch naval base at Den Helder. Some argue that the defences of Texel were responsible for bringing the plane down, suggesting that it was to the south of where it should have been – a not impossible suggestion given the conditions that night. However, experts who have studied the matter now believe that there were no gun emplacements on the north of the island that could have been responsible for bringing Byers down.[5]

The gap between Texel and Den Helder on the mainland also looked quite similar to that between Vlieland and Texel, so it would be easy for a pilot to mistake their position. The fact that Byers crashed in the sea means that it is virtually impossible to be sure who was responsible for bringing him down (a crash over land would at least allow some educated guesswork as to where the gun was fired from). However, a convincing candidate for the unit that fired the decisive shot was the aforementioned Marine-Flakabteilung 246, which was based on the western side of Vlieland.

There were fractions between life and death, surviving or not, and there were three elements in particular that were responsible for whether a crew would return. The first was the skill of the pilot, the second the intensity of the training that the men had been through, the third plain old-fashioned luck. Some of the crew later thanked their lucky stars for the pilots whom they depended on so much. Sergeant Basil Feneron, the flight engineer in AJ-F, spoke glowingly of how 'Ken Brown always kept us up to scratch. He used to take us away to knock seconds off dinghy and escape drills, while a lot of crews were more interested in the birds they were taking out.' Such skill and dedication could keep men alive.

It was only a matter of moments before another plane from this northern wave was in trouble. At 2257 Munro's aircraft was damaged by fire from a flak-ship off the coast. His radio equipment was knocked out (in fact, the transmitter, intercom and master compass were all damaged) and as he was unable to communicate with other aircraft he had to consider whether to abort his mission or not. A note was passed around to seek views from the crew – the damage meant the intercom was useless. The bomb-aimer, Jim Clay, suggested they would just get in the way of everyone else if they carried on.

Munro later insisted that his plane had only suffered one hit but it was nevertheless decisive as far as his involvement in the raids was concerned. The pilot circled his plane around at a safe distance from the flak whilst his wireless operator, Flying Officer Percy Pigeon, was sent to look at the damage and see if it could be repaired. He soon reported back that the equipment was unfixable; with no intercom between the crew, effective communication even inside the plane would be very difficult. For a higher-altitude raid, with more time to work out an alternative system, something might have been possible but on this low-level mission, where everything was happening so fast, it was impossible. The master compass unit was also destroyed. It was a litany of problems which in the end forced Munro to take the decision to abort.

Even as all this action was happening, back at base everyone was in the dark as yet as to how the raid was going. For them, it was effectively the calm before the storm. Everything that could have been done had now been done – all they could do was to wait to find out how successful they had been. At 2300 Wallis, Cochrane, Harris and other luminaries left Scampton for Grantham, where they would later be able to receive news as it was Morsed in. Several hours of tortured waiting were to follow. Only about now was there complete darkness over Western Europe as the short late May night began.

It was as well perhaps that those at Scampton were metaphorically in the dark as to what was going on as far as the wave of planes headed for the Sorpe dam was concerned. This part of the mission was already threatening to turn into an unmitigated disaster. At 2259 Pilot Officer Geoffrey Rice in plane AJ-H was about to reach the Continent. All of a sudden, panic reigned on his aircraft. Sergeant Edward Smith, the flight engineer, noted that the barometric altimeter read zero.

At almost exactly the same moment, Rice became terribly aware that the water beneath him was looming up far too closely. He had misjudged the altitude that he was flying at and was about to hit the sea. As he struggled to gain height at the last second he clipped the waves and water started to come into the plane. So much entered that the deluge threatened to drown Sergeant Sandy Burns in the rear turret as it poured down towards the back of the plane before cascading out.

Rice's instinctive reaction saved the plane and the crew as it zoomed up on an upward trajectory, but the bomb hanging from the bomb-bay was torn out and lost by the impact of the collision with the water. Burns shouted out, 'Christ! It's wet at the back …' followed by, 'You've lost the mine!' Burns was in danger of being drowned before the water drained out of the rear turret as the plane climbed higher; he was fortunate to survive.

The loss of the bomb from Rice's aircraft meant that there was absolutely no point in continuing with the mission. In addition, Rice lost both outboard engines and there was even a doubt about whether or not he could make it back to England. In the event, he limped back to England on his two inboard engines. When they eventually arrived back at Scampton, Burns had to be cut out of the rear turret in which he was trapped.

The collision emphasised the dangers of low flying. It has been suggested that perhaps the lights that were supposed to be used to gauge the correct height had been set incorrectly and caused Rice to fly too low.[6] Whatever the true reason, it was a powerful reminder of just how dangerous this mission was.

Rice would not be returning alone. At 2306 Bill Howarth, the front turret gunner in Munro's aircraft (AJ-W), felt the plane bank and realised that they were also returning home. Munro too had decided to abort his mission. Unlike Rice, he was going back with his bomb still dangling out from the callipers in the bomb-bay. This was specifically against Gibson's orders. However, Munro would not be reprimanded in any way for his actions. This contrasted somewhat with the treatment of one other pilot who returned home with his bomb undropped.

This was a terrible start for the mission on the Sorpe. There had already been doubts expressed before the raids as to the viability of breaching the dam there, and now, of the five planes deputed to attack it (already one short after Divall's late withdrawal), one had been shot down and two others were limping back to base within minutes of reaching the Continent. Further, the leader of this wave had not even crossed the coast yet. It was a sorry tale and it was not going to improve any time soon.

For Gibson at least the initial crossing of the coast had gone relatively smoothly so far. At 2303 his plane passed Roosendal. He soon after picked up the helpful signposting offered by the Wilhelmina canal below him; following this he was able to avoid the heavy AA defences of a Luftwaffe base north of Eindhoven, which was more fortunate than some of his colleagues behind him would be.

In the meantime, the next group in his wave was, at 2312, crossing the Scheldt Estuary. This was the group including Squadron Leader Melvyn Young's Lancaster (AJ-A), Flight Lieutenant David Maltby's AJ-J and Flight Lieutenant Dave Shannon in AJ-L. Unlike Gibson's flight, they had arrived on track and did not, as he had been forced to do, need to run the gauntlet of the heavy defences on Walcheren.

Yet in many ways their problems had only just begun. Whilst they had breached the first line of defence successfully, they were now flying low over enemy territory and this was an extremely dangerous part of the journey. Both the front gunner and the bomb-aimer had a crucial role in looking out for obstructions ahead as, in addition to avoiding flak positions, they also had to avoid obstacles like pylons, church towers and trees that might bring them down at any moment.

The route had been chosen with several objectives in mind. One of them was to avoid all known flak positions. The other was to have relatively short distances between waymarks on the route to enable the planes to regularly check out their position and make sure that they were in the right place. Despite this, several planes in the southern wave had to take evasive action from flak on the way in.

In the meantime, further north, Joe McCarthy had been flying flat out to catch up with the rest of his flight, unaware that, with the exception of one other plane that was ploughing onwards, it had now effectively ceased to exist. By 2313 he had reached Vlieland (this was just a minute after Young, Maltby and Shannon had crossed the coast of Europe 100 miles further south with Maudslay, Astell and Knight 10 minutes behind). This shows something of the speed he was going at. Though he had left Scampton 33 minutes after the first plane in the Sorpe wave, he was crossing the coast only 18 minutes behind; this was symptomatic of a man in a hurry.

The gunners on Vlieland were now wide awake, having been made aware of the threat by the four planes that had already tried to break through their defences, only one of which had succeeded. As a result, there was a hot reception but McCarthy was able to fly in between two sand dunes which offered some protection and allowed him to escape.

As McCarthy flew on, he spotted a goods train. Ron Batson, the front gunner, asked for permission to attack it, which was granted. This turned out to be a mistake; it was an armoured train which fired back rather more fiercely than anticipated. The plane was hit, though not badly. It was only much later, when they landed back at Scampton, that they found out where damage had been done: the starboard tyre had been burst.

Navigation for all the planes remained difficult. Don MacLean, McCarthy's navigator, did not use the roll map method whereby the maps were laid out in a long roll that was unwound as the journey progressed; he thought that it was useless if the plane went off course (only a narrow corridor on the route had been incorporated in the roll maps) so instead they took ordinary maps and used them as needed, which took up much more room but were more useful if the aircraft went astray at all.

Neither were the raiders solely in danger from flak. Night fighters from the Luftwaffe base at Leeuwarden, east of the Ijsselmeer, had been deployed to engage the bombers whose presence was now known. However, night flying was a relatively new discipline. The fighters had a very limited radar range and the fact that the British were flying at low levels meant that they were not spotted by the fighters who were flying high above them. McCarthy said that he could frequently see the planes flying about 1,000 feet higher than him but they could clearly not see him. Some of the fighters would be in the air for nearly two hours but not one would come close to intercepting anyone from 617 Squadron.

Gibson too continued to head for his target. By 2322 he had passed Beek. Here the Wilhelmina canal ended and they headed east-north-east across largely featureless countryside where, in the absence of clear landmarks, the plane once more drifted off course to the south. When he soon spotted the unmistakable outline of the Rhine below him, Gibson once more adjusted his course and tried to get back on track, but in the process he also lost contact with Martin.

Martin was also doing his best to stay on track. It was surprising, alarming even, how quite mundane matters interfered when flying at such low levels. His windscreen was splattered with spray from the sea and dead bugs; the latter were especially difficult to distinguish from landmarks on the route.[7]

By 2325 Young had passed Roosendal, distinguishable from the air by the large railway junction to the north of the town, about 20 minutes behind Gibson. He then headed slightly to the left, passing south of Breda and Tilburg, where soon after the line of the Wilhelmina canal would be followed. This should take the planes between the heavily defended airfields of Gilze-Rijen on the left and Eindhoven on the right. After Eindhoven, another canal would be reached at the village of Beek. Then from Rees the planes, by now in German airspace, would fly to a group of lakes near Dulmen.

That something was afoot was now obvious to the Germans. Even those close to the dams were alerted. At 2330 the inhabitants of Günne, the village at the very foot of the Möhne dam, heard an air-raid warning. One of the residents was a special constable, Ferdinand Nölle, who recalled that 'after the war began, for some time before the raid, people in Neheim [the nearest town downstream] started to phone in to complain. They said we should let some of the water out so as to reduce the danger if there was a raid. But nothing happened.'[8] The residents of Neheim had every reason to be nervous of what might occur should the dam be breached.

However, it was still not at all obvious where the planes in the air on this particular full-moon night were headed. At 2334 Gibson passed Rees. Near here, his flight met with a hostile reception from flak. The three planes in his flight, now separated, returned fire with interest and managed to pass the defences undamaged. Further gunfire would be experienced near Dorsten and also near Dülmen. The closer they got to the heart of Germany, the more unfriendly the reception would become.

As Gibson's crew flew on, they realised that again they had strayed off course and had come too close to the heavily defended town of Duisburg, a significant industrial centre and therefore well guarded. Taerum took responsibility for this error as he had calculated the wrong course; Gibson reminded him that this could be 'an expensive mistake'. Although this might seem harsh, in this instance it was justified as Taerum needed to be on his guard. He did not seem to be having a good night and further errors could be fatal.

They were also approaching a particularly dangerous area in terms of German defences. As they passed deeper into the Ruhr valley, the flak guns homed in on Gibson and the other planes in his flight. Searchlights lit up the sky and guns spat out at the aircraft, but their low height was a bonus, making it difficult for the gunners to get an accurate fix on a plane in time. On occasion, Gibson was even screened by the trees that loomed up beside his aircraft.[9]

They flew on, past Dortmund and Hamm, the latter a very frequent target for bombing activity with its large rail-marshalling yards. Then they moved past Soest, the main administrative centre for the region around the Möhne dam, where Gibson had almost been shot down three years before. It was sleepy now and the guns, if there were any there, were quiet – a welcome change since the last time he was in the area. Then ahead of them they saw the gentle hills above the Möhne dam. The target zone was almost in sight.

But navigation was becoming increasingly difficult. At 2342, Sergeant Vivian Nicholson, Maltby's navigator, noted that the Gee system was 'jammed something chronic',[10] which was to be expected now that the planes were moving towards the end of Gee's effective range. Other operators commented favourably on the system in the early parts of the raid, saying that it worked well until they got into Germany; but Dudley Heal, Ken Brown's navigator in the reserve wave, also later found that it jammed.[11] The German counter-defences against this equipment were proving especially effective.

Gibson's wave had at least so far managed to avoid damage from flak, but their luck was about to turn. Nearby, 'Hoppy' Hopgood was also headed for problems. One moment rear gunner Burcher was thinking of his bride-to-be – he was due to be married next month – the next moment he felt his stomach metaphorically hit the ground as the Lancaster he was in took sharp evasive action. A high-tension wire loomed ahead and Hopgood had to take a split-second decision to avoid it. He was flying so low that he actually flew underneath it.

Then the plane was picked up by searchlights. Gunfire spat out angrily at them. At 2345, whilst flying over Dülmen, 'Hoppy' Hopgood's plane was badly shot up. His rear gunner, Pilot Officer Anthony Burcher, noticed a strong smell of cordite in the plane. The port outer engine had been hit and was aflame: Flight Engineer Sgt Charles Brennan shut down the damaged Merlin and feathered the propeller.[12] Hopgood though managed to regain power and gamely headed on towards the Möhne.

But the plane had been badly hit. Burcher felt blood in his mouth, but he would be one of the luckier casualties that night. Sergeant John Minchin, the wireless operator, was hit and badly wounded; he could not move his leg. There was no response from Pilot Officer George Gregory in the front turret and Burcher assumed that he was dead. Hopgood was also badly injured: blood was streaming from his head and Charles Brennan, the flight engineer, had to tend to his wounds.

Hopgood at least managed to head on, still carrying his weapon and still able to take his part in the mission. But further to the north, the wave headed for the Sorpe was about to suffer another disastrous reverse. 'Norm' Barlow, an Australian pilot flying in AJ-E, had developed a well-deserved reputation as a survivor, having nursed back a damaged plane to base on more than one occasion. Now, though, his luck had run out.

He was an experienced pilot, unusual in being in his thirties, old for those taking part in the raids. He was the first of the 'Dambusters' to take off and had managed to fly without damage over the Netherlands. But then at 2350, when over Germany near Haldern (north of Rees), he all of a sudden found himself suddenly in danger of being ensnared by high-tension power cables. It was too late to avoid them. Staggering on for a few hundred yards into a field, the plane hit the ground and went up in flames. The impact was shattering, so much so that there were no survivors. Now, of the five planes in this northern wave, only one was left to attempt to breach the Sorpe dam: the one flown by the resilient Joe McCarthy.

Amongst the dead in Barlow's crew was Jack Liddell, the youngest crew member that night. He had previously been thrown out of the RAF as he had lied about his age when he joined up, aged just fifteen. Disappointed, he instead became a member of the Fire Service during the London Blitz. He later re-enlisted and was given the ironic name of 'killer' – he was a gunner but had never fired his guns in anger.

Barlow's bomb miraculously did not detonate and was recovered intact by the Germans, a wonderful gift for them which meant that all security measures that had been taken to keep the device a secret were largely superfluous. There would be little point in taking further measures to keep the device a secret when the Germans had a fully functional model in their hands.

Even before it was light the next day the local people gathered around the bomb, wondering what exactly this strangely shaped object might be. The mayor of Haldern was one of the crowd, the consensus amongst which was that this was a large petrol canister. This encouraged the mayor to quip that 'I'll tell the Chief Administrative Officer that he needn't send us any more petrol coupons for the rest of the war.' At one stage he even climbed on top of it and had his photograph taken. He was later reported to have felt decidedly queasy when told that it was in fact full of high explosive.

Only a few personal possessions were salvaged from the wreck site: cases, gold rings and a torch on which the number of missions that the owner had flown – thirty-two – was recorded. There were also the names of towns including Palermo scratched into it.[13] This was a pitifully small collection of objects to mark the snuffing out of seven lives.

By the following morning the bomb was being examined and within a month a preliminary report concerning it was on the desk of Albert Speer. Detailed descriptions of the bomb were distributed to, amongst others, Hermann Goering. The descriptions noted, for example, the precise dimensions of the device and the presence of the hydrostatic pistols.[14] In fact there were three of these pistols fitted so that if one were damaged on impact, one of the other two at least would hopefully work. These were based on standard Admiralty design and were what made the device a depth-charge rather than a bomb or a mine.

With the Sorpe attack now almost doomed to fail as just one plane from the designated wave was left to deliver the attack, all hopes for making a significant impact on the Ruhr industries rested on Gibson's flight. They headed on relentlessly towards their appointment with destiny. The flak as they flew through the Ruhr valley had been very active, though by weaving and jinking most of it was avoided. Searchlights had picked up planes from time to time, but because they were flying so low it was hard for the lights to stay on the aircraft; a number of the searchlights continued to be dodged by hopping behind trees.

Despite all the odds, Gibson and the eight planes behind him pushed on remorselessly. Now the major defences were behind them, and just a few miles and even fewer minutes in front of them was the dam that was their primary target. With midnight approaching, a poignant scene was even now being played out back at Scampton. Gibson's beloved pet was being interred in the cold earth of the airbase, beneath his office, buried with all the dignity that could be mustered. Nigger's grave was in front of No. 2 hangar and a simple wooden cross had been made by one of the 'chippies' to mark the spot.[15]

For all his single-mindedness, perhaps for a brief second Gibson's mind wandered back over the miles to think one last farewell to his old friend. Perhaps too he thought he might soon be joining him. Within an hour he would either be a hero or he would be dead. Perhaps after all he might be both.

8

Attack on Möhne:
Early Attacks Over Target X & Target Z
00.00 – 00.30, Monday 17 May

The first wave was now drawing close to the Möhne dam. With the exception of the damage done to Hopgood's plane, Gibson's flight had escaped relatively lightly so far. To near the dam with a full complement of planes was better than can have been hoped for and in marked contrast to what had happened to the wave headed for the Sorpe.

However, reconnaissance had shown that the dam was defended by flak and this meant that the attack was unlikely to be as straightforward as those against the others, where there were believed to be no anti-aircraft guns in place. But even for Gibson's flight, the closer they got to the heart of the Ruhr, the more resistance they were likely to experience. At 0007, John Minchin, Hopgood's wireless operator, transmitted a warning of flak over to the east of Dulmen. By now, Hopgood's crew were well aware of how dangerous the flak was.

The other two flights of this wave were continuing to make good progress behind Gibson. At 0009, 'Dinghy' Young, in the first-wave flight behind Gibson, reached the Dulmen waypoint. Here, following the pre-planned route, they turned right heading for Ahlen, where there was a prominent railway line to follow. Again, it was important to have clearly visible landmarks to point the way.

With the first wave almost at its destination, it was high time that the reserve planes were despatched from back at Scampton. They could be informed of their ultimate destination when they were en route, dependent on the success of Gibson's wave in pushing home their attack. There was no doubt that the Möhne dam was the number one objective; but after that, everything was much less clear, as would become apparent later on.

Accordingly, at 0009, Pilot Officer Warner Ottley in AJ-C left Scampton, the first of the reserve wave to take off. Two minutes later, Pilot Officer Lewis Burpee in AJ-S was next up, followed a minute later by Ken Brown in AJ-F. They made their way towards the Continent and would pick up further instructions en route. Just before take-off, Burpee had gone over to Brown, his fellow Canadian, thrust out his hand and said laconically 'goodbye Ken'. Brown took his hand and shook it; he knew that this mission was far from a 'sure bet'.[1]

It is interesting to note that all three NCO pilots were in this third reserve wave and this has led some historians to speculate that this may have been because they were considered of inferior standing, both socially and in terms of experience, to those in the first and second wave.[2] Yet both Townsend and Brown would prove themselves to be top-notch pilots during the raids. In fact, in some ways this reserve wave, which does not appear to have been as well briefed on some of the targets as the first and second waves and also had to be flexible enough to attack any one of a number of possible targets – their specific objective would only be advised later in the raid – perhaps had the hardest job of all.

Brown later recalled that, understandably, 'we were all frightened'. The nerves had had plenty of time to develop once the first two waves had left two and a half hours previously. There was so much time to brood once the fourteen planes of the first two waves had gone and for dark thoughts to enter the minds of these men hanging around with time on their hands, facing one of the most dangerous nights of their lives. But for them, at last the waiting had come to an end. Now they were taken out in a bus to the planes, three crews to each vehicle. Brown's crew were the third to disembark.

As the first two crews got off the bus and walked the few yards to their aircraft, Brown's rear gunner went very quiet and then said to him, 'You know those two crews aren't coming back, don't you?' Brown replied in the affirmative. Sadly, this information was correct; both crews would be dead within two hours. There was something in the manner of crews that knew they were about to die, a quietness in their attitude which hinted at a certain knowledge of their impending doom.[3]

Such sixth senses were not unheard of in such life and death situations and turned out to be accurate and prescient surprisingly often. Brown presumably did not suffer from the same heavy burden of a sense of his own impending doom but his departure from Scampton was difficult. There was no wind as the plane was taking off, which worried Brown as he felt they needed all the assistance going to get their heavy load off the ground. To him, the hedge at the end of the runway looked a thousand feet tall.

Flight Sergeant Bill Townsend in AJ-O left Scampton at 0014 and just a minute later Flight Sergeant Cyril Anderson and his crew in AJ-Y were the very last to take off. It was much darker now and the moon was past its zenith, which meant that it would be harder to see reflected light on the water en route and over the targets and navigation would be more difficult. As the night went on, this would turn out to be a major problem for Anderson and his crew in particular.

By now, Gibson was nearly at the primary target. Approaching the Möhne dam, his first wave had experienced difficulties with Hopgood's plane being shot up but still able to carry on. Behind, the other two flights in the first wave were still on course too. At 0012, Henry Maudslay's section, the third flight in Gibson's wave, made the turn at Rees and headed east. Les Knight turned with him but Bill Astell may have got confused at this point. It was now that the first wave hit further, more serious problems.

Flying Officer Harold Hobday on AJ-N (Knight's plane) had noticed that someone – Bill Astell – had strayed off too far to the right and moved away from him in an effort to make sure that he did not follow suit. This was a particularly difficult part of the route. Knight's plane suddenly came dangerously close to a pylon and just managed to avoid it; Astell was not so lucky.

In a farmhouse close to Marbeck, the residents were awoken by the sounds of aircraft flying at a very low altitude. Air raids were not unusual in the region and there was in fact a warning of one in force at the time. On many nights, they could see the airspace over the Ruhr lit up from the effect of the bombs that had rained down there. But this plane was unusually low and attracted their attention.

One of the residents ran out, just in time to see that a plane had crashed into a pylon and gone up in flames. It was Bill Astell's aircraft, which had been so low that it had almost scraped the roof of a farmhouse before hitting the pylon. The top of the pylon had been thrown off into a neighbour's yard. Everything was lit up by the burning plane, ammunition was exploding left, right and centre. The witness watched as a fiery ball burst from the wreckage and rolled about 150 metres away from the plane. It was a terrifying fiery inferno.

Even as the residents looked on in disbelief, there was a fierce explosion that shook the house to its very foundations. Only after half an hour was it possible to brave the heat of the inferno and approach the plane. When one of the bystanders did so, he could see a man in a crouched position, leaning on his hands. He was completely charred and stiff, a horrible sight. On the edge of the massive bomb crater, eyewitnesses saw several young airmen, all without outward signs of injury but all dead. Within a radius of 3 kilometres, roofs had been blown off houses, doors thrown off hinges and windows shattered in the terrific explosion that had followed the crash. The bomb had rolled about 100 yards away from the blazing plane and then gone up in a huge eruption.

This brought to a premature end an eventful and adventurous flying career. Bill Astell was born in 1920 into an upper-class family in Cheshire. He had spent much of his adolescence travelling. He began his RAF flying career in Egypt in 1941, where he flew Wellingtons. A crash in November of that year left him hospitalised for three months. Returning to duty in March the next year, he failed to return from a mission over enemy territory in May and was reported as missing in action in the conventional telegram to his family. However, he turned up five days later having crash-landed and been later picked up by Arabs.

Astell had been posted to 57 Squadron at Scampton in January 1943, when he started flying in Lancasters. Five of Astell's crew had trained together at 1654 Conversion Unit at Wigsley, being posted together to 9 Squadron on 23 December 1942. Three of them were Canadians. This time there would be no return from the dead: Astell and all his crew had gone. A local policeman later examined the site and meticulously listed any items that had survived: money, a ring, a watch, a cigarette case, keys – a pathetic but poignant set of relics that was all that remained along with bodies, some of which could not be identified, to evidence seven more lives now lost.[4]

But there was one object left undamaged. Just 50 metres from the bomb crater was a statue of St Joseph with the baby Jesus in his arms.

This was completely untouched by the explosion whilst buildings further away were damaged. Many of the locals were inclined to think this was something of a miracle.

Even as Astell and his crew were meeting their tragic end behind him, Gibson had at last reached the airspace above the Möhne dam (Martin was already there). His job now was not to move straight into the attack but to wait to coordinate the assault as the master bomber. So his plane settled in an anti-clockwise holding pattern 10 kilometres south of Völlinghausen and waited for the other planes in the first wave to catch up.

A few miles away, those responsible for the defence of the Möhne dam were still unaware that they were the intended target. The dam wall was defended by 3. Batterie/Leichte Flak-Abteilung 840 equipped with six single-barrelled 20-mm automatic cannon. Two of these were on top of the sluice towers, one on the balcony on the north side of the dam and three to the north below the dam. The guns fired armour-piercing high-explosive shells at a rate of 200 rounds a minute. Although the guns were theoretically effective at a range of up to 7,218 feet – just over a mile – in practice fire was normally commenced at a range of 3,280 feet.[5]

The Germans at the Möhne dam were completely oblivious of the attack that was about to hit them; it had been a quiet night and a normal watch of unalleviated mundane inactivity. There was no noise. But then the silence was broken by a phone ringing. They heard that an alarm had been sounded at nearby Lünn Castle. The gun crews were alerted and prepared to resist any attackers. They soon grew bored again, thinking that this was a false alarm, but were shaken from their lethargy by the sound of engines to the north coming from the direction of Soest. Maybe they might see some action after all.

Just a few miles to the south, also at 0015, Joe McCarthy had reached the vicinity of the Sorpe dam. The absence of other planes was a worry; he had after all been the last to leave. He was supposed to be the leader of this second wave which had been deputed to attack the Sorpe dam, but there were no other planes to lead. McCarthy's plane had been shot at by a battery of five 20-mm guns close to the Sorpe, but he and his crew now had the dam to themselves.

However, there were other problems facing McCarthy besides the lack of supporting planes. It was already quite misty when McCarthy reached the Sorpe. They were attacking the dam longways on, so that meant flying down the side of one steep hill and quickly up that of another on the other side of the dam; no easy task, this was flying that called for both skill and nerve. McCarthy positioned himself above the village of Langscheid to get into the right position for his assault. As he looked down far below onto the 2,100-foot-long earthen dam, he remarked, 'Jeez! How do we get down there?'

There was a church steeple in the way at the top of the hill on the way in, unexpected as it had not been identified in briefings (this is a surprise as it is quite an obvious landmark), which they hurriedly had to avoid. It was right at the crest and close to the run-in to the dam, an awkward obstacle but in its own way a useful marker for the final approach. It would take about three seconds from the moment that McCarthy dropped down to the dam below to the moment he reached the correct position to drop his bomb. This would be an incredibly difficult task.

Those attacking the Sorpe had a different allocated VHF radio frequency to those attacking the Möhne, but as it happened this was superfluous for there was no one there with McCarthy and anyway his reserve plane that had been delivered at the last minute did not have the VHF fitted as there had not been time to do so.

Precision was called for if there were to be any chance of breaching the Sorpe dam. The massive earth bank would cushion the explosion and even before the raids there had been much less confidence that the attack here would be a success. But it had been calculated that the bomb should be dropped as near as possible to the centre of the dam and about 20 feet out from it so that it could roll down the water side of the earthen wall and explode at 30 feet below the surface.

The design of the dam necessitated a different approach as it had gently sloping banks (though they were much steeper on the air side as opposed to the water side) rather than vertical walls. If the angle of attack had been the same as that employed at the Möhne and later the Eder dams, the high level of the water and the gentle slopes of the dam walls would probably have resulted in the bomb bouncing harmlessly over the top of the dam (though the power station below might have been wiped out as the one at the Möhne reservoir had). Therefore the approach was to be to fly along the dam rather than come in at right angles to it.

Given the drop down the hill that needed to be made when the attack was launched, and the hurried exit that would then be required once the weapon had been dropped, it would be very hard to release the bomb in exactly the right spot. To help him, McCarthy decided to use the church tower as a marker. They had been briefed to line up the port engine with the dam wall. But the task would be every bit as challenging as it appeared; it would take ten runs over the dam before McCarthy was happy with his dropping position.

The attack on the Sorpe was far less well rehearsed than those on the Möhne and Eder dams. Bomb-aimer George Johnson recalled that 'we had no practice on our type of attack on the Sorpe at all. We didn't know in fact what kind of attack it was going to be until the briefing. That gave us the style of attack, but the actual geography of it we didn't know until we got to the Sorpe. All our practising had been with the bouncing-bomb method at right angles to the objective. None of it had been running along the line of a dam wall.'[6] This suggests a certain lack of cohesion, maybe even confidence, in the attack on the Sorpe dam. The attack on the dam here was completely under-rehearsed compared to that on the Möhne.

Down below, some residents of the isolated community up in the hills by the Sorpe dam were already getting nervous. Josef Kesting, a machinist, was asleep in his accommodation at the Sorpe power station, at the base of the earth dam, when his wife woke him up. She told him, 'You'd better get up, a plane keeps flying over.'

Kesting went outside to investigate, where he found that several of his workmates had already gathered, also alerted by the strange actions of an aircraft in the area. Even as he looked he saw a plane approaching very low. It flew past him, less than 100 metres off. He could clearly see the distinctive rings of an English aircraft painted on the side. This not unnaturally alarmed him and he ran inside, telling his wife to grab their son and go down into the cellar of one of the company flats at the base of the dam.[7] This would of course be one of the worst places they could have been in should the dam walls be breached.

At the same time, the planes were now starting to assemble a few miles away at the Möhne dam even as, at 0016, Les Munro was arriving back over the English coast having nursed his damaged plane safely homewards. Four minutes later, Young identified Ahlen down below. His plane turned right (south-south-east), passing between the towns of Werl and Soest, where he was required to take more evasive action from flak.

As the planes moved down towards the Möhne reservoir, they got their first view of the challenge facing them. As well as the six guns placed on or near the dam, there were two anti-torpedo nets in front of it, some 6 feet apart and going down to a depth of 15 metres beneath the surface. The Germans clearly believed that this was more than sufficient to prevent any successful attack that might be attempted. There were no balloons over the dam to deter any planes though artificial trees had been placed on it to try and offer some basic camouflage; but this did nothing to deceive an attacking plane in practice (they were in fact a framework covered by netting to make them look like trees). The lack of searchlights at the Möhne dam suggested a degree of complacency on the part of the Germans, as if they could not believe that it would ever be attacked.

There were some interested observers who were about to get a grandstand view of the action that was about to unfold. A party of grammar school boys from Soest had spent the day at the lake and had stopped overnight at a hostel at Delecke on its northern shore. There were no adults supervising them overnight as so many of the teachers had been called up. The boys had enjoyed a pleasant evening and were listening to 'Lili Marlene' on a portable gramophone. It was as far away from a war zone as anyone was likely to be in Germany in 1943. It was a beautiful spot on the shores of the lake, where the only distraction during the course of the day had been the lazy flying of herons overhead.

The record had just finished when there was another noise that could be heard, this one more ominous and threatening: the low humming of engines. Then the noise grew louder until, almost overhead, it was deafening. The boys ran outside to watch and would look on spellbound on a succession of planes heading over them and low across the lake until the aircraft disappeared behind a narrow spit of land that hid the dam from the boys.[8] Delecke, where there was a road bridge across the lake, was in an inlet and they would not therefore be able to see the dam from there. However, they would have had a grandstand view of any planes that flew in to attack the dam until the crucial last few moments before the bombs were released.

Special Constable Ferdinand Nölle was on duty on the dam itself. He was supposed to be relieved by Wilhelm Strotkamp at 0020 but the latter was not there on time. When Strotkamp did at last arrive, Nölle asked him why he was so late. Strotkamp explained to him that 'I've been watching the show over on the water side.'⁹ Matters were about to take a dramatic turn.

At 0023, Gibson decided to make a dummy run on the dam. This might alert the defences on the dam itself but it had to be done so that the dangers of any forthcoming action could be better assessed. Having successfully completed this dry run, he remarked, 'I like the look of it.' Just three minutes later, 'Dinghy' Young had reached the vicinity of the Möhne dam, though of the planes in his flight Dave Shannon was slightly behind the others. David Maltby also arrived at about this time and soon all the planes of the first wave, minus Bill Astell and his crew, were now ready for action.

The VHF radio sets were switched on and preparations were now made to use them in the attack. They were only to be switched on ten minutes before they reached the attack area so as not to enable the enemy to get a 'fix' on them. The provision of these TR1143 VHF radios was soon to prove itself a vital development; the existing bomber radios, TR1196 HF R/T sets, were just not good enough for the job in hand as their objective was solely to contact the airbase; they had poor volume, suffered from extensive interference at night and became very difficult to hear over longer distances.¹⁰

The TR1143 sets on the other hand had a range of up to 150 miles, though it was less than this at lower altitudes. The new role of 'master bomber' could not work unless the man in charge of the mission was in charge of everyone else and he could not be so unless he had the right equipment. That which was provided would certainly prove itself on 17 May.

Now that they could at last see their objective, Gibson thought that in the silvery moon-rays 'it looked squat and heavy and unconquerable; it looked grey and solid in the moonlight, as though it were part of the countryside itself and just as immovable'. They would soon find themselves flying direct into flak, which would shoot out at them from along the dam's walls, 'like a battleship' as they seemed to him. The absence of searchlights subdued the light but the colours of the tracer would soon be shooting up like a deadly rainbow, green, yellow and red, attempting to bring down the impudent aircraft that were invading German airspace.¹¹

For the flak gunners at the Möhne, it was difficult at first to ascertain what was about to happen. Given Gibson's dummy run and the sounds of aircraft, they knew that there were planes in the vicinity but they could not at first see them, so they fired up some shells randomly to deter any would-be attackers. Within a very short space of time, the aircraft were firing back. The gunners were soon able to pick out the planes as distant, black, menacing shadows. The job of the gunners was about to be made easier as each plane would switch on its spotlights when it moved in for its attack.

The Möhne lake is aligned east–west. There are two main arms, cut in two by a wooded peninsula with a high point, known as the Heversburg, rising to 860 feet above sea level; the surface of the lake when full lies at a point that is 700 feet above sea level. The dam lies at the north-west corner of the lake and runs along an approximate line of north-east to south-west. The line of attack required the aircraft to line up over the Hevearm (the southern arm of the lake) and then dive down over the treetops on the Heversburg peninsula, pointing like a fingerpost towards the dam wall itself, at a speed of 220 mph.[12]

It has been calculated that reaching optimum height of 60 feet about a mile from the dam would, at the speed they were travelling, leave only 11 seconds before the dropping point was reached – not a lot of time, particularly when the aircraft were under heavy fire.[13] There were for the attackers some pleasant surprises in store though. Bomb-aimer Edward Johnson on AJ-N was amazed that there was no night fighter cover over the dam. Gibson on the other hand thought that there were night fighters but that the planes were too low for them to be spotted.[14]

The attack itself would be a real team effort. The wireless operator would be responsible for checking that the bomb was spinning at the required 500 rpm, whilst the navigator would line up the two spotlights on the water to confirm that they were at the right height. The bomb-aimer would of course be responsible for releasing the bomb from his prone position at the front of the aircraft whilst the pilot steered the plane. The engineer would be on hand to take over control of the plane if the pilot should be shot. He was also responsible for making sure that the plane was at the right speed as it made its approach for an attack whilst the gunners were waiting to see if any flak opened up – they would then return fire. The rear gunner would also be in the best position, given his vantage point, to assess the damage that the bomb had caused before anyone else as well as firing back at the anti-aircraft guns after the dam had been overflown.

The front gunner's task assumed greater importance than was normally the case at this point in an attack. The front turret was normally unmanned in the Lancaster at this stage in a raid as the chances of head-to-head confrontations with fighters was remote (the front gunner would by now usually have become the bomb-aimer in a conventional raid). However, on this occasion, with the planes flying at low level straight into flak, there was no chance of that happening. There were two .303 Browning guns at the front of the plane and four more in the rear turret. Rear-gunner Richard Trevor-Roper, who was in Gibson's AJ-G, was the squadron's gunnery leader. He had an important job to perform given the presence of flak positions around the dam. In the light of this need for guns at forward and rear, it was perhaps as well that a suggestion by a senior RAF officer made in February 1942, to get rid of the front turret in the Lancaster as it was never likely to be used in practice, was not taken up.[15]

Now that they were all on-station, Gibson would launch the first attack whilst the rest of the planes hid out in the hills a few miles off, waiting for their turn. Flight Officer Johnson in AJ-N looked on. This first attack would not be altogether encouraging; those involved in or observing it were surprised at the amount of flak, which was 'rather more than anyone had anticipated'.[16] Johnson thought that the defenders were quite heroic to carry on firing whilst the bombs were being dropped and he had a point – the impact of these massive bombs must have been terrifying when experienced close at hand. He and his comrades no doubt wished that the gunners' enthusiasm to fight back would diminish rather more quickly than it did.

At 0028 Gibson moved in to drop his bomb. The gunners defended the dam very aggressively. In preparation for the attack, Gibson's plane circled wide and over the hills at the eastern end of the lake. Then it dived down towards the waters now some two miles ahead. The crew would fly in over the Torhaus Bridge, behind the Heversberg. They would then have to hop up over the hill and then quickly down the other side before flying the last short leg to the dam itself.

By now they could see the silhouette of the two towers in front. The light was exceptional and they picked out virtually everything, though this was a dubious benefit as it would of course help the defenders too. And then the lights were switched on and Gibson looked for that perfect position, 60 feet above the surface. The spinning of the bomb had been started some 10 minutes beforehand. All was now ready. The attackers were about to prove that they had the guts and skill to deliver the bomb; all that remained was to see whether or not Wallis's science worked as well.

Pilot Officer Torger Taerum, Gibson's navigator, looked through the starboard blister window in the canopy behind the pilot. He was the only one who could see whether the lights were touching to form a 'figure of eight' or not, the moment at which the plane was at 60 feet, the exact altitude at which the bomb drop must take place. The bomb-aimer, 'Spam' Spafford, stared ahead at the dam and in particular at the basic bomb-aiming device that needed to line up with the towers on the dam to tell him that the dropping point had been reached.

They were able to get a good sight of the dam wall. But naturally enough, with the lights now on, the gunners could see them very well too. The tracer spat out from the anti-aircraft guns again, this time with a specific target in mind. The Lancaster moved on at a rate of four miles a minute towards the massive structure its crew wished to destroy, which paradoxically also bore the means of their own destruction: those persistent, angry anti-aircraft guns. A sense of fear pervaded the plane; even the practised nerves of Gibson were sensible to the fact that in a minute he might be dead. He told Pulford, sitting next to him, to be ready to take over control of the aircraft if he should be hit. It was a prospect, Gibson later admitted, that made him feel rather gloomy.[17]

There was perhaps a hint of irony in this statement, later made in Gibson's book. He described his flight engineer as 'a sincere and plodding Londoner', which is a blatant error as Pulford came from Yorkshire, a part of the country whose typical accent is very hard for anyone who listens briefly to it to confuse with that of the capital. In fact, these words were toned down by the censor from the original version in which Gibson's own words described Pulford as 'a bit of a dummy'. In the event, very little was said in the cockpit of Gibson's plane; it has often been suggested that this was because of their different social backgrounds and the fact that Pulford was 'only' an NCO. This has led one biographer of Gibson to say that the atmosphere in the cockpit reflected that of a 'master and servant' relationship.[18] Gibson allegedly also did not have a lot of time for front-gunner Deering, another NCO, either.

But at this precise moment, any personal prejudices needed to be put to one side. The moment of truth was at hand. Now 'Spam' Spafford was lining up his bomb-sight. The flak blazed on; Gibson had been through much worse but it was the lowness of the plane that preyed on the nerves; a mistake at this altitude and there would be no time to recover or bale out. He also felt that his plane was tiny compared to the vast bulk of the dam wall. But as the flak gunners continued their rapid firing, by some miracle Gibson was not hit.

Gibson was conscious of his own plane's guns spitting back at the gunners on the dam wall and the smell of burnt cordite in the cockpit as they attempted to silence the enemy and make the run-in easier for both themselves and those who were to follow. At the same time, they also had to concentrate on getting the aircraft into exactly the right position. Spafford told Gibson to make minor adjustments to left and right before, once they were in the right spot, telling him to hold the plane steady. Pulford crouched next to him, dreading the moment that he might have to take control of the plane if Gibson were hit. Almost before he knew it, they were reaching the moment of no return.

The time was now 0028. The spotlights underneath the plane had converged and the spot for releasing the bomb was rapidly approaching. Even as the flak continued to try and blow them out of the sky, Spafford released the weapon. Relieved of the 9000-lb bomb weight, the aircraft shot upwards, leaving the crew's stomachs down at water level as the plane ascended rapidly. As the plane soared up over the dam wall, rear-gunner Trevor-Roper fired at the anti-aircraft positions quickly receding in their slipstream.

Those of the crew who could see out of the plane peered into the moonlit night to see if their efforts had met with success. A red flare was fired from the plane, the pre-arranged signal to show that the bomb had been dropped. There was a massive explosion and a huge column of water spouted up towards the night sky. Even as they watched, they could see a huge plume of water 1,000 feet high still hanging in the air. Through the drizzly cloud, they could see that the surface of the water was now disturbed and turbulent, a stark contrast to the mirror-like smoothness of not long before. Water was seen rushing over the top of the dam but despite their initial optimism the wall was still as solid as ever.

When the surface of the water calmed down, no breach in the dam wall could be seen. Investigations carried out by the German authorities after the raid suggested that the bomb may have hit the torpedo net.[19]

It may also have veered off to the left, a major risk if the plane was not exactly level when the bomb was dropped or if it were released too far back from the dam. There was also an inherent risk in the bomb itself in that during the trials the smaller Highball weapon had performed with more consistency than the Upkeep device used during the dam raids.[20]

This lack of success was anyway not altogether surprising. Wallis had felt that several hits might be needed before the dam was breached and Gibson hoped that he had done his part in softening up the defences and paving the way for other planes to finish the job off. Now his job was to shepherd his flock through the rest of the assault until the dam was at last breached.

For the Germans, a sense of alarm was starting to hit home. The reaction of Clemens Köhler, an engineer in the power station behind the dam, was to run up the hill after telephoning a warning. This was no time to be staying down at low level in the shadow of the dam. It was clear now that it was the dam that these planes were after. He did not want to be down at low level should they succeed. The building was right underneath the dam and would be submerged in seconds should the wall give way.

Those on the dam were understandably badly shaken up by the huge explosion followed by the plume of water that resulted from the first bomb that had been dropped. The structure they were on was clearly the objective for the attackers and they were all that stood between the enemy and the massive masonry walls of the dam they were guarding. The sound of the explosion reverberated around them. As they waited to see whether or not the walls would hold, they were inundated with giant waves as high as houses battering the top of the dam wall.[21]

On a hill above the Möhne reservoir, Max Schulze-Sölde, an artist who lived in a house near the dam, watched as a bomber flew over. He was mesmerised as it passed close by and wondered what it was there for. Soon after the plane passed, there was a huge explosion, the blast from which threw him back into his house. Getting to his feet, he looked down at the dam but saw that it was still reassuringly intact.[22]

Soon after Gibson's bomb was dropped, the results of the first attack were Morsed back to Grantham, where Harris, Wallis and Cochrane amongst others were in attendance. The tension was already starting to build as everyone knew that the time for the attack on the dam 400 miles away was imminent. As this was the first time that the weapon had been used in anger, there was no certainty that it would work. The pressure on Wallis was enormous. He had argued for years that he could develop a bomb to breach the dam and now his bluff had been well and truly called.

If he was wrong, the personal humiliation would be enormous. His career could be ruined by failure and he was also very aware of the fact that men's lives would be lost because of him. Perhaps worst of all, there was the stern, searing face of Harris close by. Harris had never been convinced that the raid was going to work. His reaction should the raids not be a success did not bear thinking about.

Harris had after all been incensed that these inventors were putting the lives of his men at risk. What if Harris had been right all along and Wallis had been wrong? Lives would be lost and all for nothing. That surely was the worst thought of all.

Now, as the tension started to increase, the first message was received. It was 'Goner 58A'. This meant that the bomb had exploded between 5 and 50 yards short of its target. There was no report of any breach. Although this did not yet mean that the raid was bound to fail, it was also clearly not the initial success that everyone had hoped for. The tension went up another notch. So too did Wallis's nervousness whilst the granite features of Harris turned still sterner. Wallis's science remained as yet unproven and Harris's scepticism in contrast remained justified. This was going to be a long and trying night. And the news would get worse before it got better.

9

Breach of Möhne Dam: Nigger at Target X
00.31 – 01.00, Monday 17 May

With Gibson's bomb away and with no apparent impact on the dam, the first seeds of doubt were sown both amongst the aircrews above the Möhne reservoir and also those waiting for news back at Grantham. The bomb after all was experimental in design and had never been used in action before. With extreme precision required, there were tiny fractions of error involved. If the plane were not straight when the bomb was released, if it were too high or too low, if the bomb were dropped too early or too late, then there was no certainty that success would be achieved.

So many imponderables, so much that could go wrong. All of a sudden, it must have started to become apparent that this was after all in some ways still an experiment, as Wallis had said without perhaps realising the full significance of his statement. And the problem with experiments was that until they had been tried for real no one could be sure of their final conclusion.

In the meantime, those below the planes, the people who would be right in the line of the floodwaters should they be released if the bombers achieved their objective, remained oblivious to the danger they were in. Despite the fact that there were those in Germany who accepted the possibility of the dams being breached and argued that precautions should be developed to protect against such an eventuality, the authorities as a whole had remained complacent about the threat and no early-warning schemes had been developed in case the dams were breached. Hundreds of civilians would pay for that complacency with their lives.

What made it worse was that it was known by now that there were British planes in the area. It was at around 0030 that the first air-raid warning was received at Neheim, some 10 kilometres from the Möhne dam and right in the path of any floodwaters that might be released from the reservoir if the wall was breached. Leutnant Dicke, the duty officer in the police station at Neheim, had heard aircraft engines and gone out to see what was happening at around 0015. Not long after, he heard a muffled explosion. This was the first sign that something significant was starting to unfold in the region.

By now, Regierungspdirektor (Government Director) Niewisch, an important local official, had gone to Arnsberg town hall. Low-flying aircraft indicated a threat and he needed to try and establish what the raiders were trying to achieve. Clemens Köhler, the engineer from the Möhne dam, had phoned his superiors in the settlements of Niederense and Neheim, the first areas of significant population below the dams, expressing his fears should the dam be breached. However unlikely a breach might seem, no one was in any doubt as to what its consequences would be.

But the consistent feature about much of the German response to the attacks was its misplaced sense of security. The response to Köhler from the authorities at Neheim was not to worry them with fairy tales.[1] There was a similar reaction from elsewhere, or perhaps non-reaction would be a more appropriate description. There were, for example, night fighters at the nearby base of Werl, just a few miles away (they could have been at the dam in minutes) but none of them were scrambled during the raid. The German authorities carried on in blissful ignorance of just how much danger the inhabitants of the Möhne valley and the wider Ruhr region were in.

The fear of night fighters was a real one for the raiders, but the British planes in the vicinity of the Möhne dam remained completely undisturbed. Now that he had dropped his bomb without success, Gibson had to revert to his role of master bomber. He had to wait for a few minutes after the bomb was dropped before the next attack could be launched. First of all, he needed to establish whether the wall had been breached or not. Then he had to wait for the waters to calm down after being whipped up by the massive explosion, otherwise the bomb would not run true across the surface.

After a short wait, it became apparent that there was clearly no breach. By 0033, Gibson was happy that the time was now right for the next plane to move into the attack, that of his close confidant 'Hoppy' Hopgood. Gibson signalled the code word 'Cooler 2' over the VHF radio. This was the signal for Hopgood to launch his attack, 'Cooler' being the code to do so and the '2' being the number of the plane in the flight that was assigned to Hopgood's aircraft, meaning that in the master plan he was to move in next. As Hopgood got into position, Gibson radioed across the reassuring message that 'it's a piece of cake'.

But in the event, it was anything but. The turbulence of the water had died away but the flak gunners on the dam were now fully aware of what to expect next. Gibson had enjoyed the element of surprise; Hopgood would not. Gibson watched on with concern as 'Hoppy' and his crew followed the same route in as he had a few minutes before. Anxious minutes lay ahead.

The German defenders were ready but there was a great deal of nervousness present amongst them now that they realised that the dam they were guarding was clearly the objective of the British bombers they could dimly see without the benefit of searchlights. Nearby, Ferdinand Nölle had now been joined, and theoretically relieved, by Wilhelm Strotkamp. Nölle warned him not to go down into the galleries built into the dam. He was afraid that he would be drowned if he did so. In the event, Nölle would not be going anywhere; he could see that he was still needed where he was.

Karl Schütte, who was in charge of the guns on Tower 1, told his men to prepare for the attack. Hopgood got into position and lined up his plane for the assault. He got his plane into exactly the right spot for the approach as far as he was able, ensured that it was at the right height and set course for the dam. Aiming for the midpoint between the two towers he ploughed on as if oblivious to the flak now directed at him. The spotlights beneath his plane were now on, lighting it up as a target for the gunners.

A screen of flak was thrown up, a seemingly impenetrable barrier through which Hopgood and his men had to pass if they wished to claim their prize. It would not be easy. Long lines of shells spat up into the sky above the calm waters of the reservoir, homing in with unerring accuracy on the cumbersome Lancaster as it trundled determinedly towards the dam walls. As Hopgood hurtled closer, Schütte saw the tracer clearly hit the plane. Then a flame billowed out. Exhilarated, Schütte shouted out, 'It's burning! It's burning!' He later recalled that 'a great cheer went up, just like when you've scored'.[2]

But the exultation was short-lived, for a massive explosion soon followed, with stones flying everywhere and the gunners on the dam being thrown to the ground. When the defenders looked behind them, the power station that had once stood at the base of the massive edifice was nowhere to be seen; all that remained was a pile of smoking rubble. To the north-west, a more distant explosion told of a crashed aircraft.

All this appeared to happen in seconds, but for those involved it seemed a lifetime. The artist Max Schulze-Sölde, now wide awake, had been looking on as Hopgood approached the dam. Even as he watched the plane disappear over the hills to be followed by a violent cacophony as it crashed, the power station went up in front of him. Wilhelm Strotkamp was much closer to the action; he was on watch at the dam. When he saw the planes beginning their attack, he ran for shelter in a tunnel under the dam wall, just about the worse place he could have gone as it happened.[3]

What had actually happened in these few dramatic minutes was this. As Hopgood had been aiming his plane like an arrow for the heart of the dam, the tracer had started to hit home. Both port engines had been hit and all power to the rear turret had been lost. Then the tracer had seriously damaged the starboard wing and a fire also broke out in one of the starboard engines. These were, taken together, devastating blows and left the plane with little chance of survival, especially as it may have been damaged by flak earlier on in the raid.

But the plane had still ploughed on despite the hits that had been suffered. Now they were close to the dam wall. At this moment bomb-aimer Jim Fraser released the bomb. It was past the point at which he should have done so but it is not clear whether the late release was because of an error on Fraser's part or because he already realised that the plane was in serious trouble and the last thing they wanted was over 6,000 lb of explosive left on board should the plane crash. Better anyway to cause some damage to the dam than none at all. Dropping the bomb in the right place now anyway became an irrelevance because it was obvious that the plane would not be up to making another run in to get in the right place. It was now a question of survival for those on board.

As the bomb had been dropped later than it should have been, it bounced right over the wall (which was fairly low above the surface of the lake given the high levels of the water in the reservoir) and down into the power station that was behind it. A massive explosion followed that created chaos in the building. Fortunately for Wilhelm Strotkamp he had realised the error of his ways and had already started to make his way up the hill. As the power station blew up, great chunks of masonry showered down around him.[4] Given the proximity of the bomb strike and the large mass of explosive that the weapon had been carrying, he was very lucky to survive.

In his position in the nose of the plane as it staggered along, Fraser had been conscious of a tremendous crash on board the aircraft and a fire then breaking out. It was initially extinguished but then took hold again. As Hopgood struggled to gain height and fly over the hills behind the dam, the gunners on the wall could see the plane aflame.

Minchin, Hopgood's wireless operator, mortally wounded and with his leg virtually severed, still managed to fire off the Very light to confirm that the bomb been released which showed an incredible sense of duty and clear thinking given the state that he was in. The plane was now doomed. The fire in the starboard engine could not be extinguished and all that remained was to bale out. This was particularly difficult for Burcher who had to crank his rear turret back into position by hand as hydraulic power was no longer available to do it automatically. He needed to get back into the plane to get his parachute on as it could not be worn in the rear turret due to lack of space.

The recommended escape route would then be to get back into the rear turret and get out through there after cranking it round but that would take too long as the plane, even after attempting to gain height, was only a few hundred feet off the ground and could crash into it within seconds. Therefore he decided to take the only other practical way out; through the starboard side entry door.[5]

Burcher cranked his turret around as quickly as possible to reach his parachute back in the main fuselage. Despite the extreme seriousness of the situation, discipline and training kicked in; he got to the intercom and told Hopgood he was about to jump – 'Get out, you bloody fool!' came the reply. Hopgood's last words were, 'If only I had another 300 feet – I can't get any more height.'[6]

As he did this, a terrible sight met him. His friend John Minchin had managed to drag himself over the main spar and into the main fuselage. With his leg hanging off and having to be dragged along behind him when he did this, the strength of will required to perform this act despite the agonising pain he must have been in can only be imagined. Burcher put a parachute on Minchin before pushing him through the door, holding on to the ripcord to ensure that it opened once Minchin was out of the plane. Sadly, his heroism was in vain as Minchin would not survive his terrible injuries.

Having done his own heroic part in trying to save Minchin, Burcher could now worry about himself. It is not clear whether Burcher jumped out of the plane or was blown out by an explosion but in any event he managed to bale out. In fact, he was unconscious during the climactic following moments. His parachute failed to deploy fully but did so enough to slow down his descent sufficiently for him to survive. When he came to, he was lying on the ground. On the short journey down, he had clipped the tail-plane and broken his back. He now lay there helpless and all he could do was wait until he was captured.

Burcher's terror was not yet over, for he could not be sure that, if the dam were breached, he would not be in the line of the floods with no possibility of moving himself out of their path. But he would in the event survive and be taken into captivity, where he would be harshly cross-examined and lose several teeth in the process; he was later interred in Stalag Luft III, famous as being the setting for the 'Great Escape', where he managed to obtain some false teeth made of toilet porcelain.

Pilot Officer J. W. Fraser, a Canadian, was the only other survivor. He had unpacked his parachute as quickly as possible inside the confined space at the front of the stricken Lancaster but was horrified when he opened the hatch in the floor to see how close the treetops were. If his parachute did not open instantly he was doomed. He fell from, rather than jumped out, of the plane and his 'chute was barely opened before he hit the ground with a thud. He had witnessed the tail-wheel whistle past him as he was in the air.

Nearby, Gibson had been watching on horrified as the action unfolded. He was able to see Hopgood's plane with one of the fuel tanks ablaze. Then the plane had exploded. He had witnessed Hopgood's attempts to gain height and then at an altitude of about 500 feet saw an explosion lighting up the sky and a wing blown off. The rest of the plane disintegrated and fell to the ground, still burning like stars that had fallen from the sky.[7]

Hopgood's plane crashed into the ground a few miles north of the Möhne dam, near the village of Ostönnen on the road between Soest and Werl. It came to rest in a farmer's field, an unremarkable and mundane place to meet a hero's end. Today a small plaque still marks the spot, not far from where motorway traffic hurries past, oblivious to the drama that was played out nearby.

Five men had lost their lives and Burcher lay incapacitated on the ground. However, one man from Hopgood's plane still had an opportunity to escape. John Fraser's war was not yet over. He managed to run off after landing in a cornfield. Miraculously he had barely a scratch on him. He would stay a free man for ten days, heading for the Netherlands and living off potatoes and turnips. However, he was then captured and also sent to Stalag Luft III, where he would actually play a part in the renowned 'Great Escape'. Having been married for just seventeen days when the raid took place, Fraser returned home unannounced after the war ended. His wife Doris fainted when she saw him. It was tragically ironic that he would die in 1962 in a plane crash.[8]

Fraser would be thoroughly interrogated before being sent off into captivity. A full report of the interrogation was sent to Hermann Goering, dated 19 June 1943.[9] It suggests that Fraser handed over a lot of information, perhaps under some duress. However, it is not clear how honest Fraser was being, as he suggested that the bomb was spinning at 380 revolutions per minute though he had earlier on suggested it had been 400–500 (it was of course 500 and perhaps Fraser was being deliberately evasive).

He also told the Germans that the release point was 900 feet from the dam wall when in fact it was 450 yards, or 1,350 feet – as a bomb-aimer Fraser was probably very well acquainted with the exact distances involved. He further said that he could not give any information about where the final practice runs were held. He also gave the airspeed at release as 260 mph, which was too fast though he did give the correct height at which the bomb should be dropped: 60 feet. He said to his interrogator that Maudslay's bomb-aimer was Flying Officer Tytherleigh, which was also incorrect: he was his front gunner. The interrogating officer noted that 'F is very proud of his involvement in the raid on the dams' and it is not hard to imagine him playing a dangerous little game with his inquisitors by giving them information that was wrong but no so wrong as to be transparently ridiculous.

Fraser and Burcher's interrogation after their capture was a routine activity when aircrew were captured. The Germans built up substantial files on RAF activities and personnel (this was one reason, perhaps the main one, why Harris did not want his senior commanders accompanying their men on missions). As Burcher's experience shows, the interrogators were not afraid to dispense with niceties in the quest for valuable information. Although three men would survive their aircraft crashing that night and be taken into captivity, their ordeal was far from over.

But proper respect was at least shown to those who lost their lives. The bodies of the five dead airmen from the remains of Hopgood's shattered aircraft (which was almost completely obliterated in the crash) were later recovered and buried with full military honours at 1130 on 20 May at a cemetery in Soest. Their remains were ultimately exhumed and reburied at a military cemetery at Rheinberg on 14 August 1947.

Gibson also witnessed the explosion caused by Hopgood's bomb. Even as Gibson and his crew watched the last moments of 'Hoppy' and AJ-M, there was a massive blast from down below. It went up behind the power station with a tremendous explosion, which was followed by a large pall of smoke hanging in the air over it. This obscured visibility and meant that time would be needed to let the smoke clear before another attack could be made on the still intact dam. It was interesting that Gibson's account suggests that the bomb exploded after Hopgood crashed; presumably the 90-second self-destruct mechanism was working.

Hopgood was just twenty-two years old when he died but was already something of a veteran. He had previously been with 106 Squadron, regarded as one of 5 Group's best. He had flown his first two Lancaster sorties in thousand-bomber raids over Cologne and Essen in May 1942 and had completed forty-six missions with 106 Squadron and been awarded the DFC when he transferred to Syerston, where he test-piloted the new Mark II Lancaster. He had been awarded a Bar to his DFC and officially joined the newly formed 617 Squadron on 30 March 1943.

He became a very close colleague of Gibson, who would feel his loss keenly. But he would not be forgotten. John Fraser returned to Canada after the war and named his son John Hopgood Fraser after the man who had given him the opportunity to save his own life.[10] Hopgood's valiant last efforts had after all not been in vain.

Despite the early release of the weapon from Hopgood's plane, the blast had, however, made an important contribution which would help the other planes that still had to make their attack. The gun posted on the left-hand sluice tower was blown from its footings in the explosion that demolished the power station and was rendered useless. The crew of the now redundant flak position ran along the still undamaged top of the wall to help the crew of the right-hand tower gun with the movement of ammunition. The blast had also knocked out electricity in the valley below the power station.[11]

Whilst the rest of Gibson's flight waited their turn to attack the dam, the first plane to arrive back in England, that of Les Munro, was landing at Scampton at 0036. With his radio out of action, he could not communicate with the control tower and therefore had to use his own initiative to land. This came as something of a surprise to those waiting back at base for whom the time was passing dreadfully slowly.

Adjutant Humphries had been spending the time talking to a WAAF, Second Officer Fay Gillon. The men liked having her around. She was pretty and Humphries later noted that such qualities, despite popular perceptions about glamorous WAAFs, were in short supply. Then they heard the unexpected drone of an aircraft overhead: it was Munro returning. Seeing that his bomb was still attached, they knew that his raid had been unsuccessful. Munro was understandably furious that he had been unable to complete his mission. Munro and later Rice, who arrived back at 0047, joined those waiting anxiously for news of the rest of the squadron. They and their crews would at least live to fight another day.

For Rice in particular the return trip had been a nerve-wracking one due to the damage done to his plane and he was forced to circle around Scampton for 20 minutes whilst some of the crew hand-cranked the wheels down. Then, just as he was about to land, Munro – who was of course unable to communicate with anyone given his damaged radio equipment – had cut across in front of him, delaying Rice's landing. Without a tail-wheel, which had been damaged in the close encounter with the ocean, it was also a bumpy landing and more damage was done to the plane.[12]

Back at the Möhne, the next plane now prepared to make its run on the dam. Gibson must have been distressed by the loss of Hopgood but as a consummate professional kept his emotions in check. The crews yet to make a run now had to cope not only with the flak they knew was waiting to give them a warm reception, but also the far from welcome sight of the wreckage of Hopgood's plane burning in the hills in the near distance, a disturbing reminder of their own mortality and the risks that they were about to take.

Gibson was also of course aware that two bombs had now been dropped and the dam remained stubbornly intact. Although he would have realised that Hopgood's bomb had overshot the dam, the fact that the huge explosion had left the vast bulk of the structure unmoved ratcheted up the tension another notch.

It was Mick Martin who had the unenviable task of being next in line. At 0038 he moved in for the third attack on the Möhne dam with the moon shining on his port beam. The flak was still strong despite being one gun down by now. In order to help Martin, Gibson was flying close by, trying to give support and distract fire. However, Martin's run was not helped by the fact that there was still smoke over the target from the last attack by Hopgood.

On the dam wall, Karl Schütte and his comrades prepared to repulse the next assault. Buoyed by their success in bringing down Hopgood, they were determined to play their part in beating off the raid. At first they were distracted by Gibson's plane on the wing, but then Martin dropped down and headed straight for the wall. The flak gunners once more homed in on the plane and, according to Schütte, 'again the shells whipped towards the attacker and several hits were scored'.[13]

But the plane spat back at the flak guns, the tracer 'like a string of pearls, the luminous spur of the shells came towards the tower like large glow-worms', as Schütte put it.[14] The special night tracer lit up the moonlit sky as it spat out towards the defenders of the dam; it was so dazzling that a number of pilots expressed dissatisfaction with it after the raid and it was one part of the mission which seems to have divided opinion as to how efficacious it was.[15] Inexorably, Martin and AJ-P moved in on the dam. When bomb-aimer Bob Hay thought they were in the right spot, he released the weapon.

They waited to see what impact their weapon would have. However, it did not find its target. A German report after the raid noted that the bomb did not hit the wall but exploded near the bank about 100 metres from it – British accounts record it as 20 yards short.[16] The swell from the blast caused water to spill over the top but there was little damage to the nearby inn other than some windows blown in as a result of the blast. The starboard outer fuel tank and ailerons of AJ-P were damaged by cannon fire, but Martin managed to return safely to base despite the fact that he lost all the petrol from one of his wing-tanks.

So that was now three bombs away and still no sign of a breach. The huge plume of water when the bomb was dropped obscured the view of Martin's observer, the rear gunner Flight Sergeant Simpson, who was trying to watch how many times that the bomb bounced but could not see. Wallis was aware that the cylindrical shape of the bomb made it vulnerable to going off course if it hit the surface at the wrong angle and possibly the bomb had been dropped when the plane was not quite 'flat' in the air, causing the weapon to veer off.

It may be significant too that Martin's plane was carrying the bomb accidentally dropped on the hard standing at Scampton that morning and that might have affected the trueness of its course. However, he might also have banked slightly at the last moment to get the right bearing. In any event, the bomb veered into a narrow inlet and exploded without any real effect.

But the attacks were also taking a toll on the flak gunners. The barrels of their guns were overheating because of the fierce fire they were directing at the planes swooping down on them; but the barrels were swapped and the weapons were oiled. The attackers were of course unaware of these problems and there were now concerns expressed amongst the British crews that the dam was still apparently as strong as ever; Dave Shannon later said that there was some disappointment at this stage that the dam had not yet been breached, which must rank as something of an understatement.[17]

It was now the turn of 'Dinghy' Young to take his run at the dam. Gibson warned Young to beware of the flak, which was very hot. He moved his plane to the other side of the dam in a successful attempt to distract the gunners' attention – he even switched his identification lights on so that they would divert the attention of the gunners onto his plane, hoping to give Young a clearer run in as a result.

Young went through a similar routine to the other pilots as he prepared his run in. Martin was now flying on one side of Young whilst Gibson flew over the wall with his lights on to confuse and draw the fire of the defenders. As the moon shone down from behind the aircraft (several pilots remarked that it would have been better ahead of rather than behind them) Young flew low over the water, his front gunner Gordon Yeo exchanging gunfire with the flak gunners, who were sticking manfully to their task. In what appeared to be exactly the right spot, bomb-aimer Vincent MacCausland released the weapon at 0043. It skimmed across the surface of the water and bounced into the dam wall. There was an almighty explosion and a massive plume of water that shot up hundreds of feet.

Young was euphoric. Everything seemed to have gone like clockwork. He could not yet see through the misty veil of the water that was showering back down over the dam walls. He could not assess with certainty whether the dam had been breached or not but he was certain that it had. Gibson though, closely watching on from AJ-G, believed that it was not and that it would take at least one more attack. It was Gibson who was right. Code 78A was Morsed back to Grantham – 'bomb despatched and hit wall but no breach observed'.

No doubt the wording of Operation Chastise's operation order now started to hit home: 'Destruction of the dam may take some time to become apparent, and careful reconnaissance may be necessary to distinguish between breaching of the dam and the spilling over the top which will follow each explosion.' Plenty of water had been seen spouting up into the air and over the dam wall but there was still no breach apparent. Young's attack appeared to be textbook and the question that was now being asked by virtually everyone in Gibson's flight was whether the plan would work at all.

There was nothing for Gibson to do but be persistent and continue to send his men into the assault and continue to hammer away at the dam. At 0048 David Maltby was given the OK by Gibson to begin his run. His navigator Vivian Nicholson noted 'flak none too light'. This time Gibson would fly off his right wing and Martin on his left.[18]

By 0049 Maltby was moving in for his attack. The luck of the British pilots was about to change. Just now the AA gun fired by Schütte had jammed after a premature explosion in the barrel. His crew tried to clear it away with a hammer and a metal spike but to no avail. Whilst one other gun was still active, the other men left could only fire back with basic weapons now. During the fifth attack, some of the defenders therefore used their carbines. Now that the defenders had only one gun left, the attacking planes had things pretty much to themselves. And

Above left: 1. The Battle of Britain flight's PA474, one of the last flying examples of the great bomber left. *Above right*: 2. A Lancaster assembly line in full swing. Over 7,000 of the bombers took part in the Second World War. 3,500 of them were lost on operations.

3. An unusual profile shot of an airborne Lancaster.

4. The Lancaster cockpit, the cramped home of the pilot and flight engineer for hours at a time.

Left: 5. A cross-section of a 'conventional' Lancaster bomber from a 1940s aircraft recognition manual.

Above: 6. A ground crew, 'unsung heroes' of Bomber Command, looking over a Lancaster after it has returned from a raid.

Below: 7. A Lancaster III bomber in the air. This model was equipped with Rolls Royce Merlin 28 engines, a significant improvement on the Merlin 20 which it replaced.

Top left: 8. A large 4,000 lb bomb being loaded onto a Lancaster. As the war progressed, more and more attention was paid to the use of ever larger weapons to deliver maximum impact.
Above right: 9. A Lancaster bomber being loaded with 500 lb explosives before setting out on a raid.
Above Left: 10. A long-service Lancaster being filled up with high explosive bombs. 'S' for 'Sugar' shown here dropped over one million lbs. of explosive during the war.
Below: 11. A large bomb being loaded into a Lancaster before another dangerous mission over Germany.

12. A conventional Lancaster in flight. This photo gives an interesting contrast to the 'Dambusters' model, which can be easily distinguished by the lack of the mid-turret gun position and also the bomb which would have been dangling inelegantly beneath it.

Below: 13. The view looking out from an airborne Lancaster.
Left: 14. The rear gunner's seat, probably the most exposed, dangerous and uncomfortable of any on board the Lancaster.

Above right: 15. An impressive view of a conventional Lancaster in flight. Most, but not all, of those involved in the 'Dambusters' raids had learnt their craft thoroughly on one of these before taking part.
Above left: 16. An impressive and boffin-like Barnes Wallis at his desk.

Centre: 17. An Upkeep bomb being dropped in a practice run shortly before the raids departed. *Above*: 18. Lancaster ED817 which was used for testing bombs at Reculver before the raids.

Left: 19. The 'bouncing bomb' fitted to the undercarriage of Guy Gibson's aircraft, ED932. Some wags christened the planes 'pregnant ducks' because of the ungainly profile of the specially converted Lancasters.

Above: 22. The Petworth House Hotel at Woodhall Spa, used in the war by 617 Squadron as their mess.

Above: 20. Aircraft ED825, the last minute spare ferried up from Boscombe Down on the day of the raids and commandeered by Joe McCarthy for his raid on the Sorpe dam when his original plane malfunctioned.

Left: 21. The Chesil Beach in Dorset where many of the early bomb experiments took place.

23. A Lancaster bomber waiting to depart on another raid on Berlin; such mass attacks were at the heart of 'Bomber' Harris's wartime strategy and he saw the dam raids as an unwelcome distraction.

Above left: 24. A heavy raid over Berlin, with the sky lit up by searchlights – an insight into the dangerous lives lived by the aircrews from a period illustration. The fliers lived in fear of being caught in one of the searchlights and at least one plane flown by the 'Dambusters' may have been lost when the pilot was dazzled by one.

Above right: 25. An aircraft being shot at by flak: the low levels flown by the 'Dambusters' meant that they were immune from heavy flak but they were very vulnerable still to being shot up by lighter weapons. Period Illustration.

26. The view of the Möhne dam that the pilots had as they reached the bombing position.

27. The Möhne dam brilliantly lit up by the full moon.

28. The airside of the Möhne dam, showing where the breach occurred between the two towers.

29. The village of Günne, first in line for the Möhne flood.

30. Waldeck Castle, the marker point high above the Eder dam, giving some idea of how steep a drop faced the pilots as they moved in.

Right: 31. The airside of the Eder dam, showing where the massive breach occurred.

Below: 34. A bomb aimer, finger poised ready to release his weapon. This action called for precision during the raids on the dams as the bomb needed to be dropped in exactly the right spot if it were to be effective.

Above: 32. The shallow earth banks of the Sorpe dam. A very different proposition to the Möhne and the Eder with their massive masonry walls.

Below: 33. The village of Langscheid above the Sorpe dam. McCarthy and Brown lined up on the church steeple as they moved in for the attack.

Right: 35. Another period illustration showing the Lancaster in action on the 'Dambuster' raid.

Top left: 36. A control room in action. Coordinating the raids from a distance could be a difficult task given the difficulties of long-distance communication and for a time proved very frustrating during the night of the dam raids.

Above left: 37. Listening out for bombers on their way back from a raid. This was a tense time as those left behind in Britain waited with concern to see how many bombers would return.

Above right: 39. Wing Commander Guy Gibson in strikingly confident pose.

38. Guy Gibson's crew being debriefed on their successful return from the raids on the Möhne and Eder dams. Behind some of his crew stand Sir Arthur Harris (left) and Ralph Cochrane.

Above Left: 41. Joe McCarthy, the larger than life American who joined the RAF before the US was in the war and led a spirited, if ultimately unsuccessful, assault on the Sorpe dam on the night of the raids.

Top right: 42. Flight Lieutenant David Shannon and his crew shortly before he joined 617 Squadron. Shannon enjoyed an excellent rapport with Gibson.

Above right: 43. Flight Sergeant Ken Brown and crew shortly before joining 617 Squadron. Brown was part of the reserve force which carried out the last manoeuvres of the dam raids.

40. The crew of Flight Lieutenant Wilson who missed the raids due to illness but were wiped out during the disastrous attack on the Dortmund-Ems Canal a few months later.

Top left: 44. The diminutive David Shannon (left) towered over by Gibson's rear gunner Flight Lieutenant Trevor-Roper (centre). On the right is Squadron Leader George Holden who replaced Gibson as the commanding officer of 617 Squadron and died shortly after in the Dortmund-Ems Canal raid.

Above left: 46. Flight Lieutenant David Maltby looks over some post-raid publicity materials with Gibson. Maltby would also have his career cut tragically short by the Dortmund-Ems Canal raid.

Above right: 47. Gibson teasing Nigger with the prospect of a pint.

45. The crew of Flight Lieutenant Joe McCarthy, minus Flying Officer Rodger, the rear gunner.

48. King George VI enthusiastically goes over details of the raids with Gibson.

Top right: 50. Ken Brown meets the king at Scampton during the royal visit to Scampton on 27 May 1943.
Above right: 49. Flight Lieutenant Mick Martin, left, next to Station Commander Charles Whitworth, talks to the king after the raids. The Australian Martin went on to enjoy a successful RAF career after the raids.

51. Waiting for the medal ceremony at Buckingham Palace. The RAF crew members are (from left to right) Walker (in Shannon's crew), Deering (Gibson's), Hewstone (Brown's), Taerum (Gibson's), Oancia (Brown's), Ken Brown, Feneron (in Brown's crew) and Joe McCarthy. Some of them look slightly happier to be there than others, which given the exuberant celebrations the night before is perhaps not surprising.

Above: 52. After the medal ceremony at Buckingham Palace. Eve Gibson stands next to her husband whilst next to her whilst to her right stand Toby Foxlee, Jack Leggo and Bob Hay, all members of Mick Martin's crew.
Left: 53. Scampton airbase, now home to the Red Arrows aerobatics team, from where 617 Squadron took off on the night of 16 May 1943.

Above left: 54. Squadron Leader Joe McCarthy in later life at the Derwent Dam, an important location in 617 Squadron's training programme.
Above centre: 55. Squadron Leader Les Munro in 1993. With his plane damaged early in the raid, Munro had been forced to return to Scampton before reaching the dams.
Above right: 57. The memorial to Pastor Berkenkopf who lost his life in the flood that engulfed the Porto Coeli convent.

Above left: 56. The outlook beneath the Sorpe dam, showing the area that stood to be deluged if the reservoir banks were breached.

Above right: 58. An aerial view of the breached Möhne dam. The sandy areas at the sides of the reservoir give a vivid indication of how much water had flowed out given the fact that the lake should have been at its fullest at this time of year.

Above left: 59. A post-raid reconnaissance photo of a badly affected area of the Ruhr Valley.
Above right: 60. The massive breach in the Eder dam after it had been hit. The attack on the Eder, although an operational success, did not contribute significantly to the damage caused by the raids and was considered by some, such as Albert Speer, to be a strategic mistake.

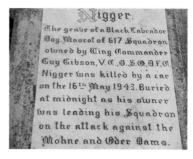

Above left: 61. The Eder dam after the raid. In the top right hand corner of the photo is the basin at the foot of the dam. Fortunately, as the area was less populated and there was a better early warning system, far fewer civilian lives were lost here than as a result of the Möhne attack.
Above right: 62. The grave of Nigger at Scampton.

DIE OPFER DER
MÖHNESEEKATASTROPHE 17·5·1943
GEORG BREDDEL   ALOIS FISCHER
BERNHARD GIERING   MARIA GIERING
LUISE GERLITZ   MARIA GRAF   ELSBETH GRAF
RESI GRAF   THERESIA HEITMANN
SOPHIA JASNIEWICZ   JOHANNES KOHLER
CAROLINE KOHLER   CHRISTINE KOHLER
HEINR. KOHLER   BERTA KOHLER   JOH. KOHLER
MARIANNE KOHLER   WILH. NEUSCHWENDER
ANNA NEUSCHWENDER   MARIA NEUSCHWENDER
THERESIA RAHMANN   FRANZISKA SCHNEIDER
FRANZ SCHNEIDER   FRIEDA SCHWARZER
ANNA STOCK   ROSA WEIDREICH
LONI WEGMANN   BERNHARD WERLEUKER

Above left: 63. The memorial to those killed at Günne, the village right below the Möhne dam.
Top left: 64. The church of St John the Baptist in Neheim where hundreds of bodies were laid out after the flood swamped much of the town.
Above right: 65. The memorial to the dead of Neheim.
Below: 66. The simple cross that marks the ruins of the Porto Coeli convent.

even this last flicker of resistance was soon extinguished by gunfire from the planes.[19]

Maltby was now charging over the surface of the water towards the dam. As he got closer, he was all of a sudden certain that he could see a minor breach in the dam. There was debris on the crest of the dam and he thought he could also see a small hole in its structure. Again his approach was textbook, though he turned slightly to port when he saw what he thought was a breach in the wall already. The bomb was released at what his bomb-aimer, John Fort, believed to be exactly the right spot. It hit the water and spun across it, bouncing true and straight. Like a dart it headed for the massive fortress-like walls of the dam in their path. The bomb hit home and a huge explosion reverberated around the shores of the reservoir.

The British pilots looked on with baited breath. But then, more disappointment. Maltby stared down through a plume of water that he estimated to be 1,000 feet high silhouetted against the moon, but as it started to settle he could see no breach in the wall and another '78A' message was sent. Neither could Gibson see anything because of the smoke and the water plumes, so Dave Shannon was ordered up to go next.

Schütte and his comrades were now virtually powerless to resist, but they had continued to look on as if they could bring down by willpower alone the attacking aircraft piloted by Maltby. Schütte had stood defiantly on his tower, with the lake in front of him, the valley behind, and under attack from all directions. It was, according to him, now child's play for the pilot whose outline he could almost see in the cockpit of the aircraft. As the bomb dropped, the lake quivered once more and a giant wave developed.

Ferdinand Nölle had stubbornly stuck around to see how the raid developed and had been going through a harrowing experience as a result. He recalled that 'each explosion in the lake was followed by a massive blast. Once I shot three metres across the duty room and bashed my head against a door. It was a good job I was wearing a steel helmet otherwise I'd have my head smashed in. This explosion was worse than anything I'd experienced at Verdun. Strotkamp arrived in the duty room out of breath from below the dam where I'd been on duty. All the windows had been blown out of the duty room and the lights had gone out.'[20]

Like Gibson and Maltby, Schütte too waited to see what would happen to the dam wall. Of course, being closer to the action than any of the attackers he was quite possibly the first to see for sure what the effect of the bomb had been. As visibility improved, Schütte looked at the dam and saw, perhaps before anyone else, that it was breached. Even as he watched, the water poured through the hole in its centre which was getting visibly bigger by the second. There was now no doubt about it – the dam had gone.[21]

Wilhelm Strotkamp had been making his way up the hill towards safety and had sheltered behind a tree when he heard another explosion, but this one was ominously different than the ones he had heard previously. As he watched he saw that the dam wall appeared to be trembling, almost as if it were a living being. Then to his horror and disbelief he had seen the wall start to split. Then the cracks began to widen and, before he could make sense of it all, what had been a small gap looked as if it were a barn door being opened.

Ferdinand Nölle was increasingly horrified by what he saw. Then a phone rang, which he answered. It was the authorities in Soest asking what was going on. He told them about the breach and suggested that they warn those in the valley; there was nothing more he could do.[22] Soest and its immediate environs would be safe due to its location but for those living in the Möhne valley a terrifying night was unfolding. The only hope was to arrange an evacuation of the narrow and confined valley as quickly as possible. But for many it was already too late. Nölle looked back below the dam but he could see nothing save a fog of spray from the water that was now pouring through the breach.[23]

The boys on the northern lakeshore at Delecke could not see the dam itself but they could work out what was happening to some extent from the noise and also from observing the planes in the early part of their run. Walter Fischer and his mates had watched as

> again and again the bombers flew at the dam wall, blazing away with all guns and churning up great streaks of vapour which were drawn along behind them. Then behind the spit of land brilliant white plumes of water shot straight up into the air followed shortly afterwards by an explosion. The fifth time there was a muffled thundering explosion. We all thought the dam had been hit.
>
> We ran over there from Delecke [a couple of miles down the road and fortunately for them above the dam] as fast as we could. A hole had been torn

in the crest of the dam and you could easily have put a block of flats into it. The water from the Möhne flowed quietly through the breach, but down in the valley it thundered up. The crashing of the water caused the roadway along the top of the dam to vibrate. I thought back to the song that we'd been listening to on our beds in the rowing club when the whole gruesome business began. There's a line in *Lili Marlene* about the whirling fog. But now a fog of doom had descended over the places in the valley which had been hit by the disaster. [24]

There was remarkable confirmation of the more or less exact time that the dam was breached. The Institut für Geophysik at Göttingen was about 120 kilometres to the north of the Möhne. The Institut had a seismograph that was sensitive enough to pick up the shockwaves from the bombs exploding under the surface at the dam. This timed the decisive explosion at the Möhne at 0049 and 40.5 seconds which, given a time lag of around 20 seconds due to the distance that the Institut was from the dam, allows an exact time for the decisive strike to be established. [25]

As the breach became obvious to those on the wall, so too did it become clear to the attackers. Gibson was just getting ready to coordinate Shannon's attack when a voice from elsewhere in the plane suddenly shouted, 'I think she has gone!'

Shannon was about to start out on his run when Gibson told him to hold off whilst he went to have a closer look at the situation. He too could see without a doubt that the dam was breached. He believed that the breach was about 150 feet in extent. He thought that the water pouring through was like 'stirred porridge'.

Others too could see the situation rapidly unfolding. The injured Burcher watched on from the hills, afraid that he would be overwhelmed by the flood whilst Schütte looked on helplessly as the water cascaded down the valley. From above, pilots could see headlights extinguished as the water rolled over vehicles trapped in its path. 'I saw their headlights burning and I saw water overtake them, wave by wave, and then the colour of the headlights underneath the water changing from light blue to green, from green to dark purple, until there was no longer anything except the water bouncing down in great waves,' Gibson said as the horror that he and his men had unleashed started to overwhelm the land below the dam. [26]

This was not the only action going on at around this time. Just a few minutes before, a very different scene had been played out at the

Sorpe dam. For half an hour now McCarthy had been flying up and down trying to get the right run in to it. He also waited in vain for other planes to join him. In fact, the scene at the Sorpe could not be more different than that at the Möhne. There were no defences and the world was sleeping. McCarthy had the skies to himself.

As well as the difficult approach to the attack, McCarthy was also handicapped because the mist that had developed over the water made it hard to see clearly. Only on the tenth approach was his bomb-aimer George Johnson happy to let the bomb go. The plan was to crack the centre of the dam and start a leak. Therefore, it might be some time before the dam collapsed rather than the instantaneous impact witnessed at the Möhne.

But the frequently aborted approaches had tested the nerves of those on board the plane to breaking point. Rear gunner Dave Rodger, who was taking the full brunt of the G-force as the plane banked away on a number of occasions, was getting increasingly fed up with these repeatedly aborted attacks and felt like throwing Johnson out of the plane. They did not have the spotlights fitted on the plane so they had to guess at the height of the bomb-drop. They were going at a speed of 170 mph when the bomb was finally released.[27]

As the bomb was dropped and they banked away, Rodger saw a huge waterspout shoot up which almost drenched him in the rear turret.[28] Wallis, according to Johnson, had said that six hits would be needed to breach the Sorpe, but there would not be six bombs available to drop on it that night. In the excitement of at last releasing the bomb, though, something went wrong; McCarthy and his wireless operator Leonard Eaton forgot to report the drop back to Grantham until 0300.[29]

Josef Kesting, the machinist from the power station at the Sorpe dam, witnessed this attack. He saw the plane drop something that looked like a 'huge septic tank' from its fuselage. An enormous explosion followed along with a plume of water 100 metres high. Kesting promised himself that he would come back with a basket in the morning and pick up any dead fish that he could find. He did not realise that it was the dam that was the target and assumed that the plane was after the power station.[30]

Although McCarthy and his crew had stuck to their task admirably, they had not succeeded in breaching the dam, though they had crumbled its crest. But despite subsequent beliefs that the damage had caused the reservoir to be drained so that the walls could be properly repaired,[31] it appears that in reality no such inconvenience was caused. The earthen core of the dam wall was simply too robust to be breached in the way envisaged. In the words of Len Sumpter, who did not admittedly witness the attack personally, 'the Sorpe was a waste of time with this bomb'.[32]

There was nothing more for McCarthy now to do except guide his men home safely. So they now set their course back towards Scampton. Because they did not have a compass deviation card loaded for their Upkeep-less state, it was hard to navigate the prescribed return route so they just returned the way they had come. With their mission accomplished as far as they were able, their duty now was to survive.

Just a few miles off at the Möhne a scene of chaos was unfolding. At 0050 a call was logged to Leutnant Dicke at Neheim, telling him that the dam had been hit and flooding had started. It would only be a few minutes before the waters were approaching the town. Dicke passed this terrifying information onto the mayor and sent one of his men to meet him. However, by the time that he arrived the mayor's house was already partly underwater. Dicke then despatched officers to the more vulnerable parts of the town, some of which was fortunately positioned above the flood. However, a floodtide of 39 feet, moving at 13 mph, was on its way towards Neheim. By 0100 the town's telephone system was out of action and the town was essentially at the mercy of the inundation that was descending on it.[33]

Frau Noller lived not far below the Möhne dam. When she heard the planes going over, she had hurried off to the air-raid shelters. She heard a bomber going over, almost skimming the roof of her house as it was so low. A deafening cacophony followed, as plane engines soared low overhead whilst the guns spat out at them. Even before the breach, the huge plumes of water spiralling up into the sky as the bombs exploded sent water pouring over the parapet of the dam. She managed to get up out of the cellars and to safety before the floods came and inundated her house.[34]

The news of the breach of the Möhne dam had not yet been received at Grantham. As far as they were all aware, the ultimate conclusion of the raid was still very uncertain. At 0050 Young's signal arrived stating that the dam had not been breached ('Goner 78A'). As Young was flying in a different order to that planned, this suggested to those at Grantham that the attack had failed. Wallis buried his head in his hands despairingly. 'No, it's no good,' was all he could find to say. He was desperate at what he believed to be the failure of the attack. He had already seen Harris and Cochrane 'looking suspiciously at me' and even he was beginning to have doubts.[35]

Wallis later wrote to Cochrane that 'the tense moments in the Operation Room when, after four attacks, I felt that I had failed to make good, were almost more than I could bear'.[36] With Harris in close proximity, the tension was terrible as Wallis's plan appeared to all of those gathered around expectantly to be close to failure.

The mood was about to change completely even as Maltby and Martin, who had dropped their bombs, were ordered home at 0053. Three minutes later, another message came across the ether to Grantham. Wing Commander Dunn, Chief Signals Officer of 5 Group, was waiting attentively to take down any messages that came in. Two, to confirm that the bombs had been released but had not breached the walls, were received from Young and Martin's aircraft at 0050 and 0053 respectively. At 0056 Dunn started to take down another Morse message. He had only taken down the three letters 'NIG' before he ran into the main ops room with the news that the dam had been breached.

With the tension now pierced, pandemonium broke out. An unusually happy Harris made his way over to Wallis and told him, 'Wallis, I didn't believe a word you said when you came to see me. But now you could sell me a pink elephant.'[37] It was not long before the news would be telephoned over to the White House in Washington by Harris, where Churchill and his staff were visiting Roosevelt. A nice legend would develop that when Harris tried to phone the White House, he was accidentally put through to a local pub of the same name instead. Sadly there is no evidence to support this rather pleasant fiction.

Then, as an afterthought, Dunn realised that he should ask Gibson to confirm the message. One wonders what the reaction would have been should Dunn have got the wrong end of the stick and relayed an inaccurate message. At 0057 Gibson was contacted by Dunn to confirm the 'Nigger' signal, which he did with a single word answer to the enquiry – 'correct'.[38] One single word but the import of it was immense.

Back over the Möhne, Gibson curbed the excited radio chatter that had started after the dam was burst and ordered the first wave to move off towards the Eder dam. As he, accompanied by Young and the remaining planes that had not yet dropped their bombs, headed south-east they could already see the Möhne dam emptying. There were little towns beneath them as they flew – Gibson called them 'the Baths and Exeters of Germany'.[39] The choice of these towns in his description was perhaps deliberate, for in the so-called Baedeker raids the Germans had been targeting towns of cultural rather than industrial significance to retaliate for damage done to German cultural sites.

Now survival on the ground below the breached dam was a lottery. It depended on where you were in the valley beneath it. Günne suffered some damage but escaped obliteration, being mostly on higher ground. That said, on this particular night everything was relative. Günne was the first to be hit, within just a minute of the dam being breached at 0050. The rifle club and three power stations in the village were the first to be overwhelmed and thirty people died.

Survival was largely a matter of luck and also keeping your nerve under enormous stress. The waves were up to 8 metres high. In the inn, Adolf Nölle had the presence of mind to guide his family from out of the cellar, where they would have all died, upstairs into the loft, where they sheltered behind a chimney breast. They survived, as did the wall clock in the bar which was later recovered. However, it did not work properly and, regardless of how many times it was repaired, it always stopped at 0050.[40]

The police and flak detachment at the Möhne dam suffered no losses at all which, given their proximity to such massive explosions, was little short of miraculous.[41] Others though were not so lucky. As a man-made tsunami started to flow, it brought terror in its wake. Now there were only minutes for thousands to make decisions that would affect the rest of their lives. For many of them, indeed, they were decisions of life or death.

10

Devastation in Möhne Valley:
Bombers Move on to Target Y
01.01 – 01.45, Monday 17 May

For years and decades, the sturdy walls of the Möhne dam had held back the accumulated rainwater that had showered down onto the hills, and it had collected the individually insignificant flow of the streams that would otherwise have carried on, almost unnoticed, down to the lands below. Trickle by trickle, shower by shower, stream by stream, the waters had been trapped until they formed a mighty man-made sea, from which flowed the lifeblood of the Ruhr industries. Now, with the walls shattered, the accumulated strength and power of the waters was released, unfettered and unstoppable, down onto the sleeping villages and towns that sheltered in the shadow of the dam. All that could stop the flood was its own exhaustion, when its momentum expired of its own volition. And that would not happen for many hours and many miles.

Survival depended significantly on where people lived. The village of Günne was right underneath the dam, a drop of many feet below where the dam walls stood. There was a compensating basin below the dam, which caressed the shores by the village, and then the River Möhne flowed down a valley into the Ruhr region. Günne was built partly up a hillside; those higher up the hill would be safe from the flood. Those by the shoreline were doomed, with just seconds' warning before the waters consumed their houses along with the three hydroelectric power stations on the banks of the waters.

Beyond Günne the valley then dropped, enclosed on either side by hills that would stop the waters from widening out and losing their power. Instead the deluge would be channelled into a fairly narrow area, where its force would build up with nowhere to go except on, forward, smashing everything in its way. Again those in the trough of the valley were often doomed; they had a couple of minutes' warning at most in which they could attempt to scramble uphill to safety, provided they knew that the waters were coming, which in many cases they did not.

For those down below, moments of blind terror were at hand. Just before one o'clock, the residents of Himmelpforten Farm were awoken by a tenant shouting for them to run, for the water was coming. They ran as fast as they could along a road up into some woods. The water threatened to overwhelm them as it overtook them and some were grasped by the waters and swept to their deaths. Others, luckier, managed to escape but watched in horror as the waters submerged houses and churches in their path.[1]

A local farm worker named Kersten had also run and given the alarm as the waters approached Niederense close by to Himmelpforten. 'Save yourselves, the water is coming,' he shouted, urging others to follow him to the high ground and safety. He ran to the road with a friend, Frau Scheven. They ran towards the woods, hoping to find some kind of refuge there. Sadly, both Frau Scheven and a visiting friend and her three-year-old son were unable to outrun the torrent.

Fraulein Muller, who owned a chicken farm nearby, saw the farmhouse and vicarage at Himmelpforten fall victim to the waters. The church and its tower stood defiant for 15 minutes before they too collapsed into the flood. As day broke a few hours later, a terrible sight greeted the eyes of the traumatised survivors. Everywhere floated the corpses of livestock – cattle, hens, pigs – as well as people. An eighty-three-year-old woman had tied herself to a chimney and clung on there for grim life. She would be there for two days until she was rescued.[2]

With the restraining wall of the dam gone, the deluge continued to pour down on the often unsuspecting inhabitants of the towns and villages below the dam. The residents of Niederense were in particular danger, being so close to the dam and with little chance of warning reaching them (though fortunately there were steep hills nearby where a number of people lived). One of those living further down was Elisabeth Hennecke, who had hidden in the cellars when she heard the air-raid alarm go some time before. Elisabeth was in a very positive frame of mind, having been earlier in the evening to the Apollo cinema in Neheim, a few miles down the valley, where she had seen a film called *Die goldene Stadt* (*The Golden City*). She had not been home long when the alarm went.

The people in the shelter were, however, uncertain as to what exactly was going on. After a while, curiosity kicked in and Elisabeth had gone outside with others to have a look. Whilst they were there, they heard a heavy blast. Returning to the cellar, they found that there was no light: the noise they had heard had occurred when Hopgood's bomb had taken out the power station. A little while after this, the residents heard 'an ear-splitting roaring, cracking and crashing'. They went outside soon after, to find that the yard was already knee-deep in water. They rushed back in to the cellar to fetch out the elderly and children who were still there when the roof caved in.

Running upstairs, they found a ladder which they used to make their way up into the attic. From there, they climbed onto the roof to escape the rising waters. They signalled out with their pocket torches to those who had escaped to the surrounding hills. They were amongst the lucky ones. About six hours later they were finally rescued, to be greeted with dry clothes and warm drinks.[3]

Whilst on the roof, they witnessed some harrowing and terrible sights:

> With the children in front of me I sat on the ridge of the roof; I had one leg over one side and the other leg over the other … All the joints in the house were groaning and creaking and it was rocking from side to side. Tree trunks were crashing through the half-timbered sides of the house. I just clung desperately to the roof hoping that if it gave way I'd be able to swim off with the children. The lightning conductor had got stretched out from all the pulling. The water carried a little timber-framed house past us towards Neheim and in a window on a table in one of the rooms there was a candle giving off a peculiar kind of light. Tree trunks from the saw-mill kept crashing down in front of the house; dead cows were carried along past the roof.[4]

It was a scene from a nightmare set in a valley of normally idyllic beauty. It changed the lives of those who lived through these terrible events. Given her experiences, it was understandable that Elisabeth later said that 'I wouldn't want to live in a valley below a dam any more. I can't escape the fear; it's always with me. I wouldn't want to go through that again.'

Another who witnessed the deluge that hit Niederense and the nearby tiny hamlet of Himmelpforten was Karl-Heinz Dohle, who had been watching the raid unfold with his father from their garden. They could clearly see the 'birds of death' and the tracer streaking across the sky. They heard explosions and then a rumbling sound.

Just before Niederense was a marvellous building, the Porta Coeli convent. It was in a wonderful, peaceful location, beside the normally placid River Möhne which day by day made its way lethargically down the narrow valley. It was a beautiful spot in an out of the way place, which hinted at its Cistercian origins. Seven hundred years before, the 'white monks' who loved places of solitude and grandeur had built a sturdy church here.[5] Over the centuries it had accumulated some glorious art to beautify it until it was a very different building to the one it had started life as.

Now this place of solitude and contemplation became the home of terror and death. Hemmed in by the hills on either side, the waters crashed into the buildings. Dohle felt impelled to climb a hill from which he and his father saw the Porta Coeli convent inundated. For a few minutes the spire stood defiantly above the waters. Then it leaned over and plummeted into the swollen river. As it did so, Dohle could hear one last muffled clang of the bell, a final knell for the wonderful church which stood at the head of what would become known as 'Todestal' – 'Death Valley'.

Another youth, sixteen-year-old Werner Hellmann, watched on in horror from 200 metres away as the waters inundated the convent. He later recalled that 'I could clearly see the weathervane on top of the steeple sticking out of that thundering flood which by then had reached its highest point. After a while the steeple tipped over to one side and went under. The bell gave a single, dull clang.'[6] It was a simple, solemn knell for those who were about to die.

Some of those in the path of the flood were saved by the heroism and self-sacrifice of others. One of them, Pastor Berkenkopf, the local priest, rang the bell of the convent to warn others; he gave his life to save his flock.[7] Strangely, the Pastor seemed to have predicted his imminent death in his last sermon on Sunday 16 May when he spoke on the subject, 'In a short while you will see me no more, for I am going to the father'.

Berkenkopf was later found in the cellar seeking shelter along with others (which must call into some question whether it was him ringing the bell at all; an air-raid shelter was a strange place to run to if a flood could be seen approaching). Later, after the deluge, the local Hitler Youth were given the task of digging bodies out of the rubble (the church had been totally swallowed by the waters). They eventually dug their way into the cellar and found the pastor's body. It was reverently taken away on a stretcher for a Christian burial.[8]

When daylight came a few hours later it brought with it a realisation of the terrible damage. 'Himmelpforten had simply ceased to exist ... Some of the trees on the road into Günne had railway lines wrapped round them like corkscrews. The flotsam had stripped away all the bark; they were standing there like white ghosts.'[9]

The breach at the Möhne had already caused havoc. Neheim, a few miles from the dam, was overwhelmed in the early hours at about 0110. It was the first significant population point below the Möhne dam. Industrial buildings stood on its banks close by the water, whilst from slightly higher up – very fortunately as it turned out – the impressive facade of the church of Saint John the Baptist stood guard on the streets and the square below.

When the floods hit Neheim, its coalfields and ironworks were swamped. Most of the inhabitants affected spent the night out in the open, camping out in the hills. Fifty-one men, sixty-six women and thirty children lost their lives in the town. In addition, 444 livestock were killed. Dortmund, further off and therefore better placed to receive warnings, later experienced major problems. The city's air-raid shelters were flooded and nearly half the citizens were forced out into the night. For a time the only way to get around many of the streets of the city was in a flat-bottomed boat.[10]

One of the problems in Neheim was that, despite several telephoned warnings, the authorities there refused to accept that the dam had been breached. There were no organised flood-warning measures in place and this undoubtedly added to the loss of life. One resident, Hermann Kaiser, went down into the air-raid shelter in the cellar when warnings of enemy activity in the area were received about midnight.

Kaiser was there with his three sisters, the housemaid and a Russian cook, Anna: his parents were away visiting as Sunday had been Mother's Day. Anna, the cook, was a widow who had been brought in as a conscripted worker by the Germans. After the noise from the planes flying over the town had died down, she went back to her room.

The others were down in the cellar when they heard the phone ring. The housemaid went to answer it but hurried back down to tell them that she could hear a terrible splashing and rattling noise. Then their nerves were shattered as their gardener, Josef Greis, burst in, shouting, 'Get out! Get out! Everyone out of here now!'

Greis then rushed to Anna's room and hammered on the door but she would not answer it. The others ran out of the house in a panic. They managed to make their way up a hill where hundreds of others had also gathered. It all happened in a matter of minutes and there were very narrow margins determining whether an individual survived or not. Kaiser looked on with disbelief as he saw a river 'as wide as the Mississippi' rolling down the valley making a noise 'like 25 express trains'. The cook, Anna, was found drowned in the laundry room the next morning having been washed there from her room. There were no signs that she had tried to save herself.[11] Perhaps the misery of a conscripted labourer's life meant that there was nothing much left for her to fight for.

Ferdi Dröge was a sixteen-year-old apprentice living in Neheim. Like many others, when he heard the air-raid warnings he had made his way to the shelter, where he reckoned there were about 200 others present. They had sat on planks and beer barrels, playing cards and eating snacks, waiting out the boredom of the raids. Then an acquaintance, Johannes Kessler, ran in and told them to get out at once, shouting that 'the Möhne's had it'. They made their way out as quickly as possible and had enough time to reach higher ground and safety.

The civilian loss in Neheim was bad enough but would be surpassed by a scene of even greater horror. In the town there was a labour camp just above the river with a number of Ukrainian female inmates. As the war progressed, the Germans had found it increasingly difficult to obtain enough labour to run the war economy. Eventually they had turned to the expedient of forcibly recruiting labour from the territories they had occupied in the east.

About 1,200 women from Ukraine and Poland had arrived at Soest railway station in the early summer of 1943 and had then been transferred to Neheim. The camp on the edge of Neheim was established to support an armaments factory. It was at the foot of the Wiedenburg, a hill above the Möhne. That night, the alarm had gone off about midnight and shortly thereafter low-flying aircraft had passed over and shot up the barracks. Even before this night, some had wondered whether the camp was too close to the river and might be susceptible to floods. They were about to have their suspicions confirmed with terrifying effect.

Just over an hour after the alarm had been heard, a fearsome roaring was heard approaching the camp. Then, as eyes began to focus in the bright moonlight, a wall of water could be seen descending on the camp. Some of the inmates were ordered out of their buildings and told to run towards safety. They began to panic and had to be threatened with pistols to keep them in check. Some though did manage to escape the floods by moving out of their way. But many it seems never made it out of their barrack blocks.

One of the workers was a Ukrainian woman, Darja Michajlowna Moros. When she heard the air-raid alarms she took no notice; in this period of intensive RAF activity, they were a regular occurrence and she was getting fed up with them and the disturbance to her sleep that they resulted in. However, when it was realised that the dam had broken, the inmates were let out and ran for their lives.

The camp was surrounded by barbed wire, which meant that there was a bottleneck by the gate where all the women were trying to get out. There was an old guard there, a man with a limp. The inmates knew him as Robert. He got out a pair of pliers and cut the barbed wire so that more of the women could get out and try to outrun the waters. Sadly he himself could not and this unsung hero was lost in the floods.[12]

Amidst the tragedy, there was one remarkable story that shed a small ray of light on the gloom. Karl Josef Stüppardt was a guard at the camp and whilst he was there he fell in love with one of the women, named Elena, who came from Siberia though she had lived most of her life in Ukraine. His feelings were reciprocated and the unlikely couple used to meet regularly, occasionally even having illicit nights out at the nearby cinema, where Elena learned German.

On the night of the flood, Stüppardt ran into the camp trying to rouse the women. Many of them did not take him seriously but eventually some did try and make their escape. Elena was one of them and she managed to get away dressed only in a slip with an overcoat on top. She survived though Stüppardt found himself in a different kind of deep water when it was discovered that he had been fraternising with one of the foreign workers, something that was strictly against Germany's race laws.

Nevertheless, he managed to stay in touch with Elena and this story did have a truly happy ending. On 16 June 1945, barely a month after the war ended, Stüppardt and Elena were married in the church of Saint John the Baptist. The church was overflowing, with many of the congregation being recently released Russian prisoners.[13] Many surely remembered that in the very same building, just over two years before, the pews had been moved to one side so that the interior could be used for the terrible business of laying out the dead whose bodies had been recovered after the deluge.

Any thoughts of romance or joy lay far in the distant and uncertain future on this most awful of nights. Now, Ferdi Dröge looked on in horror as he heard the screams of the women workers trying to get away from the floods. He could see a huge wave surging down:

> [It] looked like a black block of flats with terraces; it was full of trees, pieces of wood and animals. That pitch-black wall of water coming towards me was at least 12 metres high; in it, and looking as if they were stacked on top of each other, were sections of wooden huts and people screaming. Dotted around in amongst those whirling bits of weed were little lights which went out in the spray. I was no more than 200 metres from the leading edge of that wave.[14]

A few hundred women at least were saved but hundreds of others died. Residents later insisted that the barracks had been swept away with their residents still trapped inside, but they were smashed to pieces on a concrete bridge downstream; the screams of the doomed could still be heard as their flimsy protection was torn apart and they met their deaths.[15]

Dröge, an articulate witness who gave a vivid account of what he had seen, spoke of how the floods overwhelmed a transformer station and a colossal flash lit up the valley. As he managed to escape further uphill, he followed the tragedy down in the valley: 'the crashing, the roaring, the smashing and the death cries. Seen from the side, the first giant wave looked like steps. Each wall of water rose up above the one in front as the torrent thrust its way down the valley.'[16] The marks made by the floodwater suggested that in places it was 45 feet deep. A huge mass of rock, some 18 metres long by 5 metres high, was gouged out by the floods.

One of the residents of Neheim, Josef Rösen, had seen the sky in the north-east glowing brightly just before the deluge descended and at once thought of the dam. He ran into the house and woke his sister, having the presence of mind to ask her to collect some drinking water and candles. Then he heard a roar in the distance; over it he could hear people screaming and animals bleating. He went down to the town which was already a scene of chaos. Bodies were already swirling around in the waters that were deluging the town.

Rösen heard voices coming from the mist that had formed as a result of the huge volume of water. Looking up in the branches of a tree, he saw several completely naked women – survivors from the Ukrainian women at the nearby camp. He got them down from the tree and then to safety. He then made a basic raft out of doors and timbers and ferried those he could to safety.

He too was a hero, though he would in the aftermath witness the evidence of the horrific end that some of those in the area had suffered. There was, for example, the devoted mother who had gone down to rescue her six-year-old son from the waters after she had safely got her other children to the attic; neither of them could escape the rising waters and they both drowned in their living room. In another case, fifty people had been trapped in an air-raid shelter and had been unable to open the door because of the rising waters outside. They all drowned.[17]

The German authorities were already putting a picture together, though at the moment it was fragmented and unclear. By 0108, Hilse, the chief of police at Soest (although only a few miles away, the town was safely protected from the floods by a screen of hills), reached the Möhne dam and saw that the wall was already seriously damaged. Just a few minutes after the breach, Oberföster Wilkening had run to the Ruhr-Lippe Railway, the site of the nearest telephone that he was aware of, to phone through a flood warning; there was a phone system at the Möhne direct to Soest but it had been destroyed in the attack; it had maybe been destroyed by Hopgood's blast.[18]

As the drama continued to unfold, the main focus of the activity shifted. In contrast to the sense of triumph felt by those who had successfully breached the dam, now came the tragedy. The main actions were now being played out in the valley below the Möhne dam as cataclysmic events unfolded, bringing death and destruction in their wake.

In the skies not far above, the planes either made their way back towards safety, though their peril was as yet far from over, or pushed on towards the next objective if they had not yet dropped their bombs. Back at Grantham, after the elation following the receipt of Gibson's confirmatory message that the wall at the Möhne dam had been broken, a waiting game began once more. Following that message, there would be no further communication with the raiders for 48 minutes. But the mood was lightened as the senior figures at Grantham knew for sure that one of the three major operational objectives had been achieved.

But the evening's toll was far from over. At about 0115, the residents of Hemfurth, some miles to the south-east of the Möhne reservoir, were woken by the noise of low-flying aircraft. Gibson and the other planes that remained behind had flown on from the Möhne dam to the Eder reservoir, which was about 43 miles away. Unlike that at the Möhne, the Eder dam was unguarded – flak guns, until recently sited on the wall, had been removed just a week before.[19] However, it had extremely strong natural defences. The position of the dam would make it very difficult indeed for the attackers to get into the right position to release their bombs as it was surrounded by very steep hills.

It was at about 0130 that the attack on the Eder dam really began. There were five planes remaining, though only three of them were carrying bombs. Both Gibson and Young were bomb-less. Gibson's job was to act once more as the master bomber and Young's to take over should anything happen to him. Those with bombs were the planes flown by Shannon, Knight and Maudslay (AJ-L, AJ-N and AJ-Z respectively).

The dam had not been easy to find as fog was now starting to build up. It took Gibson five circles around the area to locate the structure. The Eder dam was surrounded by dark hills guarded by platoons of pine trees, sentinels ready to do their part in repelling all uninvited intruders. But the fact that there were no anti-aircraft guns there was reassuring as reconnaissance photos had suggested there might be – but the objects seen from the air were in fact trees.[20]

Gibson radioed Shannon to make his run first, using the message 'Cooler 6'. This was, however, easier said than done as Shannon was not sure where he was. This was not surprising as the dam was hidden away amongst hills and forests and was not easy to find. Gibson therefore told Hutchison, his wireless operator, to set off a red flare, which he did. Shannon could see it at once and moved into position.

Shannon had found a target not long before but it was in fact the wrong one. After making the short flight from the Möhne dam, Shannon's bomb had been left spinning. Those who were to attack the dam were faced with a formidable proposition. There were several challenges facing those attacking at the Eder, including the fact that there was no model of the dam available until after the raid. There were only reconnaissance photos to go from and estimates of height from these were out by up to 125 feet.

The fog was growing thick over the Eder dam too and it was hard to tell a valley filled with water from one filled with fog, especially in the enclosed landscape surrounding the reservoir. Gibson had become separated from the other planes on the way in and now called them up. Gibson's Very light over the dam alerted not only Shannon but the others in the flight too.

At the far end of the dam, and high above the water, was a magnificent Gothic castle. As the dam was surrounded by hills, the planes would have to fly in over this castle at 1,000 feet and would then have to drop rapidly to 60 feet for the final approach for the attack. Much greater flying skills were needed for this raid than the one on the Möhne dam, even though there were no defences in situ.[21] Once passing hard a-port over a spit of land in the lake, there were just seven seconds left to get into the right position for an attack on the dam and the Lancaster was a big, heavy plane that it was difficult to get into exactly the right spot.

Shannon moved in for his approach. At least there were no enemy gunners to distract him here, which was just as well given the extent of the challenges facing him. He flew over the castle on the hill at Waldeck and then dropped sharply to 60 feet. He then had to turn sharply to port to complete the final, short approach to the dam wall. However, his bomb-aimer, Sergeant Les Sumpter, was not happy with the approach so they circled again. As Shannon ascended again rapidly, forced to pull up to fly over the hills at the far end of the dam that were covered in a blanket of trees, he had to do so at full boost; Gibson could see sparks coming from his engine as the plane strained upwards. Shannon came back for four more attempts and was unable to make a suitable approach on each occasion.

Unsurprisingly, these repeated aborted attempts to get into just the right spot were very unsettling for Shannon, who later recalled that 'to get out of the valley after crossing the dam wall we had to put on full throttle and do a steep climbing turn to avoid a vast rock face'.[22] As Gibson looked on, he decided that it might be better to give someone else a go and see if they had better luck.

So as Shannon was about to line up another run, Gibson told Maudslay to take his place and make an attempt. It did not, however, make any difference, for Maudslay also took two approaches and was unsuccessful. Shannon was then directed to try again. He was finding the approach very difficult and he still could not get his aircraft in the right place to drop his bomb.

The problem was that the route to be followed called for real precision flying and there was very little margin of error. The descent from Waldeck castle was not directly towards the lake but over a spur of land called the Hammerberg. Once beyond the dam there was a sizeable hill, the Michelskopf, over which the planes would have to climb sharply. This would be no mean feat, especially if the planes had to abort an approach with a bomb still on board; it would in the end take eleven attempts to drop three bombs at the Eder.[23]

Some way behind the planes over the Eder, the third wave was starting to arrive over the Continent. At 0130 Ken Brown flew over the Dutch coast in AJ-F. He was, however, a long way off course – his compass may have been wrong.[24] He was followed over the coast by Bill Townsend, just a minute behind. They pushed on towards their objectives, though at this stage they were still not sure exactly where they would be. It depended to some extent on how well Gibson and the remaining crews got on at the Eder.

In the meantime, closer to Gibson's next target it was now becoming clearer that something was amiss. At 0132 the telephone rang in the local air-raid defence office near the Eder dam. It was answered by Leutnant Saahr of the SS. He was told that there were British aircraft circling over the dam. He rang the Third Company of the 603rd Regional Defence Battalion (SS) at Hemfurth, the village below the dam, to get confirmation of the fact, which was duly given. Saahr then rang Colonel Karl Bürke of the SS Flak Training Regiment to tell him that a flood may well be imminent. Bürke put 100 men on standby with lorries. Saahr phoned back almost at once to say that the planes were dropping flares so they had had searchlights switched on.

At 0139 Shannon moved back in for his attack on the Eder. Sumpter was this time happy with the approach and the bomb was dropped, bouncing twice and sinking as it hit the dam wall. The fact that it bounced twice may suggest that the bomb was released too early. About a minute after the bomb was released, there was an explosion and a spout of water about 1,000 feet high. A gap about 9 feet wide was seen on the east side of the dam by Shannon. Wireless officer Brian Goodale signalled back 'Goner 79B', which meant a small breach in the Eder dam.

However, Gibson was not convinced and later reported back that he could see no apparent damage from this strike. Shannon was just glad to get out of there; he later described the attack as 'a bugger of a job'. The exit over the Michelskopf, with the bomb still attached on three occasions, was described as 'bloody hairy'.[25] He had at least survived the attack, but so too had the Eder dam. Now Gibson had just two bombs left to drop (ignoring any that might be available from the reserve wave) to complete the task at the Eder and return home in veritable triumph.

Despite the success at the Möhne dam, Gibson cannot have been confident at this stage of repeating the trick here. Extreme flying was called for if the bomb were to be dropped in the right spot and, if it were not, then he could not be sure of success. Each dam had its own specific challenge; at the Möhne it was the flak guns, at the Eder the difficulty of the approach. The mission was proving every bit as difficult a challenge as expected and costs had already been high (though Gibson at this stage only knew of Hopgood's loss for certain). The sacrifices had not ended yet, either for those in the air or those on the land beneath them.

11

Breach of Eder Dam: Dinghy at Target Y
01.46 – 02.00, Monday 17 May

Even as the attack on the Eder dam was intensifying, the effects of the Möhne breach in the meantime were continuing to worsen. From Wickede, a few miles further downstream from Neheim, the planes flying over for earlier attacks on the dams could be clearly seen in the bright moonlight. There were though no reports of any serious breaches for a while and when Clemens Mols, the postmaster, went to find out if anything of significance had happened, all he heard was that planes were now flying low over the Eder. He therefore assumed that the danger had passed. Mols returned to his family, amongst whom the mood was now calm.

However, urged on by his wife, Mols went back to the post office to see if he could find out more and whilst he was there the phone rang. When he answered it, he found that it was the postmaster from nearby Arnsberg (also close to Neheim but safe from the flood as it was not on the river) on the line. He asked Mols incredulously why he was still there when the water was now in Vosswinkel, just 5 kilometres away from Wickede. Mols at once hurried back home and told his wife to get up to the high ground whilst he tried to wake people up by phone.

He tried to do this but with no success. In the meantime, his wife returned and begged him to come up to the high ground with her. He agreed but they had barely started on the journey when a fog appeared. Mols recognised this as a forerunner of the water and realised that they could not outrun it so they rushed back into the house and hurried upstairs. They were barely in time as the foaming waters followed them into the house.

They managed to carry bedding and clothes up into the attic, hoping that the walls would not give way against the weight of the water and also that the waters would not rise high enough to submerge it. Above them, the moon shone down brightly whilst the terrifying sound of low-flying aircraft could be heard, though no further bombs were dropped. Frau Mols was beside herself and all her husband could do was try and reassure her to keep her calm.[1]

Off to the south-east and some miles away, at 0146 Henry Maudslay ('Cooler 7') began his attack on the Eder dam. His aircraft had possibly been damaged on the way in as something had been seen hanging under the bomb-bay. The approach was difficult and the precision required to drop the bomb in the exact place pinpoint. The reservoir was in fact a long, serpentine lake with inlets and tree-girt promontories sticking out like long fingers of land into the water. It was impossible to get a straight run into the dam and very easy to be past it before you knew it. This was certainly a far harder attack technically than that on the Möhne dam.

Maudslay manoeuvred his plane into position as well as he could and swooped down towards the dam. It was a great boon that there was no flak, but the sheerness of the hills round about more than compensated for the lack of opposition. Here nature was the greatest enemy and the sculpting of the hills would prove the most significant obstacle that had to be overcome.

Gibson watched closely, silently urging Maudslay and his crew on, willing them to succeed, inwardly telling them to maintain the right height, hold their course, keep their nerve. Even as he did so, Maudslay's plane briefly climbed, as if trying to avoid something, perhaps a treetop, before dropping back down again.

Maudslay would have very little time to get his plane into the right position and split-second timing was called for. In the event, his bomb appeared to leave the aircraft late. The bomb bounced too high and bounced over the parapet rather than hitting the dam. It detonated seconds afterwards as the plane was still over it. 'There was a slow, yellow, vivid flame which lit up the whole valley like daylight for just a few seconds,' Gibson remarked later.[2]

Maudslay's plane was illuminated by the explosion, the shock from which may well have hit his plane. Given the late release of the bomb, Gibson's comments concerning Maudslay's sudden unexpected, albeit temporary, climb on the approach may assume extra significance. Perhaps it broke Maudslay's concentration and this led to the mistimed drop. Maybe it is even possible that he had clipped something that had caused some damage. As neither plane nor crew members would make it back to England to tell the tale, no one will ever know.

What exactly happened to Maudslay's plane is veiled in mystery though it did not crash at the dam. However, it may well have been damaged and this could have affected the performance of the aircraft, either on the way into the final approach or as a result of the blast – very possibly from both events. It was always regarded as a risk that a plane might be affected by the blast should it be in the wrong place at the wrong time: two planes had after all been damaged late on in the training stage because they had been hit by the columns of water thrown up during practice. It would be no surprise if the impact of a bomb blast had seriously damaged Maudslay's plane.

The plane limped on in the direction of Emmerich, close to the Dutch border near Nijmegen. Gibson tried to make contact over the radio but the signal from Maudslay's plane was very weak; when asked if he was alright, the reply faintly came, 'I think so.' Gibson had in fact lost sight of Maudslay: he was also worried as even now the sky was starting to subtly brighten as dawn drew closer and they were running out of time to complete the raid and certainly to return to England without a gravely increased risk of being intercepted. Maudslay flew off, now on his own, whilst Gibson returned to the immediate task of coordinating the raid on the Eder dam. However, Maudslay's 'Goner 28B' message (attack at Eder dam, bomb overshot, no apparent breach) was received at Grantham at 0157, confirming that he and his crew were still very much alive at this time.

Even with their VHF radios, communication between the crews was still fragmentary. At 0151 Gibson tried to raise Astell but there was no response as he had been dead for nearly two hours. As well as being worried about his fellow pilot, Gibson would also have been very aware that there was only one bomb left and it had to work if the Eder dam was to be successfully breached (though there was always the option of deploying planes from the reserve wave should the dam remain unbreached).

At 0152 Les Knight prepared for his attack on the Eder. As he had the last bomb remaining from the first wave, this was a particularly high-pressure moment. Like the other pilots who had attacked the Eder, Knight had great trouble negotiating the right angle for his approach. He tried the approach once but the run was aborted as the plane was not in a satisfactory position (it was in fact going too fast at 240 mph).[3]

There was a flow back and forth of chatter over the radio with advice, more or less helpful, being given by those who had already made the run or watched one being made. Shannon was especially voluble – Les Sumpter recalled that 'Dave was talking to him, telling him how to do it, and Les Knight told him to get off the air'.[4] Knight wanted no distractions as he concentrated fully on ensuring that he and his crew were working together seamlessly to get the plane where it needed to be to drop the bomb in perfect position.

Knight and his crew were effectively on their own, with the last bomb on board and the Eder dam before them still standing firm and defiant. He did though have perfect visibility with the moon to starboard. But the dam was proving very hard to attack and even Gibson was beginning to think that the approach was too difficult.

Gibson was on the point of giving up when Knight made one final run. Once more he hopped over a high hill on the way in towards the dam, an interruption to a clear run in that greatly added to the complexity of the approach. Knight took an approach route slightly to the east of that planned, where the hill known as the Hammerberg was lower and the distance to the dam beyond it greater. This gave him vital extra seconds to ensure that he was in the right place to drop the bomb.[5]

This time the approach was perfect and the calculation of the dropping spot for the bomb precise. Gibson, alongside, saw the bomb bounce three times and then explode. Flight Sergeant Robert Kellow, the wireless operator in Knight's plane, AJ-N, looked back at the dam. 'It was still intact for a short while, then as if some huge fist had been jabbed at the wall, a large, almost round black hole appeared and water gushed as if from a long hose.'[6]

To Gibson it was 'as if gigantic hand had punched a hole through cardboard'.[7] In fact, Knight's last run was the best Gibson had witnessed of the whole night. It had indeed been a masterclass of split-second timing and perfect positioning. Knight had dropped his bomb and there was what seemed like a tremendous earthquake soon after. Then the whole dam collapsed like a pack of cards. Knight was in no mood to celebrate just yet; at the end of the run, Knight 'had to climb like buggery to get out' because of the steep hills behind the dam.[8] Celebration could come later; at this particular moment survival came first as Knight and Ray Grayston, his flight engineer, pulled hard on the controls to get the plane climbing as quickly as possible.

On this occasion, there was no confusion or delay in the relaying of information back to Grantham. Pilot Officer Bob Kellow radioed back 71B, 'large breach in dam'. Those on board could see a spout of water 800 feet high shooting up above the dam. Then a tide of water 30 feet high was seen travelling down the valley, smashing buildings and bridges in its path. The workers on the steps of the generator plant below the dam felt the building shake. They ran down to the main room but the lighting had failed. Masonry fell from the ceiling and water started to rush in but they managed to reach the stone steps up before the dam burst completely open.[9]

Werner Salz was a fitter at the power stations named Hemfurth I and II right by the dam, down at its very foot. He had been out on the Saturday night but was not long in bed when he heard planes flying over. Getting up, he could see that four-engined aircraft were flying so low that he claimed that the crews could be seen in the cockpit.

He witnessed several explosions before, following a third, he felt the ground shake. He realised that the dam had been hit, a belief that was confirmed when he heard the sound of rushing water. Thinking that the power stations had been hit, he ran back to Hemfurth. When he arrived there he could see that water was already lapping around the houses.

'I ran to the dam to see how big the breach was. It was huge. Masses of water were thundering out – a catastrophe.' He was worried about his workmates. He wondered if they had drowned. He could see two men flashing lights from the roof of the control room at Hemfurth I. Of his four workmates, three would survive but Jakob Kurtze, a machinist, could not be found. His body was found in August that year under a mass of gravel.[10] The survival of the other three, who were right underneath the huge breach, was quite extraordinary.

Below the dam, Karl Albrecht was the engineer of one of the two power stations. Water and debris began to pour through the roof of the building he was in. He rushed up the steps to the parapet of the dam, just in time to see the breach widen and the water pour through into the valley below (the key to his survival perhaps therefore appears to be that the breach progressively got larger, giving him time to make good his escape, rather than the wall collapsing at once). The phone lines were cut by the deluge soon after, though some early warning was possible before this happened. The postmaster at Bad Wildungen, to the south of the Eder reservoir and out of harm's way, was able to phone warnings further down the valley and saved a number of lives in the process.[11] By now, a wave 30 feet high was raging down the valley.

Again the topography of the area was important in the sequence of events that followed. The water which poured through the shattered dam wall had a steep drop into the valley below. Once it hit the valley floor it would be hemmed in for some way by very steep, almost precipitous, rocky hills on one side and less steep but still significant contours on the other. This meant that, trapped as it was, the water would build up tremendous force as it surged down the valley. Fortunately, the Eder valley was less populated than the Möhne and this would result in a far smaller loss of life here.

At 0154 the 'Dinghy' signal was sent, the code word to tell those back at Grantham that the Eder too had been broken. Interestingly, Kellow's 'Goner 710B' message confirming that AJ-N's plane had dropped its bomb and caused a large breach at the Eder dam was not sent until 0200, six minutes after Gibson's 'Dinghy' message had been sent. This hints at one of the less successful elements of the raids, that of long-distance communications, though this element of it is often overlooked. Nevertheless, the problem may have had some significance, especially in the coordination and targeting of the third wave. It certainly also suggests that discipline concerning this element of the raids was more lax, and perhaps the training less effective, than other elements of the mission: Joe McCarthy's wireless operator, Flight Sergeant Leonard Eaton, would not report the dropping of the bomb at the Sorpe dam until several hours after it had happened.

There was nothing further for Gibson to do now but to try everything he could to get everyone back to base safely. His offensive mission was over and it was up to the reserve planes to do as best they could with, in the event, little coordination between them. Gibson ordered all the remaining planes in his flight home and promised them he would meet them in the mess afterwards 'for the biggest party of all time'. 'Good show boys, let's all go home and get pie,' were the words he remembered.[12]

As the crews who had breached the Eder dam headed home, they followed the now-released waters down the steep valley in what looked like a 30-foot wall of water. It obliterated power stations and submerged roads as it went. They saw lights being extinguished, 'like a great black shadow had been drawn across the earth', a vision of hell that a number of the crews looking on witnessed.[13] Down below, the pilots could see car headlights being submerged and extinguished beneath the unstoppable torrent that was now cascading down the valley.[14] According to Leonard Sumpter 'down there somewhere we could see cars going along and the water went over the car headlights and just drowned them.'[15]

However, for all the euphoria there was still great danger for those pilots who had not yet managed to return to British airspace. At 0157 Henry Maudslay's wireless operator Aiden Cottam sent a message back to 5 Group. It was very weak but gave the code 'Goner 28B', which means 'special weapon released, overshot dam, no apparent breach'. It was the last communication received from the plane.

There were now two dams successfully breached, but there were in all three main targets and three secondary ones identified by the British as potential objectives. The night's action was not yet over. There was still a third, reserve wave heading for the Ruhr. At around 0145 a flak warning was transmitted to this third group. The German defences would have been well on their guard now, something that was about to be proved with dramatic effect.

Going the other way, at 0153 David Maltby flew out to safety over the North Sea. At almost exactly the same time as Maltby and his men could start to relax to a certain extent, Lewis Burpee and his crew in AJ-S were shot down whilst heading towards Germany, an act witnessed by Ken Brown in AJ-F. This happened near Tilburg between Breda and Eindhoven in the Netherlands.

Burpee was about a mile off course, making his way towards the Sorpe dam (again emphasising the difficulty of exact navigation and the potentially fatal consequences of a small margin of error). When only 25 metres above the ground, Burpee's plane was caught in a searchlight at the Gilze-Rijen Luftwaffe base in the Netherlands, a heavily defended spot. Gilze-Rijen was a Dutch army airfield taken over by the Germans earlier in the war when they had overrun the Netherlands. There were nine Messerschmitt Bf 110G night fighters based there and seven Junkers JU-88Cs.

Dazzled by the searchlights that caught him as he approached the base, Burpee tried to avoid the flak at the airfield by flying still lower but his plane clipped the trees. He lost control and crashed into the airbase, ploughing into a Military Transport post where fire and other trucks were stored. There was a huge explosion; all the crew in the plane were killed instantly. Windows and doors around the base were blown in. Ammunition explosions added to the cacophony. Burpee had at least succeeded in disabling the radar base on the station but had paid the ultimate price for it.

Lewis Burpee was a Canadian, born in 1918. He had flown his first mission in October 1942 in a raid on Cologne and went on his first raid in charge of his own plane a month later in an aborted foray to Genoa. Being in the last reserve wave he had, like others in that group, followed the same southerly route taken by Gibson's wave on the way out to the region of the dams. He had been looking for a known gap in the air defences between two night-fighter bases at Eindhoven and Gilze-Rijen. As the defences would have been on alert after the earlier waves had flown their missions, members of the third wave were in especial danger. Burpee's wife was pregnant with their first child, who would be born that Christmas. He would also be named Lewis after the father he would never see.

Ken Brown, a fellow Canadian, witnessed Burpee's demise. There was at least one more positive outcome from what had happened. Seeing Burpee hit alerted Brown to danger and he was able to steer clear of trouble. When he flew over, the whole valley where Burpee had crashed was lit up by an orange flame. Brown dived to avoid danger and followed the course of a road when all of a sudden two turrets loomed ahead, either side of a castle. Brown managed to fly between them and on towards his target.

Stefan Oancia was the bomb-aimer in Brown's plane, which was about 10 miles behind Burpee's, and saw that 'Burpee's Lancaster ahead of us flew over a German airfield and was hit by ground fire, fuel tanks exploding and a ball of flame rising slowly – stopping, then dropping terminated by a huge ball of flame as it hit the ground and the bomb exploded' – a succinct but informative description of what had happened.[16]

Oancia could see quite clearly what was happening. He could see the tracer rising up from the airfield, he saw it stop when it hit the aircraft and then he saw the plane in flames. He believed that Burpee had been hit, as he witnessed the plane start to climb before it then plummeted to the ground as if the plane were completely out of control.[17] But not all witnesses saw events this way.

Herbert Scholl was a wireless operator at the base. He said that the night-fighter crews were on standby in front of their barracks when a plane flew over (the second one that had flown over the base that night). Suddenly it was lit up by a searchlight. The plane, already low, dropped even lower into the trees, where it crashed to the ground, slamming into an empty military vehicle garage.

There was then a tremendous explosion. The shockwaves knocked the night-fighter crews 600–700 feet away off their feet. Scholl was adamant that no flak had been fired (in contrast to Oancia's account) and that this was a rare account of 'kill by a searchlight'. But another eyewitness mentioned the flak too, though also accepting that it was the searchlight's blinding light that caused the plane to crash.[18]

The next morning, those on the base inspected the wreckage. The body of the rear gunner in the plane, Warrant Officer Joseph Bradley (another Canadian), showed hardly any sign of injury. Those there noticed that he was dressed in lace-up shoes with worn out soles and thin, unpressed uniform trousers.

Brown though had managed to get through without damage. Later, as they moved on, Brown instructed his gunners to open up on a train moving up a gentle slope in order to ensure that everything was in working order with the guns. But not everyone was happy with the way things were going; Basil Feneron, the flight engineer in AJ-F, felt that they were not flying low enough and were therefore at risk of being shot down.

Brown and his crew had though survived and carried on to their designated target. This was to be the Sorpe dam, still standing defiantly after having so far suffered only one hit. Brown was at least now approaching it and could do his best to succeed where McCarthy had failed. The scene was set for the final acts of this extraordinarily dramatic night. To be a complete success, the Sorpe needed to be breached, adding significantly to the chaos already unleashed on the Ruhr and its vital infrastructure.

12

Chaos in the Möhne & Eder Valleys
02.01 – 03.00, Monday 17 May

The scene of the drama now switched once more from the pilots who had released their bombs to the victims of the terror that had been put in train when the dams were burst asunder. Now, there were two dams breached and millions of gallons of water had been released with no possibility of stopping the deluge until it had worn itself out. A number of towns were under water within an hour of the breach – some within minutes. For many the horror would last through the entire night and beyond.

Freed from the walls that had held them in check, the waters surged down the valleys beneath the dams, searching out the line of least resistance and overwhelming anything or anyone in their path. After the raids, there would be much debate about how effective the mission had been. These discussions tended to look at such matters at the strategic level, ignoring their personal impact on those in the way of the waters. There is no debate whatsoever about the scale of the horror that overwhelmed all those unfortunate enough to be in the path of the inundation.

The water of course was indiscriminate as to its victims, young or old, male or female. In Hemfurth, a mile or so down a steep and winding road from the Eder dam, fourteen-year-old Wilfried Albrecht had been woken by his mother and rushed out into the street. He saw not only boats but also boathouses coming through the gap in the dam wall. One of the first to die was his workmate at the power station who had sought shelter in the cellars there, not reckoning that the dam wall would break. His body was found months later 20 kilometres downstream.[1]

Nearby, Elise Schäfer was also woken by her mother. The day before had been Mothering Sunday, a lovely, sunny day which, according to her father, promised a bumper harvest in the autumn. Her father peered out of the window and saw something, suggestive of a cloud, in the distance. He was not sure what it was but he knew it was not a normal cloud and he was worried. They went out into the street and in the distance they heard the distinct sound of rushing water. Two schoolboys appeared, spreading the alarming tidings that the water was coming. Unsure whether to believe them or not, they had their worst fears confirmed when a soldier approached them, telling them that it was all too true.

Elise went up the stairs to fetch her grandfather, who was on the upper floor. By the time she got down again, everyone else was gone and she was on her own. She rushed back in and went back upstairs to join her grandfather. Fortunately, the water did not rise high enough to submerge the house, which also stood firm against the buffeting it received from large chunks of wreckage that were hurled against it by the water.[2]

Emma Becker was sheltered in an air-raid shelter nearby. She had been to a civil defence meeting on the previous evening where ironically the subject of a raid on the dam had been broached. A warden had assured them that the dam would never be hit and on no account should anyone leave a shelter during a raid. It was poor advice and it could have cost Emma her life. It was also another example of the complacency and tunnel vision that characterised the German authorities' approach to the possibility of a raid.

Suddenly, Emma's neighbour, Herr Kohl, rushed in saying that everyone should evacuate the cellar at once as the dam had been hit and rushing water could be heard moving in their direction. She ran out of the shelter with her son, only to find that she had been parted from her daughter. Running back into the house she found the child was still there, so terrified that it was as if she were frozen to the spot. She dragged her out of the house behind her like a sack.

Then I saw the first wave coming across the nearby playing field. It was about six metres high and as white as snow. We ran up a hill behind our house, but there was a fence in the way. We lifted the children over and were pulling and tearing at the fence when the floodwater caught up with us. What a miracle! The fence gave way and we were safe.[3]

For the civilian population in Germany, the deluge was starting to hit home. It was around 0200, soon after the Eder was breached, when the phone rang in Colonel Bürke's office (Bürke was the officer of an SS flak unit in the area). It was Leutnant Saahr of the local air-raid warning office saying that he had received a message that the dam had been destroyed. The village nearest the dam had already been alerted. A motorcyclist tore up the main street of Affoldern, a couple of miles down the valley from Hemfurth right on the banks of the Eder river, telling people 'the dam has been hit, the water is coming, everyone out of the cellars quickly'. The villagers got out of the cellars as quickly as they could and headed for the nearest high ground. The water sped through and soon after demolished the suspension bridge at Hemelfort.[4]

The villagers of Nieder-Werbe, who lived right by the reservoir, had naturally been alarmed whilst the raids were on. They were at least very fortunate in living above the dam rather than below it. Now they were startled to see the lake level dropping in front of their very eyes. One of the villagers, Fritz Fesseler, a soldier home on leave, jumped on his motorbike and roared along the road that ran alongside the lake. He had the presence of mind to take his camera with him, but he was so overwhelmed by the scene unfolding before him that after taking one magnificent photograph he forgot to wind it on and ruined the rest of the film.[5]

The residents of Mehlen lived about 8 kilometres downstream from the Eder dam, just past Affoldern. One of them was August Kötter, a soldier who had only returned from the Russian front the night before and must have been looking forward to some peace and quiet and blissful domesticity compared to the horrors he had been used to. He had gone to bed at midnight after an evening with family and friends when he was woken by shouts that the dam had been hit.

At first he was disbelieving; he did not think breaching the dam would be easy and before he had left for Russia there had been anti-aircraft guns in place defending it and he was unaware that they had been moved. Having got up to see what was happening once the planes flew off, he went back to bed. He was not there long before screaming outside told him that the dam had been breached. Whilst those already up started to run for cover up the nearby hills, Kötter went to fetch his pig from the sty and brought it into the house with him.

His children had run off up the hill but he now realised that it was too late for him and his wife (and the pig) to escape. He could see a wave coming on, 'like an avalanche', about 3 metres high. A great wave smashed his front door open and he struggled, up to his chest in water, to the staircase to the upper storey of his house. He could hear the pig squealing in the water and it was washed out of the house through an open window.

He and his wife made it to the attic. He managed to remove some roof tiles so that he could look outside and see what was happening. The experience became progressively more terrifying; the pressure of the water washed the side of the house away and then the front of the building caved in. Fearing that the rest would follow, Kötter tried to cobble up a raft with which to float across to a nearby house which was relatively undamaged. However, it did not function effectively and they had to stay put and take their chances where they were. Remarkably, the house did not completely collapse; photographs taken after the waters subsided show the remains of a building seemingly perched half in mid-air as if held up by nothing save matchsticks.

Fortunately, this particular vignette had several happy endings. Kötter and his wife were both rescued and even the pig survived, rescued by a nearby farmer and put in his sty for safekeeping. The pig and Kötter's wife were reunited soon after, the animal running joyfully back to her when it recognised her voice. Whether or not this affected the pig's long-term survival prospects is sadly not recorded, but given food shortages in the area in the aftermath of the devastation it seems highly unlikely.[6]

In the meantime, the crews who had caused the damage were now focused on making their way back to England. The reserve wave, however, ploughed resolutely on. Their targets were flexible but, though in some ways such flexibility was not only desirable but essential, the lack of a clear briefing on the reserve targets would prove problematic. This would prove one of the weaker parts of the plan developed by Bomber Command.

With both the Möhne and the Eder dams gone now, clearly the next priority was the Sorpe. (In fact, economically it was a much higher priority than the Eder and the fact that it was not attacked more systematically by either the remaining planes from the first wave once the Möhne had been breached, or en masse by the reserve wave, was odd.)

Hindsight would suggest that this dam could in fact not be breached using the technology available on the raid but this was not recognised in the official orders, although conversations in advance of the raid suggested that it was always recognised as a tougher nut to crack due to its construction. Indeed, the fact that the Sorpe was still considered a prime target was hinted at when at 0210 Gibson was asked to confirm if there were any first-wave aircraft left to attack the Sorpe dam (which of course there were not).

Yet that some confusion existed was suggested when at 0221 Bill Townsend in AJ-O was ordered to attack the Ennepe dam by 5 Group. This was at best a minor target and it appeared that breaching it would not make any appreciable difference to the impact of the raids. Nevertheless, it was for the Ennepe reservoir that Townsend now headed. This was odd too given the radio message to Gibson at 0210, which asked him how many aircraft he had left in his wave to attack 'Target C', the Sorpe dam. Gibson had of course replied that he had none but clearly HQ considered the dam an important priority, which does beg the question of why they had not sent all the reserve aircraft there rather than to a purely incidental secondary target like the Ennepe dam.

In any event, at 0224 Ken Brown in AJ-F received the 'Dinghy' message to confirm that the Eder dam had been breached and set off for the Sorpe dam instead of the one at the Eder. It had been a harrowing journey for Brown and his crew so far, having experienced heavy flak over Holland and also witnessing some of their comrades being shot down on their journey to the dams.

As they passed over the town of Hamm, which was known to be well defended, they experienced very heavy fire. The planes were flying so low that the German gunners were actually firing down on them from the lip of a small hill. This was not the only problem for the aircrews either. The high-tension cables en route were a constant menace; a tangle with them would be fatal as other crews had already discovered. Brown's plane had also passed over the Möhne dam, where the gunners whose weapons had not been knocked out in the raid earlier were still quite active.

Down below the Möhne reservoir, the destruction that had been unleashed was still spreading. Further downriver from Neheim, parts of which had been under water since 0120, was Wickede. Hermann Kerstholt was a patient at a military hospital in Arnsberg but had spent the weekend in Wickede, though he had decided to spend Sunday night at Echthausen, closer to the dam. He had a good view over the valley and had been awoken by the sound of low-flying planes. He was later alerted by a rumbling noise and, looking into the distance, saw a 'grey wall' that he quickly realised was a foaming flood rolling down the valley.

As he looked on disbelievingly, he could see, floating on top of the waters, sections of huts with people on them signalling with lights. He could also see from time to time lights flare up and then as quickly be snuffed out, as would happen when a match was being lit. He ran to phone his relatives in nearby Wickede to tell them to get to high ground as quickly as they could. Fortunately, they all survived the inundation.

Hanna Maria Kampschulte was a sixteen-year-old girl in Wickede. She was woken by her mother at 0220 – she had been disturbed by the sound of rushing water and a distant fog even though the moon was bright. The family managed to reach the attic quickly but within minutes the water was up to the level of the top floor. Looking next door, they could see that their neighbour's house had already been washed away.

Soon after, they felt their own floor start to sink. They were forced up against the roof timbers. Hanna managed to push some tiles out and pushed her head through the roof. The next she knew was when the roof was being carried along by the current. Before long, the roof disintegrated around her and she then managed to grab hold of another piece of wreckage which she used as a makeshift raft. She eventually managed to haul herself out of the flood having been carried nearly 10 kilometres away from the site of her home before getting out of the deluge.

But she was still not safe. She hauled herself up into a willow tree, where she found herself in the presence of a cow nearby in the water. The cow was so close that it started to lick her feet. At around 0800 a man waded out to her, up to his shoulders in the water, and at last carried her back to safety. When she went back to her house later that afternoon, it was just a pile of stones and rubble. Tragically, the rest of her family, apart from her father who was away because of the war, were wiped out. Her mother was later buried with her infant son in her arms. Much has rightly been made of the heroism of the raids; less so of the devastation and personal loss that they caused. In war, there is never glory without death.

In the meantime, at 0226 wireless operator George Chalmers (in Townsend's plane AJ-O) reconfirmed a repeat order that had been received to attack the Ennepe dam, the original message not having been responded to – one of several occasions during the raids where communication had not always worked as well as it ideally would. Douglas Webb, the front gunner in the plane, could not speak highly enough of Bill Townsend's flying skills though: according to him they owed their survival to the pilot, who simply got lower and lower in a successful attempt to avoid any problems with flak. 'Bill was the best pilot I ever flew with,' he later said.[7] Despite his best efforts, they still experienced heavy flak on the way in, which Townsend avoided by throwing his 'heavily laden Lancaster around like a Tiger Moth'.[8]

Communications were still coming across the North Sea from England, giving the other pilots in the reserve wave their instructions as far as their targets were concerned. At around 0230 several messages were sent. One was intended for Flight Sergeant Cyril Anderson's plane (AJ-Y). With the Möhne and Eder dams both gone, he was to head for the Sorpe. Pilot Officer Warner Ottley in AJ-C was ordered to target 'Gilbert', the codename for the Lister dam.

But just a couple of minutes later, Ottley too was also ordered to head for the Sorpe, with HQ presumably realising that there were not enough planes headed for it; that it was a hard nut to crack was well known and given its importance it was crucial that as many planes as possible were sent to it. The same message was sent to Burpee in AJ-S but he of course was in no position to respond to it. Belatedly, though, Bomber Command realised that, with the exception of Townsend, focus should be on the Sorpe dam.

In the meantime Gibson's flight was going in the opposite direction, towards England and safety. On the way back, they re-engaged the still active flak positions at the Möhne dam; their instructions were to stick to low-level flying on the return journey as well as on the route out. This of course gave Gibson and his fellow surviving pilots who were with him the chance to inspect their handiwork from earlier on in the night.

As Gibson's plane flew back over the Möhne dam, the impact made through the efforts of 617 Squadron was already very apparent. Pleasure boats lay stranded on the now exposed banks of the dam whilst bridges peeked up through water like islands in a vast sea that now lapped at the base of the shattered dam. A lake had formed below its broken walls, one that was not stationary but moving clumsily down the valley drowning everything and everyone in its path.[9]

As Edward Johnson looked out from his prime position as bomb-aimer in AJ-N (Les Knight's plane) sand was showing all round the edges of the rapidly emptying lake. The power station in the shadow of the dam wall had disappeared. There were large lumps of masonry scattered around the valley below. All in all it looked a complete mess.

Joe McCarthy had already flown over the Möhne dam and the area below it on the way back from his solo mission to the Sorpe. To him it looked like an inland sea. There was nothing but water visible for miles. McCarthy was experiencing navigational problems on the way back and he had therefore decided to fly back the same way they had come in. They flew by mistake over Hamm but were so low that the guns there were unable to depress their elevation enough to fire at them. McCarthy was lucky to escape from this heavily defended area.

Gibson and his crew passed the Möhne flak positions safely and continued on their homeward journey. As they flew on, Trevor-Roper, his rear gunner – who had a few incendiary bombs left – asked if he could drop them out of the aircraft over any village that happened to be in their path. Gibson assented. Trevor-Roper had got through 12,000 rounds of ammunition during the course of the night and this was all the ammunition he had left.[10]

Front gunner Frederick Sutherland, one of Les Knight's crew, unleashed a hail of bullets at the cab of a train in a small town but the bullets just bounced off. No doubt tensions were high, especially following the death of 'Hoppy' Hopgood, but these actions contrasted with Gibson's own assertions that they were not out to harm civilians but to wipe out industrial targets – 'no one likes mass slaughter, and we did not like being the authors of it. Besides, it brought us into line with Himmler and his boys,' he said.[11]

However, there is evidence to the contrary in Gibson's uncensored account in his *Enemy Coast Ahead*. Here he quoted the story of a Sergeant Knox, whose mother had been killed in a German raid. Knox wished to fly on a raid over Germany as a way of obtaining revenge; in the uncensored account one of the deputy flight commanders was quoted as saying, 'Don't bother about the target tonight chaps, a stick across the town will do for all, and may we kill as many people as possible to avenge Sergeant Knox's mother.' This version of events was removed from the censored version released to the public whilst the war was still on.[12]

In fact, there is plenty of evidence that 'Hun hate', as it was euphemistically known, was widespread during the war years. Given a civilian population that had endured either first-hand or vicariously episodes like the London Blitz or the bombing of Coventry, there was understandable resentment in many quarters at the devastation that the Luftwaffe had brought to Britain. Not everyone was of this bent of course, but an article in the *Sunday Express* that asked the question 'why all this bosh about being gentle with the Germans after we have beaten them when ALL THE GERMANS ARE GUILTY'[13] would have found a sympathetic hearing amongst widespread elements of the population.

On the way back from the dams, night fighters were much more active but they still struggled in vain to locate and intercept the bombers flying at low altitude. At one stage, Gibson's plane was followed by a night fighter but he managed to shake it off as he had the advantage of the light being behind him.

However, the death toll for the night was not yet over as far as the British were concerned. At 0235 Ottley's plane (AJ-C) crashed; again this event was witnessed by AJ-F, Brown's aircraft, for whom these several reminders of the frailty of aircraft over enemy territory must have been very disconcerting. Ottley had climbed to 500 feet to get his bearings, another demonstration of the difficulty of keeping on course when flying at low levels.

Ottley's journey had already been eventful. When crossing the Scheldt, rear gunner Frank Tees had exchanged fire with flak positions from his rear turret. At one stage he had noticed the plane pass a church spire which towered above them.[14] However, Ottley's decision to now climb to see where he was could not have been worse timed; he was picked up by several searchlights and immediately found himself the target of a fierce flak barrage.

Frank Tees would normally have been the front gunner but for this raid had transferred to the rear gunner's exposed billet in the back of the plane, an action that would save his life and would cost the man who was normally rear gunner, Harry Strange, his. When the flak started, Tees had felt the shells strike the plane and saw flames streaming from the inner port engine. He heard Ottley say, 'I'm sorry boys, we've had it.'[15]

Ottley had in fact turned south towards the Sorpe dam too early and straight into the heavy defences to the north of Hamm. When the plane was hit, a fierce fire broke out in the fuel tank. The explosion blew off a wing and the plane went crashing into the ground. The bomb on board blew up on impact at the edge of a wood, creating a large crater.

In what appeared to be nothing short of a miraculous escape, Tees had been thrown out of the rear turret and was found some 4 kilometres away from the crash site. He was badly burned and was taken first of all to a hospital and then, when sufficiently recovered, to a POW camp. He would survive the war and return home, living until 1982. When he died, his ashes were interred alongside the graves of the rest of the crew, all of whom had died in the crash on the night of the raids.

A nearby resident, sixteen-year-old Freidrich Kleiböhmer, had been woken by light flak several hours before Ottley's crash. He was roused again when the flak started up once more and got up to see a low-flying plane with an engine ablaze flashing past. He was then aware that the plane had crashed at the edge of some woods. There was an explosion followed 30 seconds later by a much larger one as the bomb self-destructed. Although he was he reckoned 3 kilometres away at the time, the explosion was so strong that he was blown off his feet.

He had an irresistible urge to go and see the damage for himself. It was much further away than he thought. On the edge of some woods he bumped into a school friend. Whilst they were there, they were approached by a figure coming out of the woods. They spoke to him but he did not reply. It suddenly dawned on them that the man – it was Tees – could not speak German and was obviously a survivor from the crash.

Showing commendable nerve, Kleiböhmer managed to give the impression that he was armed and Tees put his hands up whilst the young man's friend ran into a house and phoned the police. They moved off and a farmer gave Kleiböhmer a hunting gun in case Tees tried to escape. However, he was in no position to do so as he was injured and Kleiböhmer had to help Tees along.

As they walked along, Kleiböhmer started whistling a song. Tees joined in. The image of the British airman and his German captor singing along to 'We're Going to Hang out the Washing on the Siegfried Line' is one of the more incongruous of that extraordinary night. They eventually reached a farmhouse where they went in and Tees sat down. Only then could the extent of his wounds be seen. His hands were badly burned and his chest was hurting. The farmer came in and berated Tees for the damage the RAF was causing. Tees just sat there, too exhausted to care.

A policeman arrived in a taxi about half an hour later to take possession of the prisoner. He asked him in Low German (similar to English) how many men were in the plane. Tees, understanding well enough, said seven. The policeman then said that four bodies had been found and that therefore there must be two men on the run. Tees was taken off, now violently shaking, whilst the search was on for the two presumed runaways.

However, there were no other survivors of Ottley's crew. Ottley himself was an experienced pilot. Despite being one of the youngest members of 617 Squadron, Ottley had already completed a full tour of operations with 207 Squadron. Hamm was well defended because of the rail-marshalling yards and the anti-aircraft position there had already been alerted by McCarthy's plane searching out a route home, although McCarthy had managed to get through unscathed.

Ottley's plane came down to the north of the village of Kötterberg near Hamm. Brown had seen the aircraft crash with a large explosion; in his own words 'he immediately blew up. His tanks went first and then his bomb … the whole valley was just one large orange ball.'[16] As well as witnessing the loss of several planes, Brown had already had an exciting trip, attacking three trains, killing five enemy soldiers and wounding eight others. Brown's plane had also received a number of hits from flak. The crew continued to head for the Sorpe dam, hoping to complete the spectacular successes enjoyed by the squadron that night.

Brown and Basil Feneron, his flight engineer, had divided their responsibilities for looking through the windscreen with Brown taking the port side and Feneron the starboard. They then passed information back to Heal, the navigator, to plot his position. Brown continued to fly at very low heights to avoid sharing the fate of some of his comrades, at one stage following the course of a road behind some trees to do so.

At virtually the same time, Henry Maudslay's plane, AJ-Z, was nearing Emmerich in the Netherlands. It was now on fire. Though the anti-aircraft post there had orders not to open fire in case they hit a night fighter in error, the gunners could clearly see that this was an enemy aircraft as it was so low that the markings could be seen. The guns opened up on the plane which went down in flames at Netterden. There were no survivors.

Again, Maudslay was unlucky. Minor errors in navigation could have fatal consequences. Emmerich contained significant oil facilities and was defended by a ring of flak. Several men from gun positions in the town later reported that Maudslay's plane tried to fly directly over the town but was hit by gunfire.[17] There were twelve guns trained on the plane, firing so low that they shot off the tops of nearby poplar trees as they tried to bring the aircraft down.[18]

The other survivors from the first two waves ploughed on determinedly towards England. Just before 0300, Gibson and those with him were in sight of safety. Before them, just a few miles off now, was the North Sea and then the homeward run to Scampton. Gibson flew over first, catching the flak gunners off-guard and roaring overhead and on across the sea, with Shannon not far behind.

When Gibson and Shannon approached the coast, they had adopted classic rapid escape techniques. They had climbed to 800 feet and then put their planes into a steep dive; this gave them the maximum possible speed to optimise their chances of avoiding flak on the coast. Gibson flew out over the golden sand dunes, lightly lit in pastel shades with the approaching onset of morning. The plane whistled over anti-tank ditches and beach obstacles and on towards safety.

However, 'Dinghy' Young, close behind, was not so fortunate. At 0258 he had been heading for a gap in defences but was possibly flying too high. He was following close behind Gibson and was unlucky as the gunners were now alerted. As he climbed to gain speed, he was perfectly silhouetted against the lightening sky. Young tried to veer away to the north but he was unable to do so.

The flak gunners homed in on him and opened up. The shells struck home and Young lost control. His plane plummeted downwards and crash-landed on a sandbar about 100 yards offshore. The plane broke up on impact and everybody on it was killed. The wreckage remained on the sandbar until 1953 when a fierce storm broke it up.[19] The gunners at Castricum-aan-Zee to the north of Ijmuiden reported shooting down an aircraft they believed to be a Halifax but this was probably Young's Lancaster.

The body of Charles Roberts, Young's navigator, was washed ashore and recovered on 17 May. Several others were recovered during the next two weeks. Having survived both the raid on the Möhne and then that on the Eder, Young was particularly unlucky. It was both poignant and sadly ironic that he had earned his nickname through his skill in surviving crashes at sea. This time, he had simply been too low to do anything about the loss of control when his plane was hit. One of the losses was particularly poignant. Sergeant Nichols, Young's wireless operator, was born on 17 May 1910 and therefore died on his birthday.[20]

There were suggestions later that Young had been flying too high before this. After the raid Maltby and Shannon remarked that they had used Aldis signal lamps to warn him that he was flying at too high an altitude. There were perhaps reasons to wonder whether or not he was a bit ring-rusty; he was not used to Lancasters, had not flown operationally for a time and was accompanied by an inexperienced crew, all factors that might have made him overcautious about flying too low. Whether or not these factors had played on his mind will never be known. He was unlucky; others had better fortune, like Les Knight, who at 0259 also flew to safety over the Dutch coast.

Behind the aircraft, parts of Germany were waking up to scenes of utter chaos. As the day was starting to lighten over Wickede, some miles beneath the Möhne dam, Clemens Mols reassured his wife that the water levels outside were starting to recede. They made their way gingerly down the stairs. On the ground floor there was a deposit of mud about 40 centimetres deep. They struggled to get the ground floor door open but could not do so without the help of others outside as the water had jammed it in. Outside the water was still a metre deep and it would be hours before it receded completely.

There was devastation all around. A metre-deep layer of the railway embankment was gone whilst a railway engine had been carried away. Two big factories had gone, along with a number of houses. The latter was a dramatic illustration of the human cost of war; not just the balance sheet of war production was affected by the raids.[21]

The residents of the two valleys struggled to come to terms with the immensity of the catastrophe they had experienced. It was hard to take it all in and the damage had not ended yet – the floods did not reach Fröndenburg, further downstream, until 0245. Many bodies were later recovered here, more than 160 of them, having been washed downstream and 26 of them, victims who were never identified, were buried in the town.

But those living below the Eder dam had on the whole fared much better than those beneath the Möhne reservoir. In part this was because the Eder valley was more sparsely populated, but also because there had been a surprisingly effective informal early-warning system that had sprung into action whereby news of the imminent flood had been phoned ahead more effectively; this contrasted with the ineffective arrangements in place in the Möhne valley. But even then it had been awful; the flood levels recorded in the Eder valley, which had been prone to flooding before the dam had been built, were nine times higher than anything seen previously.

In the aftermath of the raids, reasons for the lack of effective early warnings were sought. District President Lothar Eickhoff from one of the main local towns in the area below the dams, Arnsberg, wrote a report and, although one must recognise that he would have good reasons to try and exonerate himself by putting the best spin on things, there is an element of credibility in what he said. He claimed that an early-warning system had been in place by which the watchman at the dams would telephone a warning to Soest to the immediate north of the Möhne dam. From here, the message could be passed on to other towns in the region to warn them.

The fatal flaw was that when the plans were drawn up no one could envisage how devastating the bombs delivered by the British would be. Instead of an envisaged leak of 625 cubic metres per second (based on a breach near the top of the dam) the actual rate was 8,800 cubic metres per second and the speed of the waters released simply overwhelmed the communications network.[22] Yet however convincing this might seem, it of course assumed that a warning would only be given after the breach. If one had been delivered before the fatal moment, when an attack was under way but had not yet been successful, many lives might have been saved. But that would assume the German authorities thinking the unthinkable and accepting that the dams might be breached and moving those in the path of any inundation away from air-raid shelters and up onto higher ground.

Scenes of devastation lay all around. Later that day, another Wickede resident, Max von Booselager, went on a recce trip on his bike. He saw frightened cattle on the embankment and in the woods. In fact, the bellowing of the cattle, which according to some evidenced a certain sixth sense, had alerted a number of residents in the night to the imminent deluge and some owed their lives to them. In Vosswinkel, the first warning had come from a herd of horses stampeding through the town just before the water arrived.[23]

Now a once verdant valley was a wasteland. Meadows and pastures had been washed away or were covered with rubble or sand. The carcasses of animals – cows, sheep, chickens, horses and other animals – were strewn around everywhere. Most people in Wickede had been asleep in their beds when the floods hit and many had died. Perhaps the most poignant and macabre memorial was a child's arm that von Booselager saw sticking up through the mud.

It was ironic that the effect on agriculture had not been considered in the planning for the raids by British strategists, but the impact locally was in fact very significant. The effects of this would be longer term than those of the floods on local industry, which would soon recover. Lost animals could not easily be replaced and lost crops would not return until the following year.

In time though, even the effects on agriculture could be coped with. Crops could be re-sown and the land restored to fertility once more. Animals could be replaced, though with difficulty in the wartime economy. The impact on human beings and their lives, however, could not be so easily dealt with. For some of the inhabitants of the towns and villages affected by the deluge, the effects of these terrible events would last for a lifetime, played out in tortured dreams and tragic remembrances of loved ones who had not survived the fateful night when the dams were burst.

13

Final Attack at the Sorpe:
The Last Manoeuvres at Target Z
03.01 – 04.00, Monday 17 May

By 0300 the flood had reached the town of Fröndenburg and was starting to move beyond it. In the town, the waters were so fast flowing that a girder bridge there was washed away. But thoughts of the damage they had caused were far from the minds of the returning British aircrews now. For those who had not yet reached the relative safety of the North Sea, time was running short. Day was now breaking and this disadvantaged the British in two ways. First of all and most obviously, it made the planes much easier targets for both German flak gunners and fighter pilots. But there was also another problem. In the early morning mist, visibility lower down was extremely poor in some places and this would make it much harder for the bombers to identify their targets.

Cyril Anderson had been flying around for some time trying to spot the Sorpe dam without success. At 0310, he gave up and made the decision to turn back after being unable to find it. In addition to his problems in sighting the dam, he was also limited in his ability to fight off any attackers as the rear turret guns of his plane were not working. He had had an uncomfortable approach to the dam. Over Dulmen he had been picked out by searchlights and jamming in the rear turret gun had limited his ability to respond to the defences. He now felt that he was left with no option but to put the safety of his crew first and head back to Scampton. Just as Les Munro had done, he was going against the letter of Gibson's literal orders not to return with a bomb still attached. However, the reaction to his return was rather different.

Back at Scampton, confirmation of the details of the raid was about to be delivered in the best possible way, via the first-hand accounts of a pilot and his crew returning from the raid. At 0311 David Maltby's aircraft (Aircraft AJ-J) successfully touched down at Scampton, the first successful raider to do so. Others were well on the way but despite the existence of three prescribed routes for the return journey, no one really followed them.[1]

For many people back at Scampton there was little sleep that night whilst they waited for news of what had happened on the raids. Tension was high. There was an intense awareness that something special had been happening overnight even though for all but a select few details were still scarce. Sergeant Jim Heveron later recalled that when they heard that the planes were back in British airspace, they went out to dispersal to count them back in. For the next hour or so they would keep their eyes peeled on the lightening horizon, touched by the rays of the early morning sun, until it was obvious that no one else was coming back.

Another of those there was Ruth Ive, who left her Nissen hut at the crack of dawn to see what was going on. She noticed, as she could not fail to, that there was a number of fire engines and ambulances around – this had clearly been a big raid and no one knew what condition the planes would be in when they made it back. As planes started to arrive, Ruth could see that many of them were in a terrible mess.[2]

But there were still a few pilots flying above the heart of the lion's den and for them a successful homecoming was still a long way off. At around 0300 Ken Brown began his attack at the Sorpe. The valley was now in swirling mist, confirming the visibility problems that Cyril Anderson had experienced. Like Joe McCarthy, Brown would find it very difficult indeed to position his plane correctly for the bomb-drop.

The approach to the dam was extremely challenging. They had to fly in over the village of Langscheid directly above the target at a height of around 1,000 feet above sea level. From here they had to descend rapidly towards the dam. They then had to reach the optimum height of 60 feet above the target (unlike McCarthy, who had to do this visually, they did at least have the lights to help them). When they had reached this height, the flight engineer (in Brown's case, Basil Feneron) had to adjust the throttle to the lowest practical speed, ideally 180 mph.

To compound their difficulties, on the far side of the dam there was a large hill, unimaginatively known as Hill 321, which they had to climb over rapidly. This required that as soon as the bomb was dropped maximum power was called for, which would – hopefully – enable the plane to pull up sharply and to safety. Once the run had been completed, either successfully or not, the plane would circle back to a point above Langscheid, either to see the results if the bomb had been dropped or to have another go if not.

To make a successful drop required significant skill. If a pilot and his engineer left the escape manoeuvre just a fraction too long then the outcome might be catastrophic. Brown could see the church tower protruding through the fog, which gave him some kind of marker to get his bearings on. However, although he adopted McCarthy's tactics and tried to line up his attack using the church tower initially, it did not work. He came in for his first run but overshot the optimum release point. He had to climb hundreds of feet as quickly as he could in a successful attempt to find a safe escape route. 'It didn't do my nerves any good at all,' he later recalled[3]

Several accounts of Brown's attack on the Sorpe dam state that he did not adopt the same approach as McCarthy but instead flew down the lake. However, this contradicts the account of Dudley Heal, his navigator. He stated that 'the only way we could attack the Sorpe was to fly as near the dam as possible, at the prescribed height, and fly along the dam instead of at right angles to it as with the others, hoping that the nearer we could get to the dam and the nearer to the centre of it the better'. The bomb would not be spun though as it needed to sink quickly into the water when it dropped.

Brown's first designated target had been the Möhne dam but, with that gone, it was always the intention that he should divert to the Sorpe. Heal stated quite categorically that 'we knew if we had to go to the Sorpe Dam, we'd have to adopt a different technique'.[4] Arguing that Brown attacked the dam from across the lake also makes little sense given Brown's approach; the position of the church on the hill at Langscheid is only useful as a marker when approaching the dam wall from the side, yet Brown categorically stated that he used its spire to line up his attack.

In any event, the definitive version comes from Brown's own official account. All the returning pilots were required to respond to a questionnaire on their return to Scampton. One of the questions was whether their weapon bounced on being dropped and how many times. Brown's answer to this was 'N/A (line bombed)', confirming that he was following the approach of attacking along the dam, as McCarthy had earlier, rather than across the reservoir at right angles to it.[5]

The first attempt to get in the right position for an attack failed. A number of similarly unsuccessful attempts to approach the wall followed. Dudley Heal, Brown's navigator, thought there were six whilst Sergeant Stefan Oancia thought that there were between six and eight. Becoming increasingly frustrated, and presumably nervous too now that the morning was getting brighter, Brown decided to drop incendiaries to help visibility. They were duly dropped and achieved some success in setting light to some trees and providing some form of illumination.

Whether or not it was this that made the difference, Brown now set out on a run that he was happy with. When just past the midpoint of the dam, bomb-aimer Oancia let the bomb go. As it was not spun it dropped straight down onto the shallow sloping earthen bank and rolled into the water. Seconds after, it erupted with a massive explosion that sent a huge geyser of water into the air. The time was now 0314.

The crew of AJ-F looked on hopefully as the enormous explosion reverberated through the hills but, although the damage was greater than that seen before (which had been caused by McCarthy's attack), the dam was clearly not breached. A 'Goner 78C' message was transmitted from Sorpe ('exploded in contact with the dam, no apparent breach'). The crew could, however, see a crumbling along some 300 feet of the dam.[6]

This last attack was also witnessed by Josef Kesting, who was back inside the power station just at the foot of the air side of the earthen wall. He did not see the plane until it was over the middle of the reservoir – unlike McCarthy, who did not have them fitted, this plane, Kesting noticed, had spotlights shining out from underneath. There was another large explosion and all the windows in the power station were blown out. However, for the time being the turbines carried on working. Stones from the parapet were blown across into the compensating basin behind the dam.[7]

Another witness, Josef Brinkschulte, also saw both explosions. In his view this second one was much larger. The tiles were blown off the roofs of the houses about 500 metres below the dam. All the windows in the immediate area were shattered and all the telephones were cut off.[8]

Post-attack analysis by the Germans showed that the two bombs dropped at the Sorpe fell within 100 feet of each other but exploded just 10 feet below the surface. In actuality, about 230 feet of the crown had crumbled but there were no visible signs of cracks.[9] At the pre-raid briefing Wallis had said that six hits might be needed to break open the dam; only two bombs had been dropped on it.[10]

This was the Germans' one stroke of luck during the night of the raids. The Sorpe dam was positioned at a height of about 1,000 feet above sea level. If the wall had been breached – and given the construction of the dam this would probably have been a slow, drawn-out process rather than the relatively instantaneous explosion seen at the Möhne and Eder dams – then the water would have cascaded down the steep air side into the compensating basin below.

The power station at the foot of the dam would have been overwhelmed at once. The water would then have poured down another relatively confined valley, demolishing several small towns and factories along the way. It would finally have flowed out and added to the deluge created by the breaching of the Möhne dam, uniting with the already devastating flood formed by its destruction to create a massive swollen river that would then have obliterated everything in its path. Towns like Neheim (near where the released waters from the Möhne and Sorpe reservoirs would unite) and others further downstream would then have had an even bigger problem to cope with. But that outcome, at least, was avoided.

There is often overlooked evidence that, in the build-up to the raid on the Sorpe, Wallis was becoming increasingly nervous about the ability of his weapon to breach an earthen dam like this one. He had written in a memo to Bomber Command that it might be necessary to crater the dam on the 'air side' (i.e. the opposite side to that by the reservoir, the 'water side') before attacking it from the water. This might help to weaken it. In the event no such attack was launched and the solid earth banks that protected the concrete core of the dam, whilst crumbled, stood firm enough to prevent a collapse from occurring.[11]

A reconnaissance flight over the Sorpe dam three days later reported that 'no vital change can be seen except for violent activity on some sort of repair work and clearance of the road over the crest of the dam'. The Sorpe dam had held firm against all that had been thrown against it.

Now, having done what they could, Brown and his crew set their course for home. They would fly back over the nearby Möhne dam and see two breaches, confirmation that there had been happy hunting for at last one group of pilots that night: navigator Heal and bomb-aimer Oancia also thought they saw a third breach on the north-east end of the barrier.[12]

More planes were now starting to arrive back at Scampton. At 0319 Mick Martin and his crew landed safely. Then 4 minutes later it was Joe McCarthy's turn to bring his plane in. Because of his faulty compass equipment, he had successfully retraced his route out back to base. McCarthy had a rough landing due to his damaged starboard tyre. The right wing was very low as a result and struck the ground as they came in. When they finally came to a halt and inspected the aircraft there was also shrapnel damage underneath the navigator's feet which could have been very much worse for him if it had only been a few inches further over. Then it was in for a cup of tea.

The raids were now almost over. There was just one plane left still looking for a target. Bill Townsend was having trouble locating his target and at 0330 was still orbiting around looking for it. His objective was one of the secondary targets, the smaller Ennepe dam. As Townsend had flown in, the floodwaters from the Möhne attack could clearly be seen. In places, only treetops and the roofs of houses could be seen breaking through the floodwaters. Like Brown and his crew, Townsend's team had also seen the disturbing sight of several planes going down on their way in.[13]

As they neared what they thought was the Ennepe dam, they saw a bunch of trees on a hillside looming out of the mist. The bomb-aimer was having difficulty lining up his attack and there was some concern about whether or not they had got the right target. In any event, the spinning action was started and the plane began to shake violently.[14]

There were a number of other dams around the Ennepe so it was hard to be sure that they had found the right one. There was a big lake surrounded by land and trees, being quite hilly in parts in the surrounding countryside. There was little flak to worry about in the area, except for when they flew over a canal whilst trying to find the right approach.

With the thick mist it had been very hard to find the dam. Then they spotted it, identifying it by a distinctive hill in the vicinity. Townsend made three runs before he was satisfied that he should drop his bomb. On the last of them, the bomb was released. It bounced twice before exploding, creating a spectacular wall of water, about 30 seconds after release but well short of the dam.[15] It was now 0337 and the last bomb of the dam raids had been dropped.[16]

More recent research has suggested why the bomb may have bounced short. Quite simply, according to some historians, it appears that Townsend had attacked the wrong dam, another hint that the pre-raid briefing had not been all that it might have been as far as the reserve wave was concerned. According to these historians, instead of the Ennepe, it was the nearby Bever dam that Townsend attacked.[17] The Bever dam was completely different than the Ennepe, with an almost completely opposite dam-to-reservoir orientation and being an earth rather than gravity dam, the same type as the Sorpe, which had proved so stubbornly obstinate.

It has even been suggested that both dams were attacked that night. There were nuisance raids by Mosquitos over Dusseldorf only some 35 kilometres away from the Bever dam and one suggestion is that one of these dropped a bomb at the Bever. Paul Kaiser was a watchman at the dam and saw a plane attacking the dam there. He was convinced that it was a two-engined plane, which would mean that it could be a Mosquito but not a Lancaster.

Kaiser claimed to be quite knowledgeable about aircraft, which would add credence to his view that this was a Mosquito. But he also noticed that the plane was flying at a low level and it came over three times before it dropped its bomb, which does accord closely (though not completely) with Townsend's own account. And it does seem remarkable that an unidentified 'Mosquito' should be attacking a dam on exactly the same night that the other dams were hit by Lancasters – especially when no Mosquito had been briefed to attack a dam but, judging by its actions as reported by Kaiser, was taking great pains to ensure that it did so. This evidence points strongly towards the Bever being attacked in error by Townsend.

Yet there is still an element of doubt as Kaiser asserted that the bomb was dropped a distant 800 metres from the dam wall (it did not bounce and exploded where it fell) whilst Townsend's crew claimed that their bomb exploded 150 feet from the dam wall – a vastly different distance. Kaiser described the explosion as if the bomb just went 'phut' in the water. George Chalmers, Townsend's wireless operator, described a 'quite spectacular ... wall of water' after the explosion[18] whilst Kaiser described it as being 'no higher than the trees on the bank – it was like the way that fizz goes up when you open a bottle of sparkling wine'.[19]

Kaiser also claimed that he could see no lights on the plane (it was, he remarked, a very clear night) whilst Lance Howard, Townsend's navigator, made a specific mention of how he had great difficulty because of the shaking 6-ton bomb in managing to line the plane up with the two lights.[20]

Most likely the explanation for these contradictions is nothing more than the confusion that sometimes attends witnesses to great events when two witnesses looking at the same scene can actually experience what sound like two very different events. Trauma, fear, the confusion of witnessing something out of the ordinary – all help make bad witnesses out of well-meaning people. Interestingly, there were certainly contradictions between the accounts of crew members who were debriefed on the very morning after the raid.

That there are irreconcilable differences between these two accounts must be accepted, but the most probable explanation for events that night, short of finding a witness at ground level at the Ennepe dam who saw a bomb being dropped, was that Townsend had mistakenly attacked the Bever dam.

That there was a bomb dropped at the Bever that night seems clear enough (unlike the Ennepe dam, where only one bomb was recorded as being dropped during the entire war and that was on the other side of the dam and not on the water)[21]. The next morning Kaiser and his wife went down to the reservoir by the Bever dam and raked out red bream and perch that had been killed by a bomb blast. Other locals soon joined them, happy to take advantage of a free top-up to their limited rations.

Kaiser pickled a number of the fish that he had picked up and took them with his troops (he had been home on leave when he witnessed the attacks) on a leave train to Wilhelmshaven. His companions were drinking French cognac and Russian vodka and were soon very drunk. They helped themselves freely to the fish that had been so effectively but unwittingly supplied by the RAF.

For the British, this was a disappointing anti-climax after the spectacular results of earlier in the night. But it was after all only a minor target and the major one, the dam at the Möhne, had been breached, so there was plenty to be pleased about as far as the results of the raid were concerned. But the time for post-raid analysis would have to wait as far as Bill Townsend was concerned. Now his job was to fly his crew safely back across enemy territory at the conclusion of one of the most extraordinary air raids in history.

Daybreak was now not far off. Karl Schütte was still on duty on the Möhne and noted that, as it got light between 0300 and 0400, another aircraft flew over. He later related how 'the last serviceable gun on the approach road fired at it but in vain. This Lancaster shot up a barn in Günne with its machine guns and set it on fire. Our guns below the dam could only engage the aircraft while they were flying away from us otherwise they might have hit us on our towers.'[22] Schütte's active involvement in these extraordinary events was over. For the British raiders who had survived, a safe end to this incredible night was in sight. But for the German civilians in the path of the floods, the horrors were still unfolding.

14

The Return to Scampton
04.01 – 10.00, Monday 17 May

The raids were now over, as least as far as the British pilots were concerned. The last bomb had been dropped and the final plane was on the way home, though the deluge that was descending down the valleys in Germany would not spend itself for several days and the clean-up operation would run for months after that.

The top brass had spent the night at Grantham listening to news coming in from the raids. After the initial frustration and tension, the mood had become exuberant. Although they could not be sure of the full extent of the success or otherwise of the raids, the fact that two dams had been confirmed as being breached gave clear evidence that important and possibly vital results had been achieved. Reconnaissance flights in the morning would be despatched to assess the extent of the damage and then a reasoned judgement as to the mission's success could be made.

With everyone having dropped their bombs and either back at Scampton or on their way, there was nothing else to wait for at Grantham. At 0400 Harris, Cochrane and Wallis decided that it was time to return to the airbase at Scampton and greet the conquering heroes on their return. They would have been pleased to hear that at the same time a state of emergency was declared in Westphalia. A steady procession of planes continued to arrive back at the base even as the top brass started their short journey back to the airbase, with Dave Shannon landing at 0406.

Whilst the mood in England was jubilant (the extent of the losses suffered by the aircrews was not yet clear and would not become so until the planes had returned to base – this would dull the mood somewhat), in Germany it was anything but. At about the same time that Shannon landed, Friedrich Kleibōhmer had returned to the crash site near Hamm where Pilot Officer Warner Ottley's plane was still fiercely ablaze, emitting a shimmering blue light that lit up the woods. Bodies were lying around, one horribly impaled with a tree stump protruding through the stomach. Some of the parachutes still attached to the bodies had just caught fire. There were flak gunners searching the wreckage but no one could be bothered to move the bodies out of the way of the flames.[1]

The Germans not surprisingly wanted to extract any measure of revenge they could from the returning bombers and were on the lookout for those planes that had not yet made it to the relative safety of the North Sea. At 0410 fighters were scrambled from the Luftwaffe base at Bergen in the Netherlands to try to intercept any of the bombers that were still in the area. However, they did not realise that their targets were flying at low levels even on the return leg and at nearly 20,000 feet they were way too high to spot anyone. Townsend's plane was the only real target left and he was flying lower than he had ever done before, even in training. He had also fortunately changed course to the north to avoid any flak and this also helped throw the Luftwaffe off his tail.[2]

At 0411 Townsend sent the message 'Goner 58E' back to Scampton ('bomb exploded 50 yards short, no apparent breach, at the Ennepe dam'). Flying over the Möhne valley, the aircrew could see a vast lake. Houses could be identified only by their roofs sticking through the water. Townsend's journey back was relatively uneventful. They attacked some greenhouses in Holland in an attempt to 'stop the Germans getting their tomatoes'.

However, they would be wise not to attract too much attention to themselves. Townsend was understandably nervous on the way back as it was daylight and they were still over Germany. In a successful attempt to outfox the enemy, he kept the aircraft 'on the deck' and flew at 240 mph. The crew eventually made it back to the coast of Europe successfully.

They flew out between the islands of Texel and Vlieland. Although there was some flak, they were not hit. Marine-Flak 246 opened up on the plane but they could not get a low enough elevation and the spent shells ricocheted harmlessly over the low-flying aircraft, a neat symmetry almost for the 'bouncing bombs' that had pierced the dam walls earlier on.[3] George Chalmers felt that 'the fact that we were so low saved our bacon'.[4] The drama was not quite finished for them though; over the North Sea flight engineer Dennis Powell had to shut down one engine due to an oil problem.[5]

Ken Brown had flown back from his bomb-drop somewhat earlier. His crew had also flown above the Möhne dam and had opened up on the flak positions there from a range of about 500 yards in revenge, they said, for the death of Hopgood. As Brown's aircraft reached the coast, it was starting to get light. It was hard to make out the horizon from the sea. Three searchlights had caught them as they crossed the coast and flak came at them from all directions. They could hear shells and bullets hitting the plane but managed to make it through by dropping still lower. They were so low in fact that the sea-wall, on which the gunners were based, was actually higher than the aircraft was.

Brown's front gunner, Sergeant Daniel Allatson, blazed back at the enemy and he was vaguely aware of the flak gunners diving for cover as the plane roared over. The starboard side of the plane was riddled with shrapnel and inside the fuselage the crew made themselves as tiny as possible in an attempt to avoid being hit.

One side of the plane was riddled with bullets – just a few feet higher and the crew would have been done for. Again, fractions had made the difference between life and death. Once safely over the sea, Brown handed over the controls to Basil Feneron, the flight engineer, whilst he went to inspect the damage.[6] Brown was amazed, and intensely relieved, that none of his crew had been hit though the plane appeared to be badly damaged and he wondered if he would be able to land it properly.[7]

At 0415, the principal character of the raid landed safely at Scampton when AJ-G touched safely down. Gibson must have been delighted at the results of the raid though also worried about the loss of several planes (he, like everyone, was in the dark as to exactly how many and would have to wait and count the planes in as they came back). Only 5 minutes after him, Les Knight too arrived back at base.

As the planes were arriving back, in Germany the authorities were already starting to assess the damage and consider what measures could be taken to counteract it. Just after dawn, Reichsminister Albert Speer, one of Germany's most important figures, landed at Werl, some way off from the Möhne dam. The floodwaters had now also started to reach Kassel, about 35 miles north-east from the Eder reservoir. Parts of the U-boat, tank and artillery factories there had been affected. A number of railway sidings were under water and it was already clear that the accumulated damage from the raids was significant. There would be a major clean-up required, a significant rebuilding effort and also an investigation into what had gone wrong to allow the bombers to infiltrate and attack the dams with relative impunity.

The sight that met Speer when he arrived at the Möhne dam was horrific. The power station at its foot had been 'erased'. Industry had been brought to a standstill and the water supply seriously threatened. Speer wrote a report for Hitler which made a 'deep impression' on the Führer. But when Speer went on to the Sorpe reservoir later that day he found that the dam wall, though hit, was intact – though he felt that the British had come rather closer to breaching it than many others did.[8]

Most of the returning pilots were ecstatically received back at Scampton but there was one exception to this general rule. At 0530 Cyril Anderson landed. Gibson was not happy with his performance and he was soon moved on to another unit. Gibson remarked to Joe McCarthy that 'he had flown up and down the North Sea the full time', which was a blatant distortion of the truth and it has been suggested in some quarters that this again reflected his bias against men who were not of the officer class.

In any event Anderson was swiftly moved back to 49 Squadron soon after, officially being posted there on 2 June. Four months later, after another fourteen missions during some of which they had been involved in very close shaves, he and his crew were wiped out in a raid over Mannheim, a bitter vindication of their bravery. They were all buried close to the graves of 'Hoppy' Hopgood and his crew in Rheinberg cemetery.[9] Death did not distinguish between officers and NCOs.

It should also be noted that Gibson's negative attitude towards NCOs was far from unique. It was one that was explicitly shared by Harris too. He stated once that in his view 'decisions in NCO-manned crews are normally the subject of a mothers' meeting, and as in all councils of war whatever decision is made is inevitably one to disengage from the enemy'.[10] The RAF was not an egalitarian organisation using modern paradigms but in this it reflected the times in which the Second World War was fought.

Gibson's harsh judgment of Anderson seems unmerited and some of the fault for his failure to deliver his bomb needs to be attributed elsewhere. In fact, all crews in the reserve wave had been poorly briefed and the way in which their plans were subject to frequent alteration can hardly have helped. Only two of the planes in the reserve wave had managed to drop a bomb and one of those was probably at the wrong dam. Two other planes had been shot down flying over areas where flak gunners were now fully aware of the fact that there was something unusual going on over Germany that night. It was hardly the most successful part of the mission.

In addition, Anderson did have genuine mitigating reasons for his return. He had tried to find the dam but the mist had prevented him from doing so (though Gibson would no doubt argue that this did not stop Ken Brown and his crew from delivering their bomb after a persistent effort to determine where they were). Without a rear turret gun, Anderson was also exposed to aerial attacks from night fighters. But this was not enough for him to escape unofficial censure. His failure to deliver his bomb to a large extent confirmed Gibson's preconceived prejudices.

It also cannot have helped that, despite being thirty years of age, Anderson was an inexperienced pilot. He had only flown nine missions[11] with 49 Squadron before joining 617 Squadron (which again disproves the theory that all Gibson's pilots were handpicked 'crème de la crème'). Anderson had only recently come through 1654 Conversion Unit (such a unit being one in which pilots were retrained to fly heavy bombers like the four-engined Lancaster). His first mission as pilot of a Lancaster had not taken place until a raid on Essen on 12 March. He had returned safely from that mission with one engine non-functional.

Anderson and his crew had carried out three more missions at the end of March before another mission to Berlin was aborted when the air-speed indicator failed. This was the sum total of Anderson's Lancaster piloting experience before transferring across from 49 Squadron to join Gibson. Anderson's choice for the mission in the first place is strange given his relative inexperience in flying these leviathans of the air.

There was another issue to consider too though, one which is important in understanding Gibson's views. There was much concern in 1943 at the number of bombers that were turning back early (or on occasion dropping their bombs before the target). The Harris Papers at the RAF Museum in Hendon contain a number of items of correspondence that refer to this matter, which was considered a serious fault as it could lead to missions being incomplete and therefore requiring future raids to be carried out to 'finish the job', thereby endangering both planes and aircrew lives as well as compromising strategic objectives.

In reply to one of these missives Cochrane defended 5 Group's performance in this respect but noted that 'the weaker brethren generally make themselves known by an early return'.[12] The fact that this correspondence was dated 11 May 1943 shows that the issue was high up the agenda of 5 Group and Bomber Command's thinking only a week before the raids. Anderson's was the only plane to return to base from the raids undamaged and with a bomb still on board. In the final analysis, Gibson was unprepared to accept this perceived failure as it set a bad example to others and also stood in contrast to the actions of all other aircrews involved in the raids.

There were still two reserve-wave fliers to arrive back at Scampton. At 0533, despite the damage his plane had suffered, Ken Brown landed. Clearly and understandably perturbed by the flak they had flown through and the general danger of the mission, Basil Feneron got out and kissed the ground which perhaps he had thought he would never see again. The returning crews were well catered for; Leonard Sumpter recalled that there was a girl on hand with an urn of coffee to pep them up though the crews were naturally all very tired.[13]

The last man back in was Bill Townsend with his crew, who landed at 0615. Townsend was so exhausted and perhaps also elated to get back alive that he did not recognise Harris and brushed past him rather abruptly, which might not have been the best career move he could have made.[14] However, it is probable that Harris would not have borne a grudge. He himself was renowned for his avoidance of what he saw as unnecessary civilities and was therefore unlikely to have been too bothered by Townsend's understandable exhaustion after what he had just been through.

Harris had more than enough to be thankful for anyway. He was constantly on the lookout for ways in which Bomber Command could justify its existence. He had been fighting an ongoing battle for publicity ever since he took over. In 1942, he had complained that the press were eager for what he called 'hot' news, which strategic bombing did not lend itself to as the results were often not apparent until weeks after the raids had taken place, by which time interest in them had passed. Now, he had the hottest of all news. Contrary to Cochrane's earlier suggestions at the briefings that no one might ever know who the crews had been, they would soon be splashed all over the newspapers.

It was a magnificent opportunity in a conflict when 'instant success' in the bombing war was rare. A British government note of December 1942 had advised that, for Bomber Command to be successful in terms of its propaganda, timing was of the essence. It noted that 'it is when Bomber Command is doing well that our Public Relations Committee can take up the running. It is no use expecting them to be able to fill up the blank periods of bad weather with boastful predictions for the future [which reads like a sideswipe at Harris] or reminders of how well we did the month before last. When the weather is bad we must be patient and let the public forget about us until it improves – timing our next publicity campaign to fit in with our next good attack.'[15]

That 'next good attack' had arrived and the 'next publicity campaign' was imminent. Harris's very presence at Scampton confirmed how important the raids were. He was a man who spent much of his time in his command centre at High Wycombe and visits to front-line bases, although not unheard of, were rare. The mere fact that he was now here to greet the returning crews, and before that had spent the night at Grantham, was indicative of how highly important the raids were felt to be.

It was by now broad daylight. Eleven aircraft had returned, four of them with damage, three from flak and one from machine-gun fire. Rice's aircraft had also been damaged when it hit the water. Despite being at the centre of much of the action at the Möhne dam, however, Gibson's plane only had three small holes in the tail.[16] Eight planes failed to return, along with fifty-six men, only three of whom were still alive as prisoners-of-war.

The destruction that the raids had unleashed had not yet ended. Schwerte was 45 kilometres away from the Möhne dam. A flood warning was received there at 0300 but, unforgivably, Nazi Party officials did not circulate it, not wanting to unleash a panic and thinking that the flood's fury would be assuaged by the time that it reached them. German complacency did not stop after the dams were breached.

The floods' fury was in fact far from assuaged. The waters arrived at 0515 and washed away a number of houses. It would take four hours for the floods to pass through and more lives were lost, these losses being entirely avoidable. The floods moved on to Herdecke, 56 kilometres from the dam, where they were so strong that they washed away a column from a spectacular railway viaduct, rendering it unusable until it was repaired. A British reconnaissance report prepared after flights made on 19 May highlighted the damage and came back with detailed photographs of the viaduct.[17]

It could have been even worse. There was a train travelling towards the viaduct when the column gave way. Passengers saw what was happening and pulled the emergency brake and the train came to a timely halt before it was fully on the viaduct. The passengers got out and walked back towards solid *terra firma*. Eventually a courageous driver reversed the train gingerly back to the nearby station, taking great care to go as slowly as possible so as not to cause further damage to the still shaking viaduct.

The train was packed and the loss of life could have been great. One of those on board, a schoolgirl named Lotte Buerstätte, had noticed that her fellow passengers had been very uneasy and the train had been going very slowly. Then 'we saw an appallingly horrifying scene outside – an immense, seething mass of water roaring and gurgling along. It was filled with trees, roofs and animals. Then a scream went through the compartment. Through the train windows we saw the masonry from one of the columns of the viaduct crash into the raging waters. Spray splashed right up, the train stopped and we jumped out of the compartment.'[18] This was indeed a lucky escape.

Back at Scampton, once it was clear that no one else was returning, the surviving officers made their way to the mess, still dressed in flying boots and sweaters. Some of them helped themselves to beer whilst Humphries ran over and shook Gibson by the hand. But Humphries had more sombre duties to attend to: fifty-six telegrams to prepare for next of kin. He was both tired and depressed as he went about his solemn business with typical efficiency and a large amount of regret.[19]

At least there would be some recognition for one of the unsung 'backroom boys' at Scampton: he would be mentioned in despatches for his efforts. However, for fifty-six families the news was about to get very bad indeed. The Canadians had suffered particularly severely; of the twenty-nine Canadians involved in the raid, thirteen were killed and another taken prisoner.

Despite the apparent jubilation of those who were partying (who were probably as much as anything just relieved to be alive and able to fight another day) there was a mix of emotions present amongst the survivors and those waiting to meet them. For some, the relief was the predominant emotion, sometimes expressed in very mundane ways; Ken Brown remembered that 'when you got back – you've never had a bowel movement as great'. He was elated but noted that a number of the ground crew were in tears at the losses.[20] Brown was luckier than some; his plane was so badly damaged that it had to go back to the factory for repairs.[21]

Dave Shannon also remembered mixed reactions back at the base of both elation and depression. There was also, he confessed, a lot of drinking: Shannon fell over and blacked his eye as a result of overindulging. He was drinking until late in the morning and then went to bed for a few hours' sleep.[22]

Humphries also remembered a lot of drinking and singing around the piano. But he felt 'bloody awful' because of all the men who were not coming back. The survivors would be invited around other messes for weeks to come with Les Knight the 'taxi pilot' as he did not drink.[23] For others, at this precise moment exhaustion was the predominant feature. Harold Hobday, Les Knight's navigator, fell asleep in an armchair.

Barnes Wallis would be generous in deflecting much of the praise he received for his brilliant science onto 617 Squadron. In his own words, 'there is no greater joy in life than first proving that a thing is impossible and then showing how it could be done. Any number of experts had pronounced that the Möhne and Eder dams could not possibly be destroyed by any known means. And then one shows it can be done – but the doing was done by Guy Gibson and 617 Squadron – not by me.'[24]

Something of a mutual admiration relationship now existed between Wallis and Gibson. For his part, the Wing Commander wrote to the inventor on 20 May from Scampton:

[N]ow that the floods are subsiding and the tumult dying (wait for the Sorpe) I've at last found time to drop you a line.

I'm afraid I'm not much of a letter writer but I would like to say just this. The weapon that you gave us to deliver worked like a dream and you have earned the thanks of the civilised world.

All my pilots and I are honoured that we have had the opportunity to take part in the last great experiment which has proved all your theories.

And now, I think I need a holiday.

Best Regards … Yours sincerely, Guy Gibson[25]

Gibson's mention of the last part of the experiment referred back to what Wallis had said at the briefing just before the raids took off. It was true that many of his theories had been proved but at a high price. Wallis was unprepared for the extent of the losses suffered by the squadron. George Johnson remarked that he didn't stay for very long as he was so distraught at the number of pilots and crew lost. Dave Shannon saw that he was very distressed and Gibson himself had to reassure him that his men knew the risks that they took and that they took them willingly.

Les Munro's view on the losses was that 'you got used to it and you didn't let the loss of individuals that you knew get the better of you and affect your ability to carry out your duty on operations'.[26] In contrast to this resignation, Flight Sergeant Grant McDonald was stunned at the number of lorries later turning up at the married quarters where the men had been billeted to take away the personal possessions of those who had been lost.

Perhaps the most revealing analysis came from Ken Brown, in whose opinion 'it was the continuation of an experiment as far as Barnes Wallis was concerned. I don't think he ever expected anyone to get hurt – let alone killed'.[27] This is consistent with Wallis's comments before the raid, when he had said that the attack was just the final of three experiments. His technology had indeed worked as he had predicted it would but the cost had been high.

Wallis had entered another world to that of the laboratory and scientific experiment, one where reality was bitter and death a constant companion. The comments of the aircrews were true enough. Right from the top down, from Harris himself, there was no attempt to hide the danger that the crews were in every time they took off for an incursion into enemy airspace. Harris was, if nothing else, someone who told it how it was; he alone made no attempt to disguise the fact that in his view enemy civilians were a legitimate war target. In this he might have appeared callous but no one could accuse him of being a hypocrite. He was equally as plain-speaking with his own crews; he would tell them that only one in three could expect to see out the war but he would look after them if they did survive.[28] He tried to be a man of his word.

But he also saw no need for sympathy about casualties amongst the German civilian population. As required, the masonry of the dams had come 'crashing down' and the 'Boche' had been killed in large numbers. He would milk the raids for all they were worth, wonderful public relations material as they were. There would be more collaboration with Wallis in the future, 'earthquake bombs' of unimaginable size and power. Harris believed in the awesome might of high explosive and here was one inventor who had proved he had what it took to deliver.

Harris's views on the morality of modern warfare could not be further removed from Wallis's world of scientific experiments, a place that with its experiments with children's marbles and rowing boats across a lake seemed almost quaint. In experimental conditions people rarely died. Wallis was even reportedly shocked at the extent of civilian casualties amongst the enemy that his weapon had caused, for which he later said he was 'deeply sorry',[29] but his regret was as nothing compared to the losses that had been suffered by the aircrews that he had, in some cases, got to know. Two worlds, incompatible and at odds with each other, had collided and left the inventor distraught. It would not, however, stop him developing more weapons of Armageddon in the future.

For those whose lives revolved around the RAF, though, life had to go on. At 0800 the ground crews returned to work on the Lancasters when a tannoy announcement ordered all 617 Squadron personnel to attend a briefing at 10 a.m. Just half an hour later, 'Mick' Martin escorted a distraught Wallis, overcome at the loss of so many pilots and crew members, to his room.[30] Wallis was inconsolable, unable to come to terms with the losses that the aircrews had suffered as a result of proving his experiment. Ann Fowler too saw him with a dressing gown on, devastated at the losses suffered by the aircrews.

But elsewhere on the base, the partying continued. Later in the morning, a group of select individuals made their way to Whitworth's house. Here a party soon got going, an extension of celebrations that had already started some hours before. It was not long before they were dancing a conga through the house, quite a contrast to the sense of loss that was being felt in some quarters. Some of the more well-lubricated drinkers present were soon assembled around a piano, singing uncomplimentary songs about Germans. During the course of the celebrations, Whitworth's house was raided and his pyjamas stolen.[31] Breakfast was bacon and eggs, which tasted especially good.[32]

At 1000 Gibson briefed the squadron with details of the raids and their results. There were some happy tidings to emerge for many of them. All personnel were now instructed to proceed to the guardroom where all ground staff would be given passes for three days' leave whilst aircrew would get seven. Not everyone was ecstatic at this news, though most undoubtedly were. In contrast, it was bad news for Humphries and his staff, who would not be getting any leave – far from it. There were three documents to prepare for each individual granted leave: a ration card, a railway warrant and a leave pass, nearly 2,700 documents in total.[33] And it was down to them to do it.

The reward of leave to the ground crews emphasised an important and often overlooked point. Bomber Command was reliant on a vast army of 'worker ants' to service the aircraft and keep them in the air. They worked in uncomfortable and sometimes dangerous conditions, putting in hours that would soon inspire industrial action in modern society. They did not question the need to do so, for this was total war. For all the criticisms that might be levelled at Harris, he for one was well aware of the debt that his Command owed to the unsung heroes and heroines in the background, as he acknowledged shortly before the end of the war when he wrote:

> It is apparent to me that few people appreciate the terrible miseries and discomfort and the tremendous hours of work under which the ground personnel of Bomber Command on the airfields have laboured for nearly six years.

There was one final administrative task for most of the participants to perform. All the crews were debriefed and provided with questionnaires to answer.[34] Then they could think about their well-earned leave and what they might do with it. Humphries, however, was focused on very different things. There were those fifty-six letters to write and the fifty-six families who were about to receive the worst possible news. In their own way, they too were victims of the raids.

Even as this briefing was taking place, a few hundred miles to the east the floodwaters from the Eder raid continued to pour into Kassel. Here the flood would continue to rise for another five hours until, that same evening, it would start to subside rapidly as the water had flown through. Kassel was luckier than some: there had been ample warning to evacuate possessions from cellars to upper floors. Nevertheless, a number of military installations were affected, as were 1,130 houses and 1,220 flats. But it had got off lightly compared to many other places.

Now the raids were over. For the British it was time to assess the damage and also to ensure that maximum publicity benefits were gleaned from the raids. A great deal of effort had gone into the planning and execution of the mission. It was now time to reap the benefits. For the Germans it was all rather different: time to pick up the pieces and try to return to normality as quickly as possible. A massive and distracting clean-up process loomed.

15

The Impact on the British & German
War Effort

On 17 May 1943, British reconnaissance planes set out to assess the damage that had been caused by the raids of the previous night. They could not quite comprehend the extent of the devastation that they witnessed. A reconnaissance plane piloted by Flying Officer Jerry Fray flew over the affected area and took photographs from 29,000 feet. Water was still pouring through the gaping hole in the Möhne dam. In the valley down below the now half-empty reservoir, bridges had been torn down as if they were made of matchwood whilst villages had disappeared beneath the huge lake that had formed. The disruption was massive: power stations, roads, railways, factories, all out of action as a result of one raid where normally it might have taken dozens.[1]

The carnage at the Möhne dam itself was particularly striking. The reconnaissance planes noted a gap in the crown of the dam that was 230 feet wide, narrowing to 130 feet at its base. The power station at its base had disappeared. In the Möhne valley the damage in Fröndenburg was particularly severe. The railway and road bridges had been washed away whilst the railway station was underwater.[2]

But if anything, the damage done by the breach at the Eder dam looked greater. The break here had in fact been wider than that at the Möhne and nearly all the water had escaped. The lake had almost dried up as the water had escaped down the valley. It was though a misleading impression. There was less to harm than there was in the Möhne valley and it was there that the practical effects were greatest.

Fray returned post-haste to RAF Benson. He got something of a surprise when he landed:

> While I was landing, I could see scrambled egg at the end of the runway. It was the station commander and I wondered if I had done anything wrong. But he was only waiting to welcome me home. When I landed he came up to me and said, 'Have they hit them?' and I was able to answer, 'Yes, they've pranged two of them properly. The floods are spreading for miles'. So he went off to telephone the news to Bomber Command.[3]

Normally the photographs that Fray had taken would have remained top secret, but the Air Ministry quickly saw that wide propaganda effects were possible if they were circulated. Within days a number of photos had been given to the press so that the public could be made aware, and hopefully inspired, by the coup that had been achieved.

The results of the reconnaissance were soon telegrammed into Scampton. At the Möhne, it was reckoned that there had been an 'immense fall in the water level estimated at 30 to 40 feet ... Valley below devastated'. It was reported that 'Ader [*sic*] Dam not photographed but lake practically empty'. The two hits at the Sorpe were confirmed. There was 'every indication that seeping has started' and the lake below the dam was discoloured.[4]

The reaction in Germany was of course rather different in tone to the congratulatory euphoria that was evident in Britain. Karl Schütte was still on duty at the Möhne dam as those there sought to come to terms with what had happened. When he and his comrades saw reconnaissance planes, they fired at them but were unable to score a hit. They then turned to tidying up the damage around their gun emplacements and accommodation. In the latter, beams had been smashed and bedrooms and wardrobes were riddled with bullets and shattered by bomb damage.

In the afternoon Iron Crosses were presented; many of the gunners after all had stuck stoically to their tasks and deserved their recognition. Schütte was happy that they had brought down a plane and he and his comrades were all satisfied that they had done their best in difficult circumstances.[5]

But what of those British crew members who had not returned home but were still alive? The injured Tony Burcher had been taken on a stretcher to a nearby police station. With his back broken, he was laid out on a wooden bed for some semblance of support. He had a raging thirst and asked his guard for a drink of water whilst he waited for a doctor to come and help tend his wounds. The guard was soon back with the unwelcome news that there was no water to drink thanks to the efforts of Burcher and his brother airmen. Burcher smiled to himself, having received the first confirmation of the huge impact that the raids had had.[6]

However, the damage caused by the flooding was not yet ended as the man-made tsunami continued its destructive course onwards, carrying a mass of flotsam with it and picking up more as it went. The floods were expected to hit Essen at around 1200 on the 17th. When the floods arrived, they carried a macabre detritus with them, human and animal bodies mixed in with household goods. Water wagons had to be brought into the Ruhr district as, with supreme irony, there were shortages of the precious liquid all over. Two companies of soldiers were sent to Essen to hand out water there. A number of factories were out of action and gas production was badly affected in the short term, leading to the need for some rationing.[7]

The effect of the Eder breach too continued to worsen, though fortunately for the Germans this was at least flowing away from the Ruhr rather than towards it. The Luftwaffe airfield at Fritzlar, 25 kilometres south of Kassel, was inundated. Hangars were flooded and huts destroyed. The spreading of the damage would go on for several days yet: at Neinburg over 360 kilometres away, the water would rise to nearly six metres above normal at midday on 20 May.

For the German authorities there was also the practical problem of what to do with the unexpected 'gift' of an unexploded Upkeep that had been presented to them. Barlow's bomb was examined that morning and made safe by Hauptmann Heinz Schweitzer of the Luftwaffe; given the device's novel design, this must have been a particularly unnerving experience for him. The Germans, having examined it, described it as a 'rotating depth charge', which was as good a description as any for it.[8]

Great care had naturally been taken prior to the bomb being defused. The German bomb disposal experts at first struggled to make sense of this unfamiliar device. Local residents were told to open their doors and windows, just in case. Political prisoners were conscripted to uncover the bomb, making their expendability completely apparent to everyone.[9]

The disarmed weapon was later taken to a research establishment at Rechlin.

It was not long before Nazi Party officials were at the Sorpe dam to inspect the damage and assess how vulnerable the dam was. Given its construction there was still the possibility of a slower seepage of water through the earthen structure, which could eventually lead to collapse. They hastily initiated temporary repairs to patch up the damage done and also instructed Josef Kesting what to do if there was another attack. They gave him instructions to telephone all the houses directly below the dam if a breach was imminent; this would be no problem for him as he knew the numbers 'by heart just like the Lord's Prayer'.

Bundles of wood were brought up to patch up any future breach that might be made or indeed to protect against longer-term damage that the bombs of McCarthy and Brown had caused. However, the dam held and although there was a small loss of water due to leakage, there was no catastrophic effect from the raid.[10]

The Germans also needed to review their defence policy as far as the dams were concerned. The lack of a viable defence system had left them wide open to attack but the ease with which this deficiency could be corrected also meant that the dam raids, at least in this form, were likely to be one-off events. By Tuesday 18 May, barrage balloons were already flying over the Möhne and other defensive measures were quickly taken to protect against a recurrence of the attacks.

Just how shaken from their complacency the German authorities had been by the raids was evidenced by the defensive measures that were later taken to protect the previously unguarded Eder dam. Twenty-four low-level balloons were installed there (compared to thirty-five at the Möhne; the Sorpe dam was also now protected by balloons) and another twenty-four higher up to provide protection against aerial attack at heights of up to 2,000 metres. Five hundred smoke-generators were installed to obscure the dam in the event of attack (as they were at the Möhne dam). Searchlights were set up to pick out any planes that might attack in the future. Thirty-two guns were emplaced, some of them of large calibre.[11]

As well as these measures, some even more innovative ones were taken. At the Möhne reservoir a deflector wall, an underwater barricade constructed of logs in a raft-like construction and then weighted down with concrete, was sunk beneath the surface to prevent any future bombs from getting through at the dam. Two 100-metre-high steel masts were erected on the slopes around both the Möhne and the Eder dams. Between them steel cables were strung, from which contact mines were hung as another form of defence against low-flying aircraft.

This was an impressive array of precautions, though of course the stable door was being shut long after the horse had bolted. The precautions now taken also served to demonstrate why the raids were likely to be a one-off event given both the nature of the weapon used and also the lack of effective counter-measures on the night of the raids. There had been few defences over the Möhne and none over the other dams and there had been eight planes lost out of nineteen that had set out on the raids (many of them as a result of flak while travelling to and from the dams of course). A repeat mission using similar tactics would lead to catastrophic consequences with, in all probability, little or no success in return.

With these precautions in place, the planes would not be able to get low enough to drop their bombs. In addition, they would not be able to see to position themselves at the right release point and also stood a much greater chance of being shot down. All of these factors precluded any realistic possibility that an attack on major dams using the same tactics would be launched again.

At the Sorpe dam, Josef Kesting found himself turfed out of his accommodation to make way for flak gunners. He moved in with relatives at Hagen. Whilst he was there, he heard a rumour that the Sorpe dam had been breached in another attack. There was no truth in it, but that did not stop it running the length and breadth of the Ruhr valley, even creating panic at some of the funerals for the Möhne raid victims.

Examining the bomb of course took some time, as did the process of collating accurate data about the raid's impact. An official German report noted that 996 were dead and 221 missing; included in this number were 557 foreigners killed in the raids as well as 155 missing. Nearly 2,000 people were involved in rescue operations, including 1,250 military personnel. The loss of water would also have a powerful impact on industrial production in the Ruhr. Another German report mentioned 1,294 people killed, 6,500 cattle and pigs lost, 125 factories destroyed along with 3,000 houses as well as nearly 50 bridges destroyed or damaged.[12] The death toll was certainly the highest yet caused by a raid launched by Bomber Command.

Some areas were particularly badly affected. Casualty figures in Neheim alone included 147 Germans and 712 Russian and Polish workers killed or missing. Many bodies were interred in Osterbir cemetery, including French and Dutch prisoners of war.[13] The loss of civilian life offered something of a propaganda opportunity to the Nazis' propagandist *par excellence* Josef Goebbels, who unsurprisingly, given his track record, blamed the planning of the raids on a Jew who had emigrated from Berlin.[14]

Ferdi Dröge witnessed the aftermath once the water subsided during the morning following the raids, saying that it 'looked as if a mower had been through it. Hundreds of dead Russian women were lying scattered amongst pieces of debris, lumps of mud, cupboards, suitcases and personal belongings – a picture of abject misery.'[15] There were also muttered whispers about the inadequacy of the defences on the dam, and the silence from local Nazi Party officials about the raids afterwards was almost deafening.

The German government tried to raise spirits by issuing special rations to the residents of Neheim, including real coffee, spirits and chocolates. Three field-kitchens had to be sent over as there were limited working cooking facilities left in the town – Ferdi Dröge later remembered them serving up goulash. Members of the Hitler Youth movement were sent into town to help clear up whilst Red Cross nurses had the unpleasant task of washing the dead bodies. The town was effectively cut into two by the floods that flowed through it as a number of bridges had been swept away so temporary ferry facilities were set up. It took months to clear away the rubble and return to a semblance of normality.

But the impact on much of the infrastructure that had been damaged was relatively short-lived. Further reconnaissance flights on 18 May showed that much of the water in the dams had flowed away though Fritzlar airfield was still submerged. The water in the reservoir at the Möhne dam had dropped from 132 million cubic feet to just over 14 million, though the problem was that once it had flowed away the damage had largely been done and the task of recovery could quickly begin.[16]

The major problems caused by the flooding were quite often unexpected ones as far as the British raid planners were concerned. The loss of agricultural production created significant local shortages whilst the silt carried by the floodwaters caused ongoing problems for such important parts of the infrastructure as electricity plants. In some areas, the topsoil was washed away and the ground was barren for some time to come.

The task of reconstruction was a major one and put a significant strain on Germany's resources. The Organisation Todt played a significant part in helping the recovery effort. Founded by Fritz Todt, an engineer, in 1938, this was the organisation (now under the control of Albert Speer and incorporated into his Ministry for Armaments and War Production) which provided the bulk of the labour force for the Reich's construction projects.

Effectively, the workers were little more than slave labourers, composed of prisoners of war, concentration camp inmates and conscripts from conquered territories. Their lot was an extremely harsh one. Now, a significant number of workers were needed to begin rebuilding in the devastated areas and this impinged on other vital activities such as the construction of Hitler's much-vaunted Atlantic Wall. This was an important side-effect of the raids.

The rebuilding of the Möhne dam was particularly necessary for the German war effort, but this would not be possible until the railway line from Neheim, which had been washed away in the deluge, was rebuilt. A decision to rebuild the dam was so vital that it was made on 17 May, the same day that it was breached, and clearance work would begin within two weeks. By 15 June, the railway line would be restored and this would be crucial in enabling supplies to be brought up and the work of reconstruction to begin.

Of course, the British would have some difficulties in assessing the damage caused with complete accuracy. It quickly became apparent though that the major impact of the raids might well be in boosting morale on the home front. The spectacular aspects of the raids, their very uniqueness and the courage required by the crew members involved gave the raids a very strong 'footprint' on public consciousness as far as their potential impact was concerned.

So too did the loss of some crew members in the raids. They provided an example of heroic self-sacrifice which could also be used as a positive example to those back home. This might seem a somewhat cynical view but instances of such heroism would certainly be of some use in strengthening morale amongst a civilian population which itself had suffered quite badly from the Blitz. It is important in the context of war to try to make some sense of the senseless in terms of the loss of life and this could be done to some extent by demonstrating that men had died heroically in a valiant and successful cause.

Yet the number of deaths had made a deep impression on those back at Scampton. Possibly the loss had been deeper than that normally felt with the losses inevitably suffered in war as the squadron had lived and breathed the raids for several months. Death was no stranger to these men. But there does seem to have been an intense poignancy connected to those who lost their lives during these particular raids.

Perhaps this explained why lunch on 17 May was a quiet affair at Scampton, though there were a few still talking enthusiastically about the results of the previous night's raid.[17] However, congratulatory messages started to pour in. Harris was particularly effusive, sending one to Cochrane and another to Wallis, who was now certainly accepted as a talented engineer of the highest order. On the very next day, good news was received by David Maltby: he was promoted to the rank of Squadron Leader. More sombrely, just two days later the first replacement for those lost on the raids arrived in the form of Flight Lieutenant Allsebrook from 49 Squadron.[18]

News of the raids' success was quickly circulated around official circles. An official 'Most Secret and Most Immediate' memo was sent by the Air Ministry to Churchill and other key leaders, including Generals Marshall and Arnold and Admiral King, in the USA on 17 May. It noted that the raids had been a success and that Gibson, who had led them, had returned unscathed. The only slight caveat included was that the 'Sorpe dam being of different construction not expected to be breached but crest damaged for 200 feet. Water flowing over, seepage hoped for.'[19]

The raids were the first item discussed by the War Cabinet in their daily meeting at 10 Downing Street at 1730 on 17 May. Chaired by the Deputy Prime Minister Clement Attlee in Churchill's absence (the Prime Minister would not fly back in from the USA until 5 June), the War Cabinet duly asked that 'their congratulations on this operation should be conveyed to the squadron concerned, and to such persons concerned with the preparations as the Secretary of State for Air and the Ministry of Aircraft Production, in consultation, might select'.[20]

The War Cabinet soon moved on to other concerns. The following day's discussions focused in particular on how to deal with a troublesome prisoner in India by the name of Mr Gandhi. This would be followed later in the week by confidential discussions about whether or not to abandon support for another troublesome character in the form of General Charles de Gaulle given the hostility he often aroused. The Cabinet decided that such a breach could not be countenanced given the negative repercussions that would ensue if such a policy were embraced. Both these other contemporary issues highlight just how welcome an item of 'positive news' like that of the raids was at such a point in history.

Some details of the raids would not remain secret for long. Selected details of them were soon to be broken to a British public that was hungry for good news stories. The first public announcement was made at the Norwegian Independence Day celebrations at the Royal Albert Hall in London by Sir Archibald Sinclair, Secretary of State for Air. Sinclair also sent a congratulatory telegram to HQ Bomber Command.[21] All of a sudden, the top brass seemed desperate to hand out their praise in generous amounts to those who had taken part.

Harris was well aware of the power of the press. Since 1942 the BBC had placed its own resident correspondent, Richard Dimbleby, with Bomber Command. Harris had immediately given him virtually unrestricted access to anyone, making him answerable directly to Harris personally. Now Harris was prominently quoted in the coverage following the raids, with the following words of endorsement to the successful aircrews:

> Your skill and determination in pressing home the attack will forever be an inspiration to the RAF. In this memorable operation you have won a major victory on the Battle of the Ruhr, the effects of which will last until the Boche is swept away in the flood of final disaster.[22]

Whilst the raids were a great coup for Harris in terms of publicity, Wallis's reputation had been firmly established by his part in the design of the weapon. The day after the raid he was in King Charles Street in Whitehall. Whilst he was there, the results of the reconnaissance mission came in. Soon after, the telephone rang. Sir Charles Portal wanted to see Wallis, who hurried off complete with photographs of the effects of the raids.

Most thoughts of secrecy were abandoned as the British High Command now saw the opportunity to boost morale by stories of the raids, though some details about the bomb's construction would be kept closely guarded for years. On the day after the raids, the British press was full of headlines about the raids. 'RAF blow up three key dams in Germany' proclaimed the *Daily Telegraph*, somewhat exaggeratedly as it turned out. A photograph of the breached Möhne dam appeared next to the headline.

'Dams were burst open by only 19 Lancasters' boasted the *Daily Express* whilst the *Daily Mirror* told its readers 'Huns get a flood blitz'. Even the *New York Times* carried a report as its front page – this would have been particularly welcomed by Churchill in his efforts to build trans-Atlantic support for Britain's war efforts.

In fact, the turnaround in attitude was remarkable. Whereas even on the eve of the raids secrecy was the byword and crews were instructed to keep their experiences to themselves, now the story was literally front-page news. Of course the story still needed to be managed. Months after the raids, concerns were still being expressed that no technical details of the bomb should be released (at least not accurate ones). But the press were now invited, within bounds, into the secret and through them, vicariously, was the British public.

The reasons for this change of heart are not hard to find. The timing for Churchill, in Washington whilst the raids were taking place and due to address Congress within a couple of days, was perfect. The sensational and innovative nature of the raids provided an almost unique opportunity for Bomber Command, and more importantly the British war effort, to trumpet its successes. Although this was useful for home consumption, the greatest beneficial impact as far as Churchill was concerned was, he hoped, to be on the occupants of the White House and the Kremlin.

Harris was quick to see the opportunity too. In response to congratulations sent from the RAF delegation in Washington on 18 May, he messaged back that 'your congratulations will be heartily welcomed by all concerned. Thanks largely to your steady belief in the bomber offensive we have now a force which can deal the enemy lethal blows. To complete the job quickly we need only the increased weight of attack which American cooperation can provide and which we hope will shortly be forthcoming.'[23] The last comment was addressed to an ongoing debate with the US Air Force as to how use its resources best; unsurprisingly Harris wanted their numbers added to the massive raids launched as part of the strategic bombing campaign, but not everyone was convinced.

Bomber Command reflected very positively on the success of 617 Squadron. Much was made of the virtues of the way in which the raids had been led by Gibson in his role as 'master bomber'. It was acknowledged too that this would not have been possible without the use of the enhanced radio equipment which 5 Group considered to be 'outstandingly efficient'. The intensive training which had equipped 617 Squadron with the right skills to carry out the raids was also lauded (the 5 Group newsletter for May 1943 proudly stated that 617 Squadron had dropped 2,288 practice bombs), though the intensiveness would clearly not be appropriate for the training of most aircrews who were not involved in special missions.[24]

To some extent, the perceived success of the raids on the dams had papered over the cracks of problems elsewhere in Bomber Command; the same newsletter was full of blatant sideswipes at the quality of air bombers for ongoing problems generally regarding the accuracy of bombing raids, to which those on the dams were an exception. Some practices used by 617 Squadron were more widely adopted in the future, including both the 'master bomber' approach and the enhanced radio equipment which would become a standard feature of Bomber Command activity.

By this time, the human cost of the raids in Germany was becoming increasingly apparent. On 20 May, Neheim started to bury its dead. There had been an unseemly spat beforehand when crosses which had been placed on the coffins of the dead by representatives of the Catholic Church were removed by some faceless official. They were eventually replaced.

The official funeral service (there was to be a mass burial) started at 1000 with a Nazi 'Party' ceremony. Just as the religious rites were about to commence at 1145 some lads ran into the cemetery, shouting that the Sorpe dam had been burst. Hundreds of overwrought people scattered at once towards the hills (though the cemetery itself was set on higher ground and would probably have been above the flood anyway). Back in the town there was terrible panic. It turned out of course that it was a false alarm, but it spoke volumes for the nerves of those living beneath the shadow of the dams.

Two days later, a mass funeral was also held at Fröndenburg. The coffins were draped in the flags of the Third Reich and a string of speakers used the occasion to pump up patriotic feelings and also feelings of rage and hatred against the British. The ceremony was meticulously choreographed, with the sound of muffled drums accompanying the dead to their last resting place whilst behind the coffins priests and family members followed on.

It proved difficult for some of the bodies to be identified as they had often been washed some way away from their place of residence or, indeed, those who might have been able to claim them were themselves dead. Numbered photographs were taken by the police and circulated to relatives and friends frantically looking for loved ones. It was like the aftermath of a major disaster at sea where some great liner had gone down taking hundreds of people with it.

Although one of the aims of aerial bombing was to break the fighting spirit of the enemy, the raids on the dams did not succeed on their own in doing this. However, it was part of a cumulative process, a gradual, slow erosion of the will to resist of the enemy population. And there were certainly localised effects on morale, of which the alarm at Neheim during the burial services there was just an example. Weeks after the deluge had hit the town, Helene Schulte wrote from her home in Fröndenburg to her brother in Berlin, describing how there had been a number of air-raid warnings since the night of the disaster and that the Sorpe dam was cracked, further adding to the pressure on already frazzled nerves.

There had also been something of a loss of confidence in party officials. Frau Schulte found it hard to come to terms with the fact that there had been two hours after the dam had been breached to warn the residents of Fröndenburg that the water was coming but nothing had been done. Lives and properties had been lost as a result. The only good news, she noted with admirable sangfroid, was that there were plenty of fish lying around in her flat for her to eat.[25]

Despite the triumphal air of the headlines written by the British press, there were also families in Britain for whom the greatest emotions were ones of sadness and loss. Fifty-six families would in the next few days receive letters from Gibson (the telegrams prepared by Humphries would have been sent before, though as yet no one in Britain knew that three of the missing crew members were still alive and two of them were prisoners of war already, whilst John Fraser was still on the run and had not yet been captured).

The letter that Gibson sent to the family of Bill Astell exemplified those received by fifty-five other families for whom a terrible tunnel of doubt had been entered when they must have suspected that their loved one was dead, though there remained an almost cruel element of uncertainty that could lead to occasional but unlikely hopes that they were either an as yet undeclared prisoner of war or, even less likely, on the run somewhere.

Astell was a very popular member of the squadron whose loss would have been especially keenly felt by other members of the crew and many of the 'fairer sex' back at base. This comes through in Gibson's letter to Astell's father, which was sent on 20 May:

My Dear Mr Astell

It is with deep regret that I write to confirm my telegram advising you that your son, Flight Lieutenant William Astell, is missing as a result of operations.

Flight Lieutenant Astell was a great personal friend of mine and his assistance was extremely valuable in the organisation of this operation. I watched him making his approach to the target and saw his aircraft in difficulties, and afterwards crash to the ground. Whether there was time to get out, we cannot possibly say, and do not like to raise your hopes too high.

If, as is possible, your son was able to abandon his aircraft and land safely in enemy territory, news should reach you direct from the International Red Cross Committee within the next six weeks. Please accept my sincere sympathy during this anxious period of waiting.

I have arranged for his personal effects to be taken care of by the Committee of Adjustment Officer at this Station, and these will be forwarded to you through the normal channels in due course.

If there is any way in which I can help you, please let me know.

Yours Very Sincerely

Guy Gibson

Wing Commander,

Commanding, No, 617 Squadron, R.A.F[26]

617 Squadron would enjoy a welcome respite from serious wartime activity after the raids. For the remainder of May and all of June, the squadron only took part in training exercises, most of which appeared

to many of the crews to be pointless. There were occasionally brawls at local pubs where jealous members of other units mocked 617 Squadron for their fame, renaming them 'One Op Squadron'. Humphries wondered whether a world record in hangovers was achieved during this period.[27]

That this period of inactivity was well merited was evidenced by the urgent requests sent around the various Groups after the raids in order to find reinforcements for the badly depleted 617 Squadron. SASO Air Vice-Marshal Oxland was writing to the HQs of 1, 3, 4, 5, 6 and 8 Groups on 26 May in such a vein, requesting that Groups should send in their recommendations to 5 Group HQ. Three conditions were attached; that the men involved should have completed two full operational tours, that they should be willing to participate in further operations and that they should be complete crews.

However, there was some reticence in response to this initial request and Harris sent out a further request in June. The high level of losses sustained by 617 Squadron seems to have discouraged volunteers from coming forward, especially considering that those who had completed two tours were entitled to a withdrawal from front-line operations. Harris's suggestion that the involvement of volunteers would be 'to continue operational flying on a reduced scale' clearly did not prove attractive enough to tempt many new recruits for 617 Squadron to come forward.[28]

Despite the losses sustained during the raids, the PR opportunities for the British were obvious and soon started to be milked to the full. Medals were soon starting to be awarded in recognition of the morale-boosting success of the dams. Gibson was recommended for the highest possible award, the Victoria Cross, on 19 May and the King confirmed the award on the 22nd. The whole of Gibson's crew was honoured. In fact, every surviving pilot who had delivered a bomb was rewarded with a medal of some description.

Gibson himself went off on leave for a few days to Penarth, the home of his in-laws. Here he spent a few days relaxing with Eve and in particular playing rounds of golf with his father-in-law. Whilst he was here, he received a telephone call to tell him of his VC. A suitably boisterous celebration then followed in the clubhouse of the Glamorganshire Golf Club. It was a welcome few days for Eve, who did not see much of her husband who lived most of his time unaccompanied on various bases whilst she stayed at her parents' home or in hotels. She eventually found a house in London, where there was much more for her to do when she was on her own, but the couple continued to spend very little time together.

Although superficially they appeared to be a very glamorous couple – the young, dashing wing commander and the actress – their marriage does not seem to have been very close. In 2010, nearly seventy years after Gibson's death, a former RAF nurse by the name of Margaret Masters was quoted in the British media claiming to have been having an affair with Gibson in 1943.[29] She was certainly an attractive woman back then, but more pertinently Gibson found a willing listener in her. She said that, 'I found that he was at a bad spot. In fact his marriage was broken and he was lonely, unhappy – but he loved his job, everything was flying.' The last part of the statement certainly rings true.

The relationship (no mention of consummation was made; there has always been a good deal of gossip concerning Gibson's roving eye but the relationship with Margaret was something quite different from a casual sexual liaison) appeared doomed, as many such trysts do, because Gibson refused to leave his wife. Just three months after meeting Gibson, Margaret Masters married another man.

Even on the day of the ceremony Margaret was unsure whether or not to – a sense of uncertainty that could not have been helped if, as she claimed, Gibson phoned her on the day to ask her not to go through with it. However, she felt there was no future in the relationship with Gibson and pushed ahead with the wedding. It even appears that there was a subsequent clandestine meeting in the period immediately before the raids when the two of them went to watch the classic film *Casablanca* together in the weeks immediately preceding the raids.

Moral judgements should be avoided; the stories give a different and important insight into another side of Gibson, a man who understandably felt the loneliness of command. He was 'a man born for war' and domesticity fitted uncomfortably with this way of life. It was understandable if an older woman who was a West End performer did not fully empathise with the pressures Gibson was under (especially when she did not live with him most of the time). Margaret Masters, an RAF nurse, was in a position to appreciate the pressures of warfare far better and perhaps gave him a shoulder to cry on that was not available elsewhere.

Yet Gibson would in all probability never have deserted his wife. He was acting out a part, and doing it splendidly, and the public abandonment of Eve would have been unthinkable. It would have destroyed his public image, the protection of which was a duty that Gibson held dear. This was a poignant otherworld story, of a parallel life that Gibson might have wished for but could never have had.

The large number of medal awards demonstrates some of the thinking behind the top brass's approach to the PR opportunities offered by the raids. Whilst Gibson had shown intense personal bravery and the award of the VC was understandable, it is unclear why, for example, his flight engineer John Pulford was awarded the Distinguished Flying Medal when no other participant in the raid in the same role received such a decoration.

Similarly, only one other front gunner other than Flight Sergeant Andrew Deering was awarded a medal. (This was Sergeant Douglas Webb in Bill Townsend's crew, who was given the DFM. Townsend's crew clearly made a good impression on the authorities as six out of seven crew members were decorated. Quite what Sergeant Denis Powell, his flight engineer, had done to upset anyone is unclear, but he was the only one in the plane not decorated.) The emphasis on Gibson's crew showed that the strategy was to focus the attention on him and his men and use the positive propaganda that the raids offered to maximum effect by focusing it in particular on them.

The decorations also revealed several apparent anomalies in the awards process. During the Second World War, Distinguished Flying Crosses (DFCs) were awarded to officers whilst Distinguished Flying Medals (DFMs) were awarded to other ranks even though the qualifying actions for each decoration were identical. The DFC was awarded to officers and warrant officers. It had been brought into existence on 4 June 1918 for 'an act of valour, courage or devotion to duty whilst flying on active operations against the enemy'. 4,018 were awarded during the Second World War, along with 214 first and 5 second bars.

The DFM, which came into existence at exactly the same time, was awarded to non-commissioned officers and men and was awarded in identical circumstances to the DFC – 'a quite unnecessary piece of class discrimination', as it has been called. In 1993, the two were effectively merged with the DFC nowadays the only medal for all RAF personnel.[30]

Another anomalous situation concerned the issuing of posthumous awards. At the time of the raids, only the Victoria Cross and George Cross could be awarded posthumously (though there was also the possibility of a posthumous Mention in Despatches).[31] Therefore, for example, 'Hoppy' Hopgood was not awarded a medal despite the fact that he and his crew had dropped their bomb on the Möhne dam before, in most cases, losing their lives.

Sergeant John Pulford from Hull, one of Gibson's crew, had one of the strangest experiences of all. On the night he was informed of his DFM, he and his brother, also an airman, went out to celebrate. They thought that they would dress themselves in 'civvies' rather than their uniform. When they got home afterwards, they found that some ignorant individual had placed white feathers, the symbol of cowardice, in their pockets, assuming that their attire meant that they had forgone their duty to fight. Rarely can there have been a more ill-advised misjudgement.

Approbation and recognition came from the highest levels. On 27 May, King George VI and Queen Elizabeth visited Scampton. For most of the aircrews the visit was to be kept informal; instructions in advance were that 'all airmen are to be at work performing their ordinary functions'.[32] It was noted in the plans for the visit that at appropriate times sherry and biscuits were to be available along with light refreshments and tea whilst 'special care is to be taken to provide suitable and adequate cloak-room accommodation' for the royal party.

The royal party would come in two cars and lunch arrangements were to cover all of the party, including the two chauffeurs and two detectives that accompanied it. The royal standard was not to be flown and the press were not to be allowed into the airbase during the visit – the visit was to be kept as secret as possible. Finally, 'all available personnel should line the route within the camp and cheer Their Majesties on departure'.

It was a typically busy day for the royals; they had visited North Coates and Binbrook airbases before arriving at Scampton and were going on to Digby afterwards. They arrived at Scampton at 1300 and were taken straight to lunch in the officers' mess, where photographs were taken (Gibson sat opposite the King during the meal). Then at 1400 the royals were driven out to the runway, where they were presented to personnel from both 617 Squadron and 57 Squadron, who shared Scampton airbase.

This public demonstration of togetherness was somewhat ironic as, because of the seeming lack of activity by 617 Squadron before the raid, 57 Squadron called them 'the Armchair Boys'[33] and there had sometimes been an undercurrent of simmering resentment that had occasionally broken out into bouts of fisticuffs in the pubs of Lincoln and elsewhere.

Barnes Wallis was also at Scampton when the royals visited and was presented to them. He was there when the King and Queen visited No. 2 Hangar at 1445 after first visiting the hangar crew room and inspecting the models of the dams that had been prepared for the briefings to the crews before the raids. They then toured the bomb store and workshops.[34]

Gibson presented two draft coats of arms to the King which were possible choices for the newly formed 617 Squadron. One of them showed a hammer parting the chains of Europe and carried the legend 'Alter the Map'. The other, Gibson's preferred option, had a picture of a burst dam with the famous expression 'Après Moi Le Deluge'.[35] The King, reflecting his understanding of the need to observe proper protocol, which was second nature to someone brought up within the royal family, deferred the decision to the luminary known as the Chester Herald, who had the best knowledge of such matters. After inspecting the workshops at 1500, the King and Queen left at 1530.

That left the important matter of the formal presentation of the medals. One of the main purposes of awarding such decorations is to ensure that a high profile is given to them, as the stories of heroism must be widely known if they are to become an inspiration to others. The medal ceremony was to be held in Buckingham Palace in June, just a month after the raids had taken place. The press would be there in force to make sure that the photo opportunities were maximised.

On 21 June, the members of 617 Squadron who were to be decorated set out for London. Buses were laid on to transport those going down to Lincoln railway station: Humphries thought it was rather amusing to see so many officers waddling along with their pockets full of supplies; the clanking of bottles as they moved told eloquently enough of what these provisions actually were.[36]

They left Lincoln station at 1420 and all of them sat in a specially reserved carriage on the London train. There was, predictably and understandably, much evidence of high spirits on the journey. Some of the men on board wanted to swap their comfortable seats for a draughty perch in the driver's cab and the alcohol flowed freely.

As the train passed Grantham, many of those aboard were increasingly 'well-oiled'. The party had split into two; one half was composed of the steadier men, usually the married ones, sitting in the quieter half of the train. In the other half, everywhere the men were playing cards and the beer was flowing. The trouble came when the men got bored with the card games or perhaps when their money ran out, for then they would turn to other distractions.

At one stage, Brian Goodale – Dave Shannon's radio operator – was seen minus his trousers, having been de-bagged. A still drunk Goodale retained enough consciousness to see the problem of being presented to the King and Queen without his trousers. Humphries sat him in the toilet compartment whilst he attempted to get them back. When he successfully negotiated their return, Humphries came back with them only to find that Goodale was fast asleep.

They eventually arrived at King's Cross station at six in the evening. No hotel accommodation had been booked. Some of the officers tried to get in at the Savoy, though most of the delegation ended up at the nearby Strand Palace Hotel. It was a predictably wild night 'out on the town'; even though London was relatively austere given the fact that the country was at war, there was still a lot more to do in the evenings than there was in Lincoln. Eventually, very late in the night, they at last returned to their hotels, where frantic staff attempted to get them back to their rooms whilst making as little noise as possible. However, this did not always work as some of the men continued the party back in their rooms.

At one stage, Joe McCarthy feared that the impetus of the party was running low. He therefore danced around the room naked except for a large bath towel that kept falling off him. This rather incongruous pose by the hero of the Sorpe raid unfortunately did not have the effect he desired and eventually the party ran out of steam and he collapsed into bed as did everyone else.[37]

The men left for the Palace just before ten o'clock the next morning, some of them (including Gibson) accompanied by wives, girlfriends and parents. It was a relatively short journey from the Strand to Buckingham Palace. There were many hangovers evident from the stares of tired men's faces. As they walked into the auditorium where the investiture was to be held, they were greeted by the sounds of an orchestra playing light music. Then, the martial sounds of the national anthem heralded the arrival of the royal party.

The medal ceremony began at 1015. The King was away in North Africa and Malta so it was the Queen who invested the men with their medals, the first to do so since the days of Victoria. Normally recipients of the VC were the last in line in such ceremonies, but today the roles were reversed and Gibson was the first to be honoured, making him the indisputable star of the show.

The Queen stood for nearly three hours handing out medals and decorations. In all, one Victoria Cross, five Distinguished Service Orders, fourteen Distinguished Flying Crosses, two Conspicuous Gallantry medals and eleven Distinguished Flying Medals were awarded. After the event, the men moved outside, where a hungry press was desperate for good shots to put in the next day's paper. The PR experts within the British government were only too happy to oblige. Gibson naturally enough was the main attraction, and most photographers were desperate for him to be in their pictures. There was also a good deal of interest in group shots of the various 'colonials' involved in the raid, Australians, New Zealanders and Canadians.

Now that the rigid formalities of the medal ceremony were over, it was time for the men to let their hair down once more. They moved on to yet another party. After lunch, Gibson gave them details of the dinner being hosted in honour of them by A. V. Roe and Company that night. At about four in the afternoon, Humphries decided to try and grab a couple of hours' sleep before resuming the celebrations again. He noted that, if a squadron celebration appeared to consist of nothing but drinking and sleeping, that was not far wrong. But such libertine behaviour was understandable from men who were most days of their life 'dicing with death'.[38]

The dinner was held at the Hungaria restaurant. On the menu cards was a new name for the squadron – 'Dambusters'. It was a name that would stick. Gibson was presented with a model of a Lancaster bomber in silver. The Wing Commander was careful to include everyone in his thank you speech which followed the presentation. Wallis was also given a memento, a photograph of the Möhne dam, signed by the crew, which moved him a great deal.

Then it was off to yet another party, this one made even more memorable by the presence of such contemporary entertainers as

Chesney Allen (part of the famous Flanagan and Allen double act, amongst whose numbers were 'We're Going to Hang out the Washing on the Siegfried Line', as hummed by Fred Tees on the night of his capture) and Arthur Askey the comedian. Eventually they managed to make their way back to their hotels, where Humphries and Munro were so overcome by the events of the day that they fell into bed with their trousers still on.

There was, however, some resentment over the decorations handed out. Sergeant Ray Grayston, flight engineer to Knight in AJ-N, commented how Knight, the pilot, and the navigator and bomb-aimer got DSOs but the rest of the crew went unrecognised. Flight Sergeant Leonard Sumpter said that it 'got up my nose' when the King and Queen visited Scampton that they didn't go anywhere near the NCOs and only mixed with the officers.[39]

It is important to recognise of course that society was not as egalitarian back in 1943 as it is usually reckoned to be in the contemporary Western world. Yet it is equally important to recognise that even at the time there were criticisms from some quarters as to the distinctions that were made between officers and other ranks. It is a criticism that was made on a number of occasions from those who came across and worked with Gibson. There is, to reiterate, little doubt that he was the right man for the job. Yet there is also no doubt that he was not universally popular. Gibson was a man who was widely respected rather than liked. And that was probably the way that he would have wanted it.

Gibson soon moved on after the raids. His success and the very public fêting that accompanied it made him a very recognisable figure. But it also meant that he would have to be kept away from danger and carefully protected; a dead hero was of limited use. He was for a while deployed to public relations and he would later have the opportunity to write his story in a book, *Enemy Coast Ahead*. His place at the head of 617 Squadron was taken by Wing Commander George Holden.

Gibson's official posting away from 617 Squadron was dated 3 August, and he was to join Churchill on a trip to Canada. The day before, Gibson and his raid crew, along with Holden, took one last spin together for 85 minutes before bringing the curtain down on a short but historic association. Then it was off on the tour, where Gibson proved himself a very convincing frontman and a PR adviser's dream.

The future of the squadron as a crack elite unit, destined to undertake a number of special missions in the future, was assured – a prospect which was also of course full of risk for the crews involved and meant that high losses were likely to be sustained on an ongoing basis. We can be certain that Gibson would have been very upset not to have shared the dangers with them.

What at this time was not assured, however, was the method of delivery of those future raids. Although the attack on the dams had been a spectacular event which ensured its place in history, it was far from clear that such an attack could ever again meet with success against an enemy that was far more prepared to defend himself against such an eventuality.

Such a reading of the situation is obvious when looking at the training record of Dave Shannon in June 1943.[40] There were a number of exercises which were very much connected with the tactics of the 'Dambusters' mission. These included dummy runs of the Derwent and Ladybower reservoirs near Sheffield on 15 June; low-level bombing and spotlight altimeter runs the day before; and night spotlight altimeter tests, also on the 15th. But tests later in the month involved dropping bombs from 20,000 feet, a very different approach to that employed against the dams. Shannon also found the time to learn how to fly a Horsa glider during June.

Wallis himself was unconvinced that Upkeep would be a suitable weapon against other suggested targets. He met Cochrane on 22 June to discuss future raids, including against ship lifts, canals, railway viaducts and river barrages. As far as the ship lift was concerned – and the Ministry of Economic Warfare believed this to be as important a target as the dams – Wallis believed that 'any attack by "Upkeep" or large bombs against the structure is out of the question'. He suggested instead that he developed a 12,000-lb 'penetration bomb'. Heavy explosives were back at the top of Wallis's agenda.[41]

Whilst the training of 617 Squadron continued, Gibson carried on with his tour of Canada and the USA to strengthen support for the war and to attract further recruits from Canada to the conflict. It was a role that with his looks, his self-confidence and his ability to interact with a wider audience, he appears in many respects to have been made for, though given his warrior instincts he would also have longed to return to action. After one lecture, he was taking questions after completing his speech when he was asked by someone in the audience how many missions he had flown. At the time it was the rule that American bomber crew who had survived twenty-five missions returned home. When Gibson responded that he had currently flown 174 missions there was a stunned silence from the audience.[42]

The rewards and recognition were not yet complete. In December 1943, Gibson was awarded the Legion of Merit by President F. D. Roosevelt. After he returned from America, Gibson was also interviewed for a BBC Home Service radio programme where he was asked to nominate his eight favourite pieces of music. The last of them was Wagner's 'Ride of the Valkyries', later made famous as the music used in the classic war movie *Apocalypse Now* when an air raid is carried out by helicopters (the choice of a German composer may not have been Gibson's most politically correct choice ever). Gibson said of the music that 'it's exciting, it's grandiose, it's – rather terrible. It reminds me of a bombing raid.' The warrior could not put down his sword forever and eventually persuaded his superiors to put him back in the firing line in 1944.

Gibson also wrote an article for *The Atlantic Monthly* called 'Cracking the German Dams' in December 1943, on which some of the material in his later book *Enemy Coast Ahead* was based.[43] The book, when it came out, enthusiastically recounted details of Gibson's career and culminated with his account of the dam raids. As the war was still on, some of the details were left deliberately obscure and others were plain wrong, including the impression created that most of the crews were hand-picked. But it was still an invaluable and very readable account from one of the main protagonists in the drama.

For two months after the dam raids, 617 Squadron was taken out of the front line. The squadron's resources of course needed to be replenished after the losses of the raids, but it would also have been especially unfortunate if more men had been lost whilst the unit was still so much in the public eye. Not until 15 July would the squadron head into battle again, this time to Italy. Amongst the pilots involved were Brown, Townsend, Maltby, McCarthy, Munro and Rice, who had taken part in the raids on the dams, as well as Divall, whose illness had forced him to withdraw late on.

Then in September 1943, 617 Squadron was to face another dark hour, this time with no redeeming features in terms of success to sweeten the bitter pill. A raid was planned on the Dortmund-Ems canal. It first took off on the 14th but was called back whilst still over the North Sea because of reports of bad weather ahead. As one of the Lancasters turned with its heavy 12,000-lb bomb aboard, it span out of control and crashed into the sea. Squadron Leader David Maltby and his crew were all lost as a result of the accident. Dave Shannon flew overhead for two hours in a vain attempt to launch an air–sea rescue operation. Maltby's body alone was recovered. He had not been long married and left behind a six-week-old son.

The following night, eight planes set out once more for the same target. This was to be another low-level assault. Wing Commander Holden led the attack but he was shot down and all his crew died with him, including Taerum, Hutchison, Spafford and Deering, who had flown with Gibson in the attack on the dams, as well as Dennis Powell, who had been Townsend's flight engineer on 16/17 May. Flight Engineer John Pulford, whom Gibson did not like, had been moved by Holden, which saved his life though only for four months.

Also lost were Flight Lieutenant Wilson and Pilot Officer Divall with their crews; both men had missed the dam raids through illness. Flight Lieutenant Allsebrook, the recent replacement who had only arrived after the raids, was also killed, as was Flight Lieutenant Les Knight. The body of Knight was found at the controls and buried with full honours at 1800 on the same day (the crash having occurred at 0246). However, the other seven members of Knight's crew survived and five of them made remarkable escapes back to Britain.

Of the eight planes (nine including Maltby's the night before), only three returned home, those of dam raids survivors Martin, Shannon and Rice. There was no significant damage to the canal and civilian casualties were light though damage to property significant. Forty-one men had been lost and the heavy casualties with no tangible results confirmed to Harris that low-level flying was not worth the losses it incurred and it was abandoned as a tactic for a while.

This disaster also created urgent problems for 617 Squadron, for whom once again new crews were required to replace those lost. Cochrane wrote to Harris on 17 September 1943 in a slightly delusional letter which claimed that but for adverse visibility the raid would have been 'an outstanding success'. Cochrane felt that the losses, however, might encourage Harris to consider the future of the squadron. Cochrane was sure that the squadron should continue but might have to be flexible on its policy of recruiting only those crews who had completed two tours. In his reply on 1 October, Harris did not object to this relaxation of policy but encouraged Cochrane to do everything he could to find crews who met the 'two tours completed' criterion. He was, however, keen for the squadron to continue in its present guise.[44]

Mick Martin was one of those to receive special mention in Cochrane's letter of 17 September, in which he was described as 'quite outstanding as a leader'. Martin survived the war, rising to become an Air Marshal and setting a speed record for flying from London to Cape Town, though his bomb-aimer Bob Hay did not live through the conflict, having been killed by flak in a raid – in which Martin and his crew participated – on the Antheor viaduct in southern France in March 1944. Martin would die on 3 November 1988, on the very same day as Eve Gibson. Dave Shannon also survived and died in 1993. Geoff Rice lived until 1981, though he was shot down on 20 December 1943 and was later taken prisoner after hiding out for six months with the Resistance. They and the others who lasted through the war, including Les Munro and Joe McCarthy, were in a minority.

In Germany, the not inconsiderable task of reconstruction of the devastated areas was undertaken, under Speer's watchful eye, with considerable efficiency. On 3 October 1943, the reconstructed Möhne dam was opened with Speer taking the leading part in the ceremonies. A congratulatory telegram was read out from the Führer publicly expressing his appreciation for the efforts of all those involved in completing the reconstruction well ahead of schedule. Only the towers were missing, with no hint of them in the reconstructed dam, just in case any future British bombing raids wanted to line up between them for the sake of an accurate drop.[45]

There was also an unexpected result in Britain. There were fears that the Germans would have discovered the secrets of the 'bouncing bomb' by examining the wreckage of the planes lost. Some suspected that it would only be a matter of months before Britain was exposed to its own 'Dambusters' raid. The Ministry of Home Security and the Air Ministry were jointly commissioned to review defensive measures that could be taken against any retaliatory attack now that the Germans were, it was noted, more 'water minded'.[46] Barnes Wallis was asked to suggest effective defences against such an attack and rather unimaginatively felt that the only effective tactic would be to dazzle an attacking pilot.

The genie that Wallis had released was spreading its shadow but there would never be another raid quite like those of 16/17 May. Their very uniqueness would seal their place in history and, in the best tradition of such epic events, the actions of the protagonists would mutate into the realm of legend and myth where they would live on long past the time when their historical impact ceased to have importance.

That did not stop a further attack being made on the Sorpe dam on 15 October 1944 but this was with a very different weapon, a massive 12,000-lb 'earthquake bomb'. This proved equally unsuccessful in breaching the stubborn earthen walls of the reservoir. On 11 December 1944, 617 Squadron attacked the Urft dam (the third attack on it in a week); they were accompanied by 200 other planes. These attacks were made with massive Tallboy bombs. Despite these intensive efforts, it was later assessed that the only damage was 13 feet blown off the top of the dam.[47] This was quite a contrast to the end result from the efforts of just nineteen planes over the Ruhr eighteen months earlier.

The only significant damage to a German dam throughout the rest of the war was caused deliberately in a vain attempt to prevent the Allies from advancing into the heartlands of Germany (although the destruction of the sluice gates of the Schwammenauel dam in February 1945 did hold the Allies up for a short time). This was a strange conclusion indeed to the story of the German dams during the Second World War, a tale that will be best remembered for the extraordinary events of the night of 16/17 May 1943.

16

The Raids in Perspective

The German writer Helmuth Euler, who has devoted a great deal of his time, effort and talent into investigating the raids, especially from a German perspective, has asked a perfectly fair question, namely, 'was it [i.e. the raids] worth the cost in time and materials, coupled with the loss of eight bombers and the lives of 53 men?'[1]

Of course, such an issue has a significant moral dimension in it, inviting the question of whether the loss of even one life is worth any gain in war. But ignoring that important but ultimately subjective question, best left to philosophers or ethicists rather than historians, analysing in other terms whether the raids were worth it requires a bi-dimensional approach.

There is first of all the operational level consideration; that is, did the raids achieve what was required of them tactically? Even the answer to that is not straightforward because four dams were attacked with very different results. Wrapped up in this dimension are considerations of not only whether operational objectives were delivered but of how did the planes perform, the crews perform and the science perform.

The second level is the strategic. Most analysts would accept that this is the one that matters most, particularly when considering the 'was it worth it' question, for however well executed a military action is, if it does not achieve the results required then it is a waste of time, effort and resource.

Having said that analysing the acceptability of losses is essentially a moral question, it is nevertheless necessary to understand something of the context in which the raids took place. The losses endured by Bomber Command during the Second World War were horrific. Bald statistics cannot do this justice but can still help to create a certain simple perspective. During the war 7,377 Lancaster bombers were built, 3,500 of which were lost on operations.

But this loss in terms of materiel pales into insignificance compared to the human cost. During the war 125,000 aircrew took part in Bomber Command operations. Of these, there were 73,000 casualties, 55,573 of these being killed (aircraft crashes of course by their very nature have a high death to total casualty ratio).[2] That equates, in cold accounting terms, to a death ratio of over four in every ten of those who took part. No wonder aircrew were entitled to an official 'breather' after thirty missions (they might then, for example, have the opportunity of taking up a training role).

Given the high losses, it was understandable that senior British officers reflected on the raids and whether they might have been undertaken in such a way that there was still a high chance of success but one accompanied by lower losses. Cochrane considered that the planes on the raid had flown excessively low on their way to and from the targets, an action that had brought them within the range of light anti-aircraft guns. His view was that,

> on balance, for any future similar operations, it would probably be far better for aircraft to fly at 2,500–3,000 feet above ground level and be prepared to get down to ground level if attacked by fighters. This height should be above the effective accurate range of machine gun fire and light flak but should be low enough to make the task of interception by fighters difficult. [3]

Of course, German non-combatant losses were terribly high too. Civilian deaths in Germany due to the overall effects of strategic bombing were estimated to be in the region of 360,000–370,000 based on a survey done by the German Armed Forces Military History Research Office in 1990 (this figure was based on the pre-war 1937 boundaries of Germany),[4] in itself a truly shocking statistic (this was almost as many deaths as were estimated in Japan, which amounted to nearly 400,000, with 210,000 from the deaths of civilians in the atomic explosions at Hiroshima and Nagasaki alone).[5]

One man who had no moral problem with this was Harris. When towards the end of the war, with the Allies on the brink of victory, it was suggested in official circles that it had never been a primary objective to target civilian populations, Harris was unrepentant. He said, rather chillingly, though perhaps also with a commendable lack of hypocrisy, that:

> The aim of the Combined Bomber Offensive ... should be unambiguously stated [as] the destruction of German cities, the killing of German workers, and the disruption of civilised life throughout Germany.
>
> It should be emphasized that the destruction of houses, public utilities, transport and lives, the creation of a refugee problem on an unprecedented scale, and the breakdown of morale both at home and at the battle fronts by fear of extended and intensified bombing, are accepted and intended aims of our bombing policy. They are not by-products of attempts to hit factories.

In the overall pattern of the bombing campaign, although one must be careful to avoid treating individual actions as the equivalent of a 'profit and loss account' approach based on human lives, again the contextual position of the dam raids can also be assessed by comparing them to other raids. The raids on the dams were part of a series during the 'Battle of the Ruhr' and the losses incurred in other missions by both attackers and civilians were also shocking.

Heavy concentrations of planes were used on a number of occasions against targets in Germany and achieved on occasion comparatively little. For example a 960-bomber raid on Bremen in June 1942 has been described as 'moderately effective' whilst the 1,000-bomber raid in the same month on Essen was called 'an abysmal failure'.[6] In this latter raid, thirty-one planes were lost. The dam raids resulted in eight planes lost, a much higher proportion of course than the losses sustained in Essen but with a much greater return in terms of damage inflicted.

By this benchmark the destruction of two dams and the infrastructural damage caused especially in the Ruhr as a result was, although the harm inflicted was far from as decisive as hoped, still a reasonable return for the losses suffered, if there can be such a thing. Of course from a human perspective every life lost is a tragedy and from a moral viewpoint little short of a crime to many. But the ethics of war are complicated and most strategists would, from the comfort of their armchairs, postulate a balance between the returns made from a particular operation against the losses incurred. Relatively speaking, the number of planes lost during the dam raids was proportionately high but it is also worth noting that Operation Chastise did not even have the highest proportional (or absolute) losses of the month.

On 3 May 1943, earlier in the month, a raid from 487 (New Zealand) Squadron set off for the Netherlands with twelve planes. These were Lockheed Venturas, one of the less notable aircraft of the Second World War. They were never popular with most fliers and this raid would evidence why. Of the twelve planes that took off on this mission, one fortunate aircraft had to return early. For the remaining eleven, which flew at low level over the North Sea, accompanied by three squadrons of Spitfires as escorts, a terrible fate awaited.

By a stroke of ill fortune there was a Luftwaffe conference being held at Schiphol airport at the time and, when the element of surprise was lost because of the earlier activity of Spitfires in the area (this was a daytime raid that relied on surprise for success), sixty-nine fighters took off to greet the Venturas. Of the remaining eleven aircraft, one was badly shot up and managed to limp back to England. The other ten were all lost – a loss rate of over 90 per cent.

This little-remembered disaster just two weeks before was a salutary benchmark to measure the dam raids against (though both raids were atypically high in terms of the proportion of losses). The target for the earlier raid was a power station; in the event only one bomb was dropped and caused only blast damage. There were certain reminders here of what might have happened to the low-level raid on the dams should the element of surprise have been lost or the night fighters have got up to challenge Gibson and his crews. It also evidences that raiding the dams was a high-risk strategy and could have gone spectacularly wrong.

There was an interesting contrast in the fortunes of the two raid commanders too. Gibson was feted as a hero and awarded the Victoria Cross in the full glare of publicity. After the Venturas' raid on the Netherlands earlier in the month, the only survivors from the planes that crashed were Squadron Leader Trent and his navigator. He had pushed on against overwhelming odds to drop the only bomb that was released on an enemy target that night before being downed (only after his gunner had shot down an attacking German fighter).

Trent became a prisoner of war and largely disappeared from public view (though he too was an unsuccessful participant in the 'Great Escape'). When, retrospectively, full details of his heroism became public, he was presented with a VC at Buckingham Palace in 1946.[7] A man who shunned the limelight, unlike Gibson, he probably found the occasion to be more unnerving than the raid he had bravely led.

A raid on the Skoda works at Pilsen in Czechoslovakia on 16/17 April 1943 was also a terrible failure. 327 bombers had set out on a raid that took place on the night of a full moon, similar conditions to those experienced by the dam raiders. Eighteen Lancasters and eighteen Halifaxes were lost in this raid, which caused little damage to the works but more to a barracks 7 miles away near an asylum which was mistaken for the primary target. Elsewhere on the same night, another eighteen aircraft were lost in other raids, a total cost of fifty-four planes in one evening.[8]

These comparisons are, to reiterate, not a 'profit and loss account' by which one can make measurements in a cold, calculating way that ignores the ethics and morality of the taking of human life in war, and they should not be taken too far. The raid involving the Venturas, for example, would be measured a failure by every account. That on the dams cannot be so easily assessed. It is a truism that nothing in war comes without human costs and that military planners in the main divorce themselves from these (moralists would of course say too much so) and look merely at the operational and strategic levels of success.

That should now be considered, and rather than do this on a dam by dam basis, it could alternatively be considered by wave of attacks. Assessment on the former basis is in fact easy; the attacks on the Möhne and Eder dams were an operational success whilst those on the Sorpe and the Bever (or, if one accepts counter-arguments, the Ennepe) were not.

In fact, using the second analysis and looking at each wave, the answer is also straightforward, though marginally less so. In the first wave, nine planes took off but only three bombs were dropped in precisely the way required; those of Young and Maltby at the Möhne and that of Knight at the Eder. These three bombs brought down two dams, which would seem to prove that the science of the bombs against a masonry dam was exceptionally sound given the mass of the targets which would have made them invulnerable to alternative and more conventional forms of attack even if the bombs could have been delivered accurately using these (which all the evidence suggests they could not be).

In terms of the delivery of the bombs, three others were delivered at the Möhne and two at the Eder. Five therefore failed to have the success desired. Both Hopgood's at the Möhne and Maudslay's at the Eder *may* have been due to human error, though other equally plausible explanations are possible, but the failure to create a breach was probably not due to any defective performance in the weapons.

On the other hand, the other three bombs delivered that did not cause a breach may possibly have failed to do so because of human error (for example, being dropped in the wrong place or from the wrong altitude) or because the weapon misbehaved (for example, going off at the wrong angle once it struck the surface as sometimes happened during trials). The latter would be ascribed to a scientific and not a human error (though armchair analysts should surely avoid being overcritical of any human error when being shot at by enemy flak whilst flying at ridiculously low levels or approaching a dam with an almost impossible angle of attack).

Nevertheless, for the cost of nine bombs and four aircraft the first wave had breached two of its three primary targets and caused great material damage and disruption as a result. Judged against other raids, it is impossible to argue that this was not an operational success. The second and third waves on the other hand were clearly operational failures. The science of the bombs against earthen dams, which was always doubted by many (even on occasion by Wallis), was proven to be ineffective. The losses incurred by the raiders were also high; four planes out of ten, a similar ratio to the first wave but for no tangible result.

One strange by-product of the raids was that some contemporary British accounts talk about a strike against the Schwelm dam. There is no such dam and none was mentioned in the briefings before the raid so this may be a simple mistake, an attempt to confuse the enemy or even, as some have suggested, a cover-up to hide the fact that the wrong dam was attacked.[9] However, this last suggestion is difficult to accept as even in 'Most Secret' documentation from the time, the Air Staff were writing to the War Cabinet stating that an attack on the 'Schwelm' dam had taken place.[10] It also continued to appear on planning maps used by the RAF.[11]

Overall, the breaching of two dams and the subsequent damage caused would seem to indicate an operational success when compared against the benchmark of the massive material resources and ordnance committed in other attacks such as the thousand-bomber raids. The loss of eight planes and fifty-three lives on the part of the attackers, whilst high, was certainly not as prohibitive as some other raids, as judged by the strange, inverted logic of the morality of warfare. The loss of enemy lives would, from a British perspective, have mattered little, one suspects, to the attackers, as indeed was the case when the Luftwaffe bombed cities such as Warsaw or London or the major cities in the Soviet Union. Morality is quickly lost sight of in war.

Harris made much of the success of the dam raids in his monthly report to the commanding officers of the various groups issued on 1 June. After listing the various large raids that had been carried out on targets in the Ruhr and elsewhere during May, he noted that 'the bursting of the dams has ruined the navigation of the River Ruhr, probably for years, compromised the water supplies to the Ruhr towns for an indefinite period and together with the bombing has reduced the railways in the most vital industrial area of Germany to virtual chaos'.[12]

It is much more difficult to judge strategic success objectively. Yet in one way at least the strategic thinking behind the planning of the raids seems somewhat muddled. The Möhne and Sorpe were always regarded as the prime strategic targets, whilst the bombs were always felt to be much more likely to succeed against the Möhne and the Eder.

This led to an illogical compromise. If the logic were that the Möhne and Sorpe dams were breachable then the first wave should have moved on to the Sorpe after their success in their first attacks. Yet they moved on to the Eder. Similarly, the reserve wave were not all sent to the Sorpe either, which they logically should have been rather than to a secondary target like the Ennepe dam.

It rather suggests a policy of hedging one's bets, as if the planners knew there was a strong chance that the attack on the Sorpe would fail and therefore built in other targets just in case. Yet those other targets were not exclusively even in the Ruhr area and the case for the Eder dam, which was not, was regarded as weak even before the raid. Therefore, unless experience was proving that the attack on the Sorpe was indeed certain to fail then attacks should have continued against that as the other main target.

In the event, no such case was proven when the key decisions were made. Only one bomb had been dropped on the Sorpe when the decision was made that the remaining first-wave planes should move on the Eder – five bombs had been needed to prove that the Möhne was breachable. This was still the case when the reserve wave was sent into action. Without the gift of hindsight, available to us but not at the time to the planners or the senior officers and scientists at Grantham on the night, it is difficult to argue that the second major focus after the Möhne should not have been exclusively on the Sorpe dam, for if that were breached then the effects on the Ruhr valley would have been far worse than they actually were.

The strategic effects, however, were in the long-term repairable, albeit after creating considerable pressure on the infrastructure. Indeed, when the news of the raids was reported to Josef Goebbels, he reflected that the results could have been a lot worse (although he noted in his diary that the raids were 'an act of war against the state, but one to be admired, for the English [*sic*] had navigated and planned so thoroughly'). Measures were taken to bring a large labour contingent across from working on the Atlantic Wall, about 7,000 men in total. Germany's production would fairly quickly be brought back to normality by the remarkable organisational skills of Albert Speer.

Speer was very impressed with the British raids. He later wrote that 'that night, employing just a few bombers, the British came close to a success which would have been greater than anything they had achieved hitherto with a commitment of thousands of bombers. But they made a single mistake which puzzles me to this day. They divided their forces and that same night destroyed the Eder Valley dam, although it had nothing whatsoever to do with the supply of water to the Ruhr.'[13]

Speer felt that the dam raids provided evidence of strategic clear-thinking in terms of air attacks that neither side involved in the war emulated very often. In the aftermath of the attacks, he urged Hitler to mimic the approach of launching concentrated attacks on key targets rather than the blanket 'area bombing' approach that was the current norm. But Hitler, who seemed surprisingly reluctant to take on Goering and other senior Luftwaffe figures, did not have the stomach for pushing the point. Therefore, Speer's desired strategy, which included the targeted bombing of British coal mines, was never adopted. He concluded by saying that 'the British, for their part, thoughtlessly copied this irrational conduct – aside from their single attack on the dams'.[14]

Speer's views were almost exactly the opposite of those held by Harris. Over time Harris would have his doubts over the raids' effectiveness. The Harris Papers, now housed in the RAF Museum at Hendon, offer a rather different analysis. As early as December 1943, he wrote that 'for years we have been told that the destruction of the Möhne and Eder dams alone would be a vital blow to Germany'. He went on to say that 'I have seen nothing in the present circumstances or in the Ministry of Economic Warfare reports to show that the effort was worthwhile except as a spectacular operation'. In fact, he listed the dam raids as an example of one of the 'panacea' missions he detested so much. In January 1945, he was writing to Portal that 'it [the raids] achieved nothing compared with the effort and loss'.[15]

These comments reflect the situation that the dam raids went contrary to Harris's espoused beliefs in area bombing. His instinct was that the key to long-term success in the bombing command, and with it the winning of war, was to flatten whole areas of Germany's infrastructure. The idea of targeting specific targets, 'panaceas' as Harris termed such plans, was in his view unrealistic and undeliverable. He quickly came to believe that the raids on the dams, however useful they might have been for propaganda purposes, did not achieve the long-term impact that supporters of the plan said that they would.

It is not clear though that this was his initial assessment. A confidential Bomber Command report covering operations between January and March 1943 (though the raids took place outside of this period, by the time the report was written they had taken place) stated that 'the breaking of the Moehne and Eder Dams and their effect on the shattered industries of the Ruhr are at present impossible to assess and are in any case outside the scope of this review, but they should prove, in every sense, overwhelming'.[16] They did not and perhaps Harris himself was secretly disappointed that his initial scepticism had not been proved wrong.

Long after the war, Harris wrote a typically vigorous response to criticisms that had been made of his actions concerning in particular the bombing of Dresden. This is a fascinating document[17] which gives a stunning insight into Harris's mentality. Included in it is a small reference to the dam raids. Harris explained that he was not responsible for the strategic planning of the aerial war (which is somewhat disingenuous as he certainly left papers on file which argue strongly for what he believed the right strategy to be) but for controlling the tactical operation of Bomber Command. At the start of his tenure as head of Bomber Command, he had been given the directive of 'the destruction of the major German cities'. This overall aim was disrupted by 'many interruptions and diversions caused by the numerous additional tasks imposed upon the Bomber Force'. The dam raids were specifically listed as one of these diversions – indeed, they appeared first in the list. The inference is clear; the raids were an unhelpful diversion and not part of Bomber Command's core activities.

There was undoubtedly disruption caused by the raids but it was mainly short-term in nature. Water supplies fell initially by 80 per cent, in the short term reducing supplies to coking plants by about 50 per cent, but they returned to 80 per cent of full production within a few days. This is because the supplies relied in the main on the aquifer and the reservoirs were only used to top up supplies as needed. Because rainfall had been reasonably high that year, the destruction of the Möhne dam was not the problem it might otherwise have been.[18] Hydroelectric power was badly affected but within a week armaments production in the area was back at about 50 per cent of pre-raid production and another week later was back at full capacity.

Disruption was caused in other ways. As well as the loss of livestock and food supplies, which was significant, there were also unexpected side-effects. For example, boundary marks were washed away; in the village of Affoldern alone 200 separate conveyances were required to bring the previous ownership up to date.[19] And the damage was also widespread. In Neinburg, 362 kilometres from the Eder dam, the waters had reached 5.96 metres above normal by 20 May. The floods also had a scouring effect, dragging up the topsoil as the water poured over it and leaving something of a desert in its wake which would take years to recover.

Speer said though in May 1945 that 'the attack on the Eder Dam had no effects except some slight flood damage. The Möhne Dam attack would have had serious consequences only if the Sorpe Dam and two other smaller dams had been broken at the same time.' The chief factor which prevented serious reduction in industrial water supplies to the Ruhr was the existence of a pumping system from the Rhine up to the

Ruhr valley designed to supply the whole district as far upstream as Essen. The pumping system was silted up by the floodwater from the Möhne but was quickly restored. Repairs to the Möhne dam were then rushed through in time for catching the autumn rains. Restrictions on water consumption were imposed on the Ruhr industry during the summer, but otherwise the attacks had no effect except that of giving the Germans 'a big scare'. That did not stop Speer from describing the raids as a potentially 'critical situation'.[20]

The limited material results compared to those hoped for means that questions about how successful the raids were are justified. Some writers on the subject have made up their own minds on this: Euler as one example states quite categorically that 'though it had been based on a series of experiments whose results had been accurately predicted, the first air raid to have been conceived within the context of engineering technology proved a failure'; in other words a scientific success but a strategic disappointment.

Given the losses suffered by other raids and the sometimes insignificant damage caused by them, I believe that the dam raids in isolation can be considered a moderate success in terms of the material damage caused. The initial damage caused was quite significant but what was underrated in the pre-raid analysis was the ability of the German infrastructure to deal with the after-effects. Considerable energy and organisation was put into the recovery operation and this was achieved with notable efficiency, though also in the process creating some strain on the resources available to the Third Reich.

A number of writers have pointed out that the failure of the British to follow up on their raid by a later attack focused on the reconstruction efforts at the Möhne dam in particular was a mistake; these critics include no less a person than Albert Speer. And the bombing of the scaffolding and other materials at the dam would not have required the same kind of precision bombing and the special type of delivery mechanism so would have been more straightforward to execute and probably less costly in terms of lives. This does seem like a lost opportunity to create further disruption without facing the same challenges that had been presented to the first dam raiders.

This would have continued to deprive the great German industrial machine in the Ruhr, as well as many households, of the water that was essential to their existence. That would certainly have added to the strategic impact. Instead the Germans were able to repair the dam and it was refilled by the winter rains in time to ensure that it was at full capacity again in 1944.

There is, however, another dimension to analysing the success of the raids and that is that it was part of a strategic bombing campaign that was ongoing and attritional. It is beyond the scope of this book to consider whether the impacts of strategic bombing were decisive in winning the war or not, but the dam raids were part of a night-after-night operation that aimed to progressively wear down both the material resources and the morale of the enemy. The dam raids formed an important part of the attritional effects of the 'Battle of the Ruhr' and cannot be dismissed without at least recognising that, however innovative the technology used in the raids was, the operation was part of the longer campaign.

Further raids on the Ruhr continued after the dams were breached. These were a return to the large-scale intensive bombing activities that had previously been the norm. Just a week after 617 Squadron's raid, 826 aircraft attacked Dortmund. Almost 2,000 buildings were destroyed but 38 bombers were lost. A raid of 700 aircraft against Düsseldorf on 25/26 May 1943 failed due to heavy cloud cover. However 500 buildings were destroyed in Essen two days later.

On 29/30 May, a massive raid on the town of Barmen left it with over 80 per cent of its buildings in ruins. 4,000 houses were reduced to rubble. Out of the six largest factories, five were gutted. Over 3,000 people died, meaning that the dubious record set by the raids on the dams was exceeded within a fortnight. This itself was surpassed when raids on Cologne on 28/29 June left 4,300 people dead and 6,300 buildings gutted (further raids in the next ten days left a further 4,600 buildings demolished).

This was a terrible war of attrition. As well as the loss of buildings the human cost was devastating. 5,500 people were killed in these raids on Cologne alone and 350,000 people were left homeless.[21] The strain on both individual human beings and the resources of the state was enormous. It was a process of grinding the enemy down, destroying both his morale and his infrastructure, authored by Harris in pursuit of final victory.

Harris had his supporters who backed up his views regarding strategic bombing. Initially, Gibson was one of them. In the book he later wrote concerning his career, he wondered how war might be stopped in the future and opined that 'the answer may lie in being strong. A powerful strategic bomber force based so that it would control the waterways of the world could prevent and strangle the aggressor from the word "go". But it rests with the people themselves; for it is the people who forget.'[22]

Overall, the 'Battle of the Ruhr' reduced German steel production by about 200,000 tons. This was significant as the armaments industry in Germany faced shortages of 400,000 tons.[23] A sub-components crisis followed (*zulieferungskrise*). Aircraft production was badly affected. However, the contribution of the dam raids to these outcomes was limited. Major targets for the raids collectively were particularly Essen, Duisburg, Cologne, Gelsenkirchen and Düsseldorf.

Only Essen was affected significantly by Operation Chastise although much of the damage caused there, especially to the large Krupp factory, had been caused by direct heavy bombing on several occasions, especially in March. Essen had been declared a primary target by the air bombing directive of February 1942 and certainly, in Harris's evocative phrase, 'reaped the whirlwind' (Harris also judged the city as 'the largest arsenal in the world').[24] Judged by their overall contribution, the raids can only be regarded as having had a useful strategic impact, far from decisive, and therefore at best a moderate strategic result in terms of the enormous resources put into them.

In the final analysis, the major benefits of the dam raids were ones of morale and these, though less tangible, are still important in a war context – no less a personage than Lord Trenchard opined that the moral effects of bombing exceeded the material by a factor of twenty to one. The tidal wave of congratulatory messages sent to 617 Squadron was as unstoppable as the floodwaters of the Möhne and the Eder. One of the first of them on 17 May was sent from the War Cabinet to Bomber Command HQ. It set the tone for what was to follow:

> The War Cabinet have instructed me to convey to you and to all who shared in the preparation of and execution of last night's operations, particular to Wing Commander Gibson and his squadron, their congratulations on the great success achieved. This attack, pressed home in the face of strong resistance, is a testimony alike to the tactical resource and energy of those who planned it, to the gallantry and determination of the aircrews and to the excellence of British design and workmanship. The Cabinet have noted with satisfaction the damage done to German air power.[25]

Taking up the baton, Harris caught the mood of the moment and was magnanimous in his communications with Wallis and in his implied acceptance that he was wrong in his initial mistrust of the scientist and his engineering credentials:

> But for your knowledge, skill and persistence, often in the face of discouragement and disappointment, in the design, production and servicing of the equipment used in the destruction of the dams the efforts of our gallant crews would have been in vain. We in Bomber Command in particular and the United Nations as a whole owe everything to you in the first place for the outstanding success achieved.[26]

Cochrane wrote to Wallis on the 17th stating that 'I must write to tell you how much I admire the perseverance which brought you the outstanding success which was achieved last night. Without your determination to ensure that a method which you knew to be technically sound was given a fair trial we should not have been able to deliver the blow which struck Germany last night.'

Gibson wrote a few days later to Wallis, admitting that he was not much of a letter writer but saying that 'the weapon that you gave us to deliver worked like a dream and you have earned the thanks of the civilised world'. He concluded with the understandable sentiment that 'I think I need a holiday'.[27]

Sir Henry Tizard, chief of the Air Staff, also caught the congratulatory mood when he write to Wallis that 'taking it all in all, from the first brilliant ideas, through the model experiments and the full-scale trials, remembering also that when the sceptics were finally convinced you had to work at the highest pressure to get things done in time, I have no hesitation in saying that yours is the finest technical achievement of the war'.[28]

There was a positive impact on morale even for British prisoners of war, including the redoubtable Group Captain Douglas Bader, who later said, 'I well remember the destruction of the Möhne and Eder dams while I was in a prison camp. It had an enormous effect on the Germans and the opposite effect, of course, on us, the prisoners of war.'[29]

However, although there is no reason to doubt the sincerity of these sentiments they were essentially self-congratulatory and insular. Much more important was the effect that the raids could have on the outside world and perhaps the most important message sent the day of the raids was a 'most secret' communication to Churchill in Washington.

This stated that 'reports confirm success of Upkeep. Photos this morning show 200 feet breach in Möhne dam, disappearance of Power Station and widespread floods reaching to Dortmund.'[30] It went on to say that the Eder had not yet been photographed but that very bad flooding had clearly taken place. Whilst it did not make extravagant claims about what damage might have been done to the industry and infrastructure of the regions affected, it was enough to present a fantastic propaganda opportunity to Churchill. He was not the sort of man to pass it up.

The timing could not in fact have been better. He was due to make an address to the United States Congress on 19 May. He made a 50-minute oration, which was also relayed to the BBC in London for a live broadcast. He made the most of the PR opportunity he had been afforded, in a way that would demonstrate to his American ally that the British were still a force to be reckoned with (Stalin had already telegrammed his congratulations to Churchill the day before) and would help to strengthen the resolve of his own people.

On the subject of the raids, he told his rapt audience that 'you have just read of the destruction of the great dams which feed the canals and provide power to the enemy's munitions works. That was a gallant operation costing eight out of the nineteen bombers employed but it will play a very far-reaching part in German military output.'

He went on to explain that 'it is our settled policy – the settled policy of our two staffs of war-making authorities – to make it impossible for Germany to carry out any form of war industry on a large or concentrated scale, either in Germany, in Italy or in the enemy-occupied countries'.

Warming to his task in a way that only Churchill could, he went on to say that 'in the meanwhile, our air offensive is forcing Germany to withdraw an ever larger proportion of its war-making capacity from the fighting fronts in order to provide protection against the air attacks'.[31]

In other words, the British air effort, of which the dam raids were a part, was a crucial factor in winning the war. It was an implied rebuff of Stalin's complaints that it was taking forever to start a second front to take the pressure off his stretched armies and also to American perceptions that Britain was a spent force. Innovative and imaginative, delivered with skill and bravery, the raids were a public relations dream.

This was evidenced by ongoing congratulations that continued to be sent. The day after Churchill's speech to Congress, the figurehead of the RAF, the venerable Lord Trenchard, telegrammed in his greetings to Scampton in the following terms:

> Many congratulations on destruction of dam [*sic*]. It is splendid. Please congratulate Gibson and all concerned from me. Wonderful work of Bomber Command is being recognised by all now.[32]

The last short sentence in particular showed how important the raids were to enhancing the image of Bomber Command in the perception of the public, both domestically and internationally.

Harris also took advantage of the PR opportunities. In reply to congratulatory messages received from the War Cabinet and the Air Ministry, he wrote that 'this accurate blow delivered by a small force of picked men is proof of the capacity of the bomber offensive to soften the enemy's resistance at vital points as well as devastate wide areas of industrial production. At last Germany is beginning to experience to the full the impact of war within her own frontiers. There is plenty more to come.'[33]

The raids also made an impact on the Soviets too; within a fortnight of the operation, the British government was approached by them asking for details of the raids and the weapons used. This created something of a headache as to how to respond. Concerns about secrecy were expressed but, as was pointed out, arguments in this respect were weak because 'the Germans know a good deal already'. The argument drifted on for several months until it was decided in August to pass on the requested information with the suggestion that it might be used as something of a 'bargaining counter'.[34]

The raids undoubtedly helped boost the image of Britain as far as the Soviets were concerned. A letter from Air Marshal Peck to Harris in June 1943 noted that 'the Russians have not only shown recognition of our Army achievements, but they have also seemed more ready of late to recognise the injury we are doing to the German war effort by our air offensive'. Peck went on to suggest that a Lancaster should be sent over to Moscow carrying an exhibition that included pictures of the damage caused by Bomber Command; that which had been effected by the dam raids would be prominent amongst these.[35]

Given the scale of the losses in Germany, it was inevitable that questions would be asked there about the lack of preparedness on the part of the authorities. This was especially the case as there had been warnings before the raids that constructions such as dams could be prime targets. A number of people in Germany had long before noted the comments made concerning the viability of such attacks in the work of a well-known French military aviation specialist, Camille Rougeron, who described attacks on dams in detail in his book *L'Aviation de Bombardement*, published in 1936. The British attacks on the dam in Sardinia were also commented on before the raids on the Ruhr, though of course in this latter case the authorities could respond that the attacks there had failed and this seemed to confirm the invulnerability of such large and solid targets.

Questions were asked about whether the raids could have been predicted and also if more measures could have been taken to avoid some at least of the casualties suffered. Justus Dillgardt, the mayor of Essen, had long before the attacks took place written to military authorities noting the correlation between the time when the reservoirs were at their fullest and the potential for serious damage and casualties. No notice was taken of this sound advice.

However, a specific problem was that no one predicted the power of the bombs that the British had available to them and the size of the breach in the dams that they would cause. Predictions in advance of the raids suggested breaches 6.7 metres wide and 7 metres deep – the actual breach at the Möhne was 77 metres wide and 22 metres deep. Water flowed down the valley at between 20 and 30 kilometres per hour, too quickly for the warning systems that had been set up to keep up with the pace of the flood.[36]

There was no doubt that the British had benefitted from the element of surprise and that the German response had been uncoordinated and completely ineffective. The flak gunners had done their job for sure, both at the Möhne dam and also on the route to and from it – men such as Karl Schütte, who had burned his hands whilst servicing the guns at the Möhne dam, earning in the process the Iron Cross, Second Class.

They had though been let down by those in authority who had not believed a successful raid possible and who had therefore allowed the malaise of complacency to influence their thinking. They ranged from the military planners who removed all the guns and barrage balloons from all of the dams except that of the Möhne (and even there left just an emaciated rump of a defence system) to the party officials who, in common with the unthinking stupidity and callous unconcern for humanity typical of all totalitarian states, insisted that the dams could never be breached and any attempt to suggest that they could be, and the adoption of appropriate defensive measures as a result, was tantamount to treason.

The performance of German night fighters was not so much inadequate as non-existent. They could at least blame this in part on technological reasons. As General Josef Kammhuber said, 'the night fighter force could not come to grips with the attackers since it was an attack at the lowest level, and the targets could not be picked up by radar, hence they offered no prey for the night fighters'.[37]

There would be a time for judgement against those who were guilty later, though again in common with many other examples of totalitarianism no one who should have been held to account at a senior level ever was. In the short term, life had somehow to be returned to a semblance of normality. In the immediate aftermath of the attacks the immediate priority was to organise rescue work. Orders were given on 18 May in the areas affected by the Eder flooding that unambiguously issued instructions in the following peremptory manner (once again typical of totalitarian regimes):

All inhabitants between 14 and 60 years not directly affected by the Eder flood disaster at home and on their farms, and not involved in work outside the area, will be formed into working parties consisting of 10–20 men or women. An able-bodied man, or woman in the case of female working parties, is to be nominated as leader. The mayor will be responsible for urgent measures locally, and for setting up and deploying the working parties.

The instruction went on to say that anyone who refused to cooperate would be forcibly conscripted into a working party. It was emphasised that personal considerations were to take second place to the rescue operation until life in the community returned to normal. Male working parties were to undertake outdoor clean-up operations and females would clean up indoors. As a final unmistakable warning, Heinrich

Orthwein, the Chief Administrative Officer of Kreis Melsungen in the Eder valley, declared that 'the mayor will be held to account for any failure and severely punished'.[38]

By July, work was beginning on rebuilding the Möhne dam. Herr Wildbrett of Heinrich Butzer of Dortmund was responsible for the enterprise. On 23 September 1943, just in time, the breach in the Möhne dam was sealed. This allowed the autumn and winter rains to be collected and water levels would be close to normal levels for the next summer.

The design of the rebuilt dam was somewhat different from its previous appearance. The towers on the Möhne dam were now reduced to virtually the same height as the parapet to reduce their usefulness for sighting. A significant change was the lowering of the water level by 10 metres, reducing capacity from 131 to 68 million cubic metres, a useful long-term strategic benefit of the raids as far as the British were concerned.[39]

The world moved on and for Guy Gibson it would never be the same again. The raids introduced unexpected tensions between him and Harris. Gibson's tour to Canada and the USA with Churchill had been something of a triumph. The alcohol-fuelled glamour of the extended tour, which included a trip to Hollywood where a film about the raids was seriously discussed (the script to be written by a young military attaché by the name of Flight Lieutenant Roald Dahl; sadly this movie never reached the production stage[40]), in the opinion of Harris turned the young Wing Commander's head. When Gibson considered a foray into politics in 1944, he was quoted as saying on several public occasions that, although bombing was a crucial part of the war, it could not win the conflict on its own – a stance that stood directly contrary to that of Harris.

The plans to enter politics eventually came to nothing, though at one stage he was selected as the prospective parliamentary candidate for the Conservative Party in Macclesfield. His role was to fight, and his destiny belonged with the war. He eventually successfully pestered Cochrane and Harris for a return to the skies, though great care would still be taken to ensure that he was as much as possible kept out of harm's way.

There was still the occasional contact with Margaret, even though they were both now married. It was mostly through letters. They had often before talked together of a mystical home, based on one remembered from Gibson's youth, called Honeysuckle Cottage. Then they would dream of what the furniture would look like in this unattainable and elusive haven in which they could live together happily in a life that could never exist. But throughout their relationship Gibson had always refrained from openly expressing what he felt about Margaret, even on that fateful morning when she was on the verge of marriage. Feelings were always left un-discussed though their intensity could not be doubted.

But then Gibson decided he had to see her. A meeting was arranged at her mother's home in Bognor Regis in July 1944. It was a wet, grey day perhaps in keeping with his mood. Margaret asked how Honeysuckle Cottage was, to which Gibson replied that he had not been there recently. The tension soon relaxed and it was before long like old times again, as if Margaret's new husband and Eve did not exist (though Margaret was by now a mother to a son that Gibson had agreed to be the godfather of, but he had missed the christening as he had been away on the other side of the Atlantic at the time).

When Gibson left, he had promised to come and find Margaret after the war so that they could set out together to look for a real Honeysuckle Cottage. A note followed shortly afterwards. Its poignancy is remarkable, for this was the last earthly contact there would ever be between the two who lived in a dream world remote from reality. There was no hiding of feelings now as far as Gibson was concerned. He said simply that 'the day was perfect. I love you now and forever' – something he had never said to her before and a heart-rending ending to the correspondence between them.

Gibson was living in more than one false world, in one of which he was in possession of the domestic bliss that he deep down craved but never found, whilst in the other fantasyland he was a hero. After the raids on the dams, Gibson became lionised so much that he became an almost mythical role model for the British. Yet, despite the eulogising and behind the sentimentality, the words of Barnes Wallis perhaps sum up Gibson best of all:

> For some men of great courage and adventure, inactivity was a slow death. Would a man like Gibson ever have adjusted back to peacetime life? One can imagine it would have been a somewhat empty existence after all he had been through. Facing death had become his drug. He had seen countless friends and

comrades perish in the great crusade. Perhaps something in him even welcomed the inevitability he had always felt that before the war ended he would join them in their Bomber Command Valhalla. He had pushed his luck beyond all limits and he knew it. But that was the kind of man he was ... a man of great courage, inspiration and leadership. A man born for war ... but born to fall in war.

It was an apt analysis. For whilst it was the war which killed him, it was also the thing that made him. There are some obvious clues to this: one biography of Gibson is 321 pages long, of which about 290 concern his role in the conflict. The writer of this book said that 'in the opinion of a good number who knew him well, he was not a born leader. Guy Gibson was a fairly ordinary, high-spirited aircrew officer who survived long enough to be given unusual opportunities. He achieved greatness because his combat experience was backed by a practical application of rules of leadership which he had learned; the need to unify his squadrons behind clear aims, to communicate those aims with confidence and to balance discipline with the enlistment of hearts.'[41]

Guy Gibson VC was killed in a raid on 19 September 1944 whilst returning in a Mosquito from Germany on a mission that he did not need to be on (Harris later regretted ever allowing him to go on it); he crashed near Steenbergen, Holland. He was flying in a plane in which he had logged very few hours and it has been suggested by some experienced wartime pilots that, due to his unfamiliarity with the plane, his engines cut out as he had failed to switch fuel tanks. It is easy from this remove in time to overlook the fact that, as the war went on, pilots were required to continuously bring their skills up to date, often in aircraft that were quite different to those that they had become used to. This may indeed have cost Gibson his life. He was buried, as he probably would have wished, not far away from the spot at which his very last flight had come to a fatal end.

The deputy burgomaster of the Dutch town, Chris Herbers, had argued with the German authorities that a small public ceremony should be allowed. The Germans, to many of whom it was now clear that the war had been lost, agreed. But the Dutch did not know whom they were burying. Whilst the remains of the two dead crew members from the crashed Mosquito were gathered together, a charred sock was found (the bodies had literally been blown to pieces and there was little left to bury). On it was a laundry tag with the owner's name – Gibson. But it meant nothing to those responsible for the burial.

There was a small impromptu gathering of some of the townsfolk in the Roman Catholic cemetery and the bodies of the two men were reverently interred (their shattered remains shared one small coffin). They may have been anonymous to those there but Gibson was also a hero to them, this time as an unknown British airman who had given his life fighting in a war to, amongst other things, liberate the Dutch from German occupation. This was a bad week for British forces in the Netherlands; at the same time, not far away, an audacious attempt by airborne forces to seize the Rhine crossing at Arnhem was going disastrously wrong.

A few hundred miles away in London, a messenger boy arrived at the flat in Aberdeen Place where Eve lived. He carried a telegram which used very few words but which in the process said everything: 'Regret to inform you Wing-Commander G.P. Gibson (39438) reported missing on operational flight on the night of 19th/20th September'. There was no such telegram for Margaret but she did not need one. She had woken up that day feeling ill and went back to bed. She became aware of a dark shadow over her and by the afternoon, without being told, she was sure that her beloved Guy was dead.

In their own way, the dam raids had killed Gibson too. They had turned him into a hero but into an ultimately unfulfilled one. What was the use of a warrior who could not fight? So he had pestered and cajoled until he had persuaded those in authority to let him get back behind the controls of a plane again. As a result he was now dead – but that, as others hinted at, was perhaps what destiny had always had in store for him.

Gibson's life after the raids was ultimately a frustrating one for him. There had been no clear role for him now that he was a hero who was too precious to lose. There were many suggestions that the tour across the Atlantic had turned his head and consistent stories that his worse traits of snobbery and superiority – which had been moderated, relatively speaking, whilst he was in command of 617 Squadron – were now as bad as ever. One pilot from 627 Squadron (Gibson's last unit) stated bluntly, 'Let me tell you, I did not like Guy Gibson.'[42]

The dam raids were destined to remain a one-off. Forty Upkeep weapons remained after the raids but they were never used and, after being kept at Scampton in storage for a while, they were dropped after the war had ended, unarmed, into the North Sea and a watery grave in what was designated 'Operation Guzzle'. In August 1943, there had been plans to use some of the bombs against railway viaducts around the Ruhr but tests had proved disappointingly inconsistent and the idea was dropped. 617 Squadron would, in 1944, get its chance to destroy the *Tirpitz*, but when it did so in Operation Catechism on 12 November, it would be with massive Tallboy bombs and not Highballs. 618 Squadron was sent to Australia later in the war to hopefully attack Japanese capital ships with Highballs but the weapon was never used in action.[43]

By October 1943, there was a flow of exchanges between Cochrane and Harris. Cochrane wanted some of the aircraft that had been specially adapted for the raids to be converted for alternative use: 'it [Upkeep] is not to be used again, which demonstrates that already, within six months of the raids, they might remain one-off events in the history of aerial warfare'. Harris replied that they should retain the 'possibility of using Upkeep again' but there was already a strong likelihood that there would be no repeat of the dam raids, at least not using the same approach.[44]

Ironically, by 26 May 1943 the Germans had their own blueprints for an Upkeep weapon based on the bomb recovered from the crash site of Barlow's plane. They developed their own version, codename 'Kurt', which was to be rocket-propelled and have a bouncing range of 4 kilometres. It experienced a number of problems, however, many of them similar to those experienced by Highball. In the end 'Kurt' was cancelled with other schemes such as the V2 rockets taking precedence.

But the British were worried. Within a month Churchill had circulated a memo asking for information about what precautions had been taken to protect against a 'copycat' raid. Five dams around Sheffield, including the Derwent, were protected by 5,000 troops, smokescreens and balloons – measures that echoed those taken by the Germans to protect against a repeat attack. A number of British dams were subsequently overflown by 'an experienced pilot of No. 617 Squadron' who concluded that virtually all the structures examined were 'vulnerable to frontal attack by day or night'.[45] Having unleashed the whirlwind, the British lived in fear that the Germans would launch one of their own in return.

A number of Provisioning 464 Lancasters were placed in storage at RAF Lossiemouth in Scotland. Three were returned to Scampton in 1947. Not long after, they were all scrapped. It seems a shame that not one plane was saved from a raid which, even then, had almost entered into folklore; but perhaps in those days of continuing austerity people just wanted to forget the war as quickly as possible and look with hope towards the future.

Other planes, however, were returned to conventional Lancaster design after the attack on the dams and took part in raids later in the conflict. These included Gibson's ED932 as well as ED906, ED909 and ED933. It has been plausibly suggested that planes returned for repair after the raid were converted back to the conventional model Lancaster for ongoing use, although the extensive modifications that had been made meant that the bomb doors which would normally be present could not be re-installed.

ED825 (McCarthy's plane on the dam raid) was shot down in an SOE mission over France in December 1943, as was ED886 (formerly Townsend's plane). The wreckage of ED825 was lost for many years but was found again in 2007 – the dig revealed that the plane had been converted back to a standard bomber configuration. ED918, Brown's plane, crashed on a training flight over Norfolk in January 1944. Brown had flown the plane after it was returned from repair and had found that it was not 'flying true'. Despite passing this information on, the problem was not fixed and the plane was taken up whilst Brown was on leave. In the crash that followed, two lives were lost needlessly.[46]

By the end of 1944, it was being noted in official circles that the ten 'Upkeep aircraft' still being maintained were 'something of a white elephant and a cause of embarrassment to 617 Squadron as they are surplus to establishment and require a certain amount of care and maintenance. All the crews who were specially trained for this particular kind of operation have either been posted or are out of training practice in the use of Upkeep.' It was therefore suggested that the planes should be sent to 41 Group for storage.[47]

After the war, the reputation of Barnes Wallis was made. He had been made a Commander of the British Empire (CBE) in 1943 and was knighted in 1968. He lived to the ripe old age of ninety-two, eventually dying on 30 October 1979. He had been given an award of £10,000 at the end of the war. He used this to set up an educational foundation for the children of RAF crew killed during operations undertaken in the conflict.

The reputation of Air Chief Marshal Harris on the other hand was far from assured. Most of the major war leaders who had contributed to the victory of Britain and her allies in the war were awarded peerages in the 1946 New Year's Honours List; Harris was a notable exception (though strong evidence subsequently emerged that Harris was offered one but turned it down as he was unhappy at the lack of recognition given for ground crews within Bomber Command).[48]

Even Churchill distanced himself from him. When a statue of Harris was erected outside the RAF's church of St Clement Danes in London in 1992, there were widespread protests. In the strange morality of war, heroes are expected to meet certain mores of chivalry, as Gibson appeared to do and Harris, in the eyes of many, did not. Yet Gibson and Harris were two sides of the same coin, in their own different ways ruthless and resolute, as they needed to be with a war to be won.

Germany of course was in the end rebuilt after the war finished. For those who lived in the shadow of the dams, not just lost homes or shops needed to be rebuilt. They had to pick up the pieces in more ways than one, but in many cases they managed to do so. After a time, normality returned to the devastated regions. To visit the dams now is an unexpected pleasure. They sit in spectacular locations with beautiful countryside around them. Small boats sail across the surface of the reservoirs whilst holidaymakers sit around the edge of the water at elegant cafés. All that flies overhead now are birds in what are now National Park areas.

There is though an occasional reminder for the observant. There are memorials for those who were lost in some of the towns, such as Neheim. In the town cemetery there are also a number of monuments that can be found by those who look closely. The most poignant are not the fine artworks but the simple square slabs used to mark the grave of someone without much influence or money to afford anything grander, inscribed with just a name and a date – 17/05/1943. What monuments there are are subtle and understated, speaking of grief and solemn remembrance rather than anger or bitterness. None though is as eloquent as the flood-gouged remnants of the Porto Coeli convent. Where once sturdy walls decorated in gold and holy images stood, there is now just the shattered stub, barely more than foundations, of the church that once stood there.

To the side of where the sanctuary once was, there is a simple stone memorial to Pastor Berkenkopf, who died on 17 May 1943. Where the altar stood for 700 years there is now only a giant cross, the eternal emblem of sacrifice, simple and lonely but more eloquent than any words. The chant of the nuns has long gone and now there is just the sound of the wind in the trees to remind one of the lives once lost here, drowned out in the screams of the torrent that deluged the hamlet and the last, despairing toll of the bell as it collapsed into the flood.

There are few reminders in Britain to recall the sacrifices made there too. RAF Scampton does, however, still live on, though its survival is currently under threat, as it has been on several occasions in recent decades, due to spending cuts. Nowadays a visit to Scampton is a crucial part of understanding something of the 'Dambusters' story, for many parts of the base are little different than they were in the 1940s. The layout, the buildings, the hangars – much of the base is still redolent of a bygone age and provides strong links to an airbase of another era.

There are ghosts here too – some would say literally. On one occasion, a group of schoolchildren were having a photograph taken at Scampton when, from nowhere, a black Labrador appeared and posed in the shot before trotting off again and disappearing.[49] No one knows who the dog belonged to. But some have their theories.

Appendix I

The Crews & Their Fates on the Raid

FIRST WAVE

ED932/G (SERIAL NUMBER) – AJ-G (CALL SIGN 'G' FOR GEORGE)
Wing Commander Guy Gibson (Pilot) – awarded VC
Pilot Officer Torger Taerum, RCAF (Navigator) – awarded DFC
Pilot Officer Frederick Spafford, RAAF (Bomb-aimer) – awarded DFC
Sergeant John Pulford (Flight engineer) – awarded DFM
Flight Lieutenant Robert Hutchison (Wireless operator) – awarded Bar to DFC
Flight Sergeant George Andrew Deering, RCAF (Front gunner) – awarded DFC
Flight Lieutenant Richard Trevor-Roper (Rear gunner) – awarded DFC

ED925/G – AJ-M ('M' for Mother)
Flight-Lieutenant John Hopgood (Pilot) – killed in action
Flying Officer Ken Earnshaw, RCAF (Navigator) – killed in action
Flight Sergeant John Fraser, RCAF (Bomb-aimer) – taken prisoner
Sergeant Charles Brennan (Flight engineer) – killed in action
Sergeant John Minchin (Wireless operator) – killed in action
Pilot Officer George Gregory (Front gunner) – killed in action
Pilot Officer Anthony Burcher, RAAF (Rear gunner) – taken prisoner

ED909/G – AJ-P ('P' for Popsie)
Flight Lieutenant Harold Martin (Pilot) – awarded DSO
Flight Lieutenant Frederick Leggo, RAAF (Navigator) – awarded Bar to DFC
Flight Lieutenant Robert Hay, RAAF (Bomb-aimer) – awarded Bar to DFC
Pilot Officer Ivan Whittaker (Flight engineer)

Flying Officer Leonard Chambers, RNZAF (Wireless operator) – awarded DFC
Pilot Officer Bertie Foxlee, RAAF (Front gunner)
Flight Sergeant Thompson Simpson, RAAF (Rear gunner) – awarded DFM

ED887/G – AJ-A ('A' for Apple)
(Note: many sources quote this as ED877G but it is believed that this is a typographical error as ED877 was a 156 Squadron bomber lost earlier in May 1943.)
Squadron Leader Melvyn Young (Pilot) – killed in action
Flight Sergeant Charles Roberts (Navigator) – killed in action
Flying Officer Vincent MacCausland (Bomb-aimer) – killed in action
Sergeant David Horsfall (Flight engineer) – killed in action
Sergeant Lawrence Nichols (Wireless operator) – killed in action
Sergeant Gordon Yeo (Front gunner) – killed in action
Sergeant Wilfrid Ibbotson (Rear gunner) – killed in action

ED906/G – AJ-J ('J' for Johnny)
Flight Lieutenant David Maltby (Pilot) – awarded DSO
Sergeant Vivian Nicholson (Navigator) – awarded DFM
Pilot Officer John Fort (Bomb-aimer) – awarded DFC
Sergeant William Hatton (Flight engineer)
Sergeant Antony Stone (Wireless operator)
Sergeant Victor Hill (Front gunner)
Sergeant Harold Simmonds (Rear gunner)

ED937/G – AJ-Z ('Z' for Zebra)
Squadron Leader Henry Maudslay (Pilot) – killed in action
Flying Officer Robert Urquhart, RCAF (Navigator) – killed in action
Pilot Officer Michael Fuller (Bomb-aimer) – killed in action
Sergeant John Marriott (Flight engineer) – killed in action
Warrant Officer Alden Cottam (Wireless operator) – killed in action
Flying Officer William Tytherleigh (Front gunner) – killed in action
Sergeant Norman Burrows (Rear gunner) – killed in action

ED929/G – AJ-L ('L' for Leather)
Flight Lieutenant David Shannon, RAAF (Pilot) – awarded DSO
Flying Officer Daniel Walker (Navigator) – awarded Bar to DFC

Flight Sergeant Leonard Sumpter (Bomb-aimer) – awarded DFM
Sergeant Robert Henderson (Flight engineer)
Flying Officer Brian Goodale (Wireless operator)
Sergeant Brian Jagger (Front gunner)
Flying Officer Jack Buckley (Rear gunner) – awarded DFC

ED864/G – AJ-B ('B' for Baker)
Flight Lieutenant William Astell (Pilot) – killed in action
Pilot Officer Floyd Wile, RCAF (Navigator) – killed in action
Flying Officer Donald Hopkinson (Bomb-aimer) – killed in action
Sergeant John Kinnear (Flight engineer) – killed in action
Warrant Officer Abram Garshowitz, RCAF (Wireless operator) – killed in action
Flight Sergeant Francis Garbas, RCAF (Front gunner) – killed in action
Sergeant Richard Bolitho (Rear gunner) – killed in action

ED912/G – AJ-N ('N' for Nancy)
Pilot Officer Leslie Knight, RAAF (Pilot) – awarded DSO
Flying Officer Harold Hobday(Navigator) – awarded DFC
Flying Officer Edward Johnson (Bomb-aimer) – awarded DFC
Sergeant Raymond Grayston (Flight engineer)
Flight Sergeant Robert Kellow, RAAF (Wireless operator)
Sergeant Frederick Sutherland (Front gunner)
Sergeant Harry O'Brien (Rear gunner)

SECOND WAVE
ED825/G – AJ-T ('T' for Tommy)
(Note: some sources erroneously give this the serial number of ED923/G.)
Flight Lieutenant Joseph McCarthy, RCAF (Pilot) – awarded DSO
Flying Officer Donald MacLean, RCAF (Navigator) – awarded DFM
Sergeant George Johnson (Bomb-aimer) – awarded DFM
Sergeant William Radcliffe (Flight engineer)
Flight Sergeant Leonard Eaton (Wireless operator)
Sergeant Ronald Batson (Front gunner)
Flying Officer David Rodger, RCAF (Rear gunner)

ED927/G – AJ-E ('E' for Easy)
Flight Lieutenant Robert Barlow, RAAF (Pilot) – killed in action

Flying Officer Phillip Burgess (Navigator) – killed in action
Pilot Officer Alan Gillespie (Bomb-aimer) – killed in action
Pilot Officer Samuel Whillis (Flight engineer) – killed in action
Flight Officer Charles Williams, RAAF (Wireless operator) – killed in action
Flying Officer Harvey Glinz, RCAF (Front gunner) – killed in action
Sergeant Jack Liddell (Rear gunner) – killed in action

ED921/G – AJ-W ('W' for Willie)
Flight Lieutenant John Leslie Munro, RNZAF (Pilot)
Flying Officer Grant Rumbles (Navigator)
Sergeant James Clay (Bomb-aimer)
Sergeant Frank Appleby (Flight engineer)
Flying Officer Percy Pigeon, RCAF (Wireless operator)
Sergeant William Howarth (Front gunner)
Flight Sergeant Harvey Weekes (Rear gunner)

ED934/G – AJ-K ('K' for King)
Pilot Officer Vernon Byers, RCAF (Pilot) – killed in action
Flying Officer James Warner (Navigator) – killed in action
Pilot Officer Arthur Whittaker (Bomb-aimer) – killed in action
Sergeant Alistair Taylor (Flight engineer) – killed in action
Sergeant John Wilkinson (Wireless operator) – killed in action
Sergeant Charles Jarvie (Front gunner) – killed in action
Flight Sergeant James McDowell, RCAF (Rear gunner) – killed in action

ED936/G – AJ-H ('H' for Harry)
Pilot Officer Geoffrey Rice (Pilot)
Flying Officer Richard MacFarlane (Navigator)
Warrant Officer John Thrasher, RCAF (Bomb-aimer)
Sergeant Edward Smith (Flight engineer)
Warrant Officer Chester Gowrie, RCAF (Wireless operator)
Sergeant Thomas Maynard (Front gunner)
Sergeant Stephen Burns (Rear gunner)

THIRD WAVE
ED910/G – AJ-C ('C' for Charlie)
Pilot Officer Warner Ottley (Pilot) – killed in action

Flying Officer Jack Barrett (Navigator) – killed in action
Flight Sergeant Thomas Johnston (Bomb-aimer) – killed in action
Sergeant Ronald Marsden (Flight engineer) – killed in action
Sergeant Jack Guterman, RAAF (Wireless operator) – killed in action
Sergeant Harry Strange (Front gunner) – killed in action
Sergeant Frank Tees (Rear gunner) – taken prisoner

ED865/G – AJ-S ('S' for Sugar)
Pilot Officer Lewis Burpee, RCAF (Pilot) – killed in action
Sergeant Thomas Jaye (Navigator) – killed in action
Flight Sergeant James Arthur, RCAF (Bomb-aimer) – killed in action
Sergeant Guy Pegler (Flight engineer) – killed in action
Pilot Officer Leonard Weller (Wireless operator) – killed in action
Sergeant William Long (Front gunner) – killed in action
Warrant Officer Joseph Brady, RCAF (Rear gunner) – killed in action

ED918/G – AJ-F ('F' for Freddie)
Flight Sergeant Kenneth Brown, RCAF (Pilot) – awarded CGM
Sergeant Dudley Heal (Navigator) – awarded DFM
Sergeant Stefan Oancia, RCAF (Bomb-aimer) – awarded DFM
Sergeant Harry Basil Feneron (Flight engineer)
Sergeant Harry Hewstone (Wireless operator)
Sergeant Daniel Allatson (Front gunner)
Flight Sergeant Grant McDonald, RCAF (Rear gunner)

ED886/G – AJ-O ('O' for Orange)
Flight Sergeant William Townsend (Pilot) – awarded CGM
Pilot Officer Lancel Howard, RAAF (Navigator) – awarded DFC
Sergeant Charles Franklin (Bomb-aimer) – awarded Bar to DFM
Sergeant Dennis Powell (Flight engineer)
Flight Sergeant George Chalmers (Wireless operator) – awarded DFM
Sergeant Douglas Webb (Front gunner) – awarded DFM
Sergeant Raymond Wilkinson (Rear gunner) – awarded DFM

ED924/G – AJ-Y ('Y' for York)
Flight Sergeant Cyril Anderson (Pilot)
Sergeant John Nugent (Navigator)
Sergeant John Green (Bomb-aimer)

Sergeant Robert Patterson (Flight engineer)
Sergeant William Bickle (Wireless operator)
Sergeant Eric Ewan (Front gunner)
Sergeant Arthur Buck (Rear gunner)

Appendix 2
Code Words

Main Targets
Objective X   Möhne dam
Objective Y   Eder dam
Objective Z   Sorpe dam

Secondary Targets
Target D   Lister dam
Target E   Ennepe dam
Target F   Diemel dam

Code Word	Action
'Pranger'	Attack Target X
'Nigger'	Target X breached, divert to Target Y
'Dinghy'	Target Y breached, divert to Target Z
'Danger'	Attack Target D
'Edward'	Attack Target E
'Fraser'	Attack Target F
'Mason'	All aircraft return to base
'Apple'	First wave listen out on Button B
'Codfish'	Jamming on Button A, change to Button C
'Mermaid'	Jamming on all R/T, control by W/T
'Tulip'	No. 2 take over control at Target X
'Cracking'	No. 4 take over control at Target Y
'Gilbert'	Attack last resort targets as detailed

'Goner'   Bomb released

The 'Goner' code word had further codes associated with it, as follows:

1	Failed to explode
2	Overshot dam
3	Exploded 100+ yards from dam
4	Exploded 100 yards from dam
5	Exploded 50 yards from dam
6	Exploded 5 yards from dam
7	Exploded in contact with dam
8	No apparent breach
9	Small breach
10	Large breach

There were also location codes associated with the 'Goner' code word, as follows:

A	Möhne dam
B	Eder dam
C	Sorpe dam
D	Lister dam
E	Ennepe dam
F	Diemel dam

For example, Gibson's report from AJ-G's attack was 'Goner 58A', which means that the bomb was released at the Möhne dam, and it exploded 50 yards short with no apparent breach.

Appendix 3

W/T Messages

Appendix 3a: W/T messages received and sent to and from Grantham regarding the Möhne raid

Time	From	Message
00:11	G	Flak warning at 51.48N 07.12E
00:12	Group	(As above – retransmitted on full power by Group HQ)
00:37	G	GONER68A
00:50	A	GONER58A
00:53	P	GONER58A
00:55	J	GONER78A
00:56	G	NIGGER
00:57	Group	NIGGER – retransmitted on full power by Group HQ. Aircraft replied 'Correct'.

Appendix 3b: W/T messages received and sent to and from Grantham regarding the Eder raid

Time	From	Message
01:45	Group	Flak warning at 51.48N 07.12E transmitted to 3rd Wave
01:51	G	Called B by W/T
01:53	G	Called B by W/T
01:54	G	'Dinghy'
01:55	Group	(Retransmitted on full power by Group

		H.Q. Aircraft replied 'Correct')
01:57	Z	Goner 28B
02:00	N	Goner 710B
02:06	L	Goner 79B
02:10	Group	To 'G'. How many aircraft of first wave are available for 'C'.
02:11	G	'None'

Appendix 3c: W/T Messages received and sent to and from Grantham regarding the third wave

Time	From	Message
02:19	Group	Group called each of the 5 aircraft of the third Wave.
02:21	O	Answered
02:22	Group	to 'O'. GILBERT
	F	Answered
02:24	Group	to 'F' DINGHY
02:25	F	Received
	Group	to 'O'. GILBERT
02:26	O	Message Received
	Group	Calling 'Y'
02:28	Y	Carry on with your message
	Group	to 'Y'. DINGHY
	Y	Received
	Group	Calling 'C'
02:30	C	Carry on with your message
02:31	Group	to 'C'. GILBERT
	C	Message received.
02:32	Group	to 'S'. DINGHY
02:33	Group	to 'S'. DINGHY
02:57	L	GONER 78B (repetition of 02:06 transmission)
03:00	T	GONER79C
03:23	F	GONER78C
04:11	O	GONER58E
04:23	Y	Returning to base unsuccessful

Appendix 4
Raid Questionnaires

On their return to Scampton, the pilots of the surviving planes were asked a number of questions in a set questionnaire. The questions, and the answers from each pilot (which may be examined at the National Archives, reference AIR 14/840), are reproduced below.

QUESTIONS

1. What could be seen of the objective during the run up? (With particular reference to the direction of the moon?)
2. At what range did you first see the target?
3. (a) Number and height of bounces of 'UPKEEP'
    (b) Was 'UPKEEP' spun? If so, what RPM?
4. Description of explosion, with particular reference to behaviour of water, height of spout etc.?
5. Description of damage to the target.
6. How many runs did you make?
7. Were you obstructed by any other aircraft during your run up?
8. What method of control was used and was it effective?
9. What was the effect of the 100 per cent night tracer carried;
(a) On the enemy?
(b) On your own gunners?
10. Pilots personal report (criticism and comments).

ANSWERS

G/617 Wing Commander Gibson GO 939 Time of Attack:
0028 hrs.
(Attacked Möhne dam)
1. Saw the whole thing.
2. 3–4 miles
3. (a) 3.   (b) Yes 500
4. Enormous column of water.
5. There are two holes in the dam.
6. One.
7. No.
8. VHF (Perfect)
9. (a) Very satisfactory effect against gun positions. (b) No dazzle. Perfect for this job.
10. River below dam to a distance of about 3 miles was several times its normal size.
<u>Note on GO 934.</u>
1st and 3rd hit. 2nd overhit.
A large hole was definitely knocked in it and a great deal of water was seen flowing out.

P/617 Flight Lieutenant Martin GO 939 Time of Attack:
0038 hrs.
(Attacked Möhne dam)
1. Smoke from previous burst obscured objective. Moon on port beam.
2. From 1¼ mile one tower could be seen. Other tower obscured by smoke from last attack.
3. (a) Not seen. (b) Yes. 480.
4. Spout formation which reached above smoke but height could not be judged.
5. No visible damage – this aircraft was 3rd to attack.
6. One.
7. No.
8. R/T Good.
9. Good from gunners point of view.
10. Very good trip. Numerous searchlight and light flak positions north of

the Ruhr against which gunners did wizard work. Rear gunner extinguished two searchlights. Front gunner shot up other flak posts and searchlights. Navigation and map reading wizard. Formation Commander did a great job by diverting the gun fire from target towards himself. Whole crew did their job well.

J/617 Flight Lieutenant Maltby GO 939 Time of Attack: 0049 hrs.
(Attacked Möhne dam)

1. All of it including the towers. Would have been easier running into moon instead of from it.
2. Saw towers at 2,000 feet range.
3. (a) 3. Height not known. (b) Yes.
4. Saw water flung up (harassed by tracer at time).
5. Saw breach in centre of dam before attacking; so went to port and made a contact.
6. One.
7. No. Clear.
8. VHF very good.
9. (a) Not known. (b) No trouble and slightly easier to aim.
10. Found VHF control excellent. In two cases a second aircraft flew alongside the one bombing and machine gunned defences on North side of objective. Good route, flak free and easy to map read.

L/617 Flight Lieutenant Shannon GO 934 Time of Attack: 0139 hrs.
(Attacked Eder dam)

1. Entire target. Moonlight good but would have been better ahead.
2. 3 miles.
3. (a) 2. (b) Yes.
4. Saw enormous spout of water about one minute after attacking. Believed over 1,000 feet high.
5. Made gap about 9 feet wide towards east side. Saw second aircraft overshoot. 3rd aircraft with contact widened gap. Water seen pouring down valley.
6. 3.

7. No.
8. VHF Control by No. 1.
9. (a) Not known. (b) Rather dazzling but gunner likes it.
10. Plan worked perfectly. Route extremely good. Shot up a train at COESFELD.

N/617 Pilot Officer Knight GO 934 Time of Attack: 0152 hrs.
(Attacked Eder dam)
1. Everything. Moon on starboard beam.
2. 1 mile.
3. (a). Three. Impossible to estimate height. (b) Yes.
4. Spout of water about 800 feet high right on the dam. Explosion must have occurred on contact with dam wall.
5. Large breach in wall of dam about 30 feet below top of dam, leaving top of dam intact. Torrent of water pouring through breach causing tidal wave about 30 feet high seen half a mile down valley from dam.
6. Two.
7. No.
8. VHF very good.
9. No opposition at target. 100 per cent tracer dazzled gunner but appeared to frighten searchlight and gun crews. Opinion of gunner – ordinary night tracer would have ensured greater accuracy because of reduced dazzle.
10. Routeing excellent. Reports from aircraft ahead re flak found to be very useful. Attack straightforward and as predicted. It was found possible to gain 1,000 feet easily after dropping the Mine. Satisfied that the raid was successful.

T/617 Flight Lieutenant McCarthy GO 960 Time of Attack: 0046 hrs.
(Attacked Sorpe dam)
1. Everything. Moon on starboard beam.
2. Five miles.
3. N/A (line bombing).
4. Half-circular swelling of water with wall of dam as diameter, followed by a spout of water about 1,000 feet high.

5. Crown or causeway of dam crumbled for a distance of about 15 to 20 feet.

6. Ten.

7. No.

8. None. Operating independently.

9. Betrayed position of aircraft to searchlights and light flak on route. No opposition at target and no guns fired.

10. Pilot not in favour of 100% tracer. Cannot say if a big breach in dam was made, but raid seemed to be successful. Route out good and easily followed (blue). Route return (red 1) failed to find pinpoints because of faulty compass, so set course as route out and headed for Zuider Zee.

F/617 Flight Sergeant Brown GO 960 Time of Attack: 0314 hrs. (Attacked Sorpe dam)

1. Everything. Moon on starboard beam.

2. 500 yards.

3. (a). N/A. (Line bombed). (b) N/A.

4. Missile dropped about 10 feet away from dam about two-thirds of way across. Semi-circular swelling of water against dam wall followed by spout of water about 1,000 feet high.

5. Crumbling of crown of dam for about distance of 300 feet.

6. Ten.

7. No.

8. No control – independent attack.

9. Very dazzling. Ordinary night tracer preferred. Appeared to have considerable effect on accuracy of searchlights.

10. Routeing good. Raid on this target seemed to be successful. Difficult to attack because of hills and trees on both banks. Went to have a look at GO 939 [the Möhne dam]. Flight engineer saw two large breaches close together between the two targets. Each breach was about a quarter width of space between the two towers. Water was pouring through both gaps, shooting well out before falling in two powerful jets. The valley seemed to be well covered with water. Report confirmed by air bomber. Front gunner reports a third breach beyond the tower on the NE end of dam. Breach about half the size of other two. Water pouring through.

N/617 Flight Sergeant Townsend GO 935 Time of Attack:
0337 hrs.
(Attacked Bever or Ennepe dam)
1. Sighted by profile of hills. Running into moon in half light reflected on mist and water.
2. ¾ mile approximately.
3. (a) One. Explosion occurred approximately 30 seconds after release. (b) Yes.
4. High column of dirt and water. Circle afterwards meeting dam.
5. No sign of damage.
6. Two.
7. No.
8. None.
9. (a) Has a good deterrent effect on flak. (b) No trouble with dazzle or stoppages and very encouraging to crew.
10. The island shown in centre of lake on target map is actually joined to the spit. Did three dummy runs and circled several times having difficulty with drifting mist and dazzle from moon. Considered timing was too light as we were still over Germany in daylight. Kept the aircraft right on the deck and cruised at about 240, this appeared to fox the defences. Had a look at MOEHNE [*sic*] DAM on way in and could not find it for some time. Found sheet of water about 7 miles long and extending to four miles wide up valleys with dam in middle. Roofs of houses could be seen sticking up above the water which was flowing very fast.

F/617 Flight Sergeant Anderson
(Did not drop bomb)
1 to 8 Not applicable
9. Very satisfactory – no dazzle and continuous line very helpful and apparently scaring the enemy.
10. Unable to find lakes near DULMEN. Mist in valleys made recognition difficult and above five miles before DULMEN we were forced off our track by searchlights being at that time unable to shoot at them owing to stoppages in rear turret. Realised we could not reach target in time so turned back at 03.10 hours bringing the mine back.

Notes

Preface
1. Arthur 260
2. In Foster 118
3. In Flower 64
4. PRO Cab 65

Chapter 1
1. Lionel Charlton, *The Air Defence of Britain* (1938)
2. PRO AIR 14/229
3. Cooper 11
4. Minutes of the meeting: see PRO AIR 14/229
5. Cooper 24
6. In Dildy 6
7. Ibid 8
8. PRO AIR 14/817
9. Flower 18
10. Ibid 17
11. Ibid 19
12. Ibid 22
13. Dildy 9
14. Falconer 6
15. Probert 202
16. See HP H59
17. Arthur 50
18. Earlier experiments at the Nant-y-Gro dam without the charge being directly against the target had led to a calculation that a completely impractical 30,000 lb would be needed at the Möhne dam.
19. Bateman 7
20. Dildy 10
21. Ibid 16
22. Minutes of the meeting in PRO AIR 14/840
23. PRO AIR 14/840
24. Dildy 16
25. Flower 28
26. See PRO AIR 8/1234
27. Dildy 16
28. Arthur 48
29. Probert 223
30. Ibid 254
31. Ward and Lee 282
32. Morris 30
33. Ibid 106
34. Ward and Lee 14

35. Morris xxiii

Chapter 2

1. PRO AIR 14/840
2. PRO AIR 14/840
3. Falconer 187
4. PRO AIR 14/840
5. Lincolnshire was a popular site for airfields, of which there were forty-nine during the Second World War.
6. Thorning 31
7. Arthur 82
8. Ibid 21
9. Martin was actually christened Harold Martin. In many accounts the nickname of 'Mick' or 'Micky' seems interchangeable.
10. Arthur 18
11. Ibid 36
12. Morris 112
13. Humphries 12
14. Ibid 4
15. Arthur 29
16. Probert 150
17. Arthur 37
18. Arthur 33
19. Arthur 38
20. Gibson 221
21. See PRO AIR 8/1234
22. Ibid
23. 'Immediate Most Secret' cipher message relayed this to Washington in April but the plan was referred to in a 'Most Secret' memo of 25 March: see PRO AIR 8/1234.
24. Morris in *Breaching the German Dams* 17. This followed on from a request to the Air Ministry on 21 March to issue a number: PRO 14/840.
25. Thorning 127
26. Ward and Lee 43
27. In fact, 618 Squadron was formed eleven days after 617 Squadron with a view to attacking the *Tirpitz* with Highball bombs. Wilson 168.
28. Gibson 228
29. Arthur 77
30. Ibid 107
31. Gibson 229. The reference in his book to models of three dams was a mistake as that of the Eder was not available until after the raids had happened. The Möhne model is still on display in the Imperial War Museum.
32. Dildy 30
33. Gibson 228

Chapter 3

1. See Cochrane's post-raid report in PRO AIR 14/2087.
2. Foster 96. In fact there were only two so modified by the end of April. See Owen

in *Breaching the German Dams* 27

3. Owen in *Breaching the German Dams* 27
4. PRO AIR 14/842
5. Arthur 119
6. Morris 156
7. Wilson 166
8. For further information on Gibson's appointment see article by Richard Morris in *Breaching the Dams* 17–20
9. Wilson 171
10. PRO AIR 14/840
11. Ibid
12. Arthur 85
13. PRO AIR 14/2088
14. PRO AIR 14/2087
15. In the National Archives, PRO AIR 8/1238. However, this information summarised arguments that had been made the month before – see memo of 21 March in PRO AIR 8/1234.
16. Wilson 167
17. HP H59
18. HP H51
19. Thorning 117
20. Ward and Lee 47
21. There is some confusion over the name. Sweetman (99) says that the name was either 'Lanchester' or 'Lancaster', while Bateman (12) calls him 'Lancaster'. Robert Owen in the RAF Museum's publication *Breaching the Dams* also calls him Lancaster.
22. Flower 35
23. See PRO AIR 14/595
24. PRO AIR 14/840
25. Flower 37
26. PRO AIR 14/842
27. One such device used at Reculver was recovered and may be seen at the RAF Scampton Museum. It is significantly smaller than the actual devices used in the raid.
28. In fact the devices used were Highballs to be used against capital ships. A single Upkeep version of the bomb was dropped at Reculver on the 29th.
29. Probert 192
30. See *Hansard* for 24 July 1941

Chapter 4

1. PRO AIR 14/840
2. Ibid
3. PRO AIR 14/842
4. Euler 40
5. Wilson 171
6. See article by Robert Owen in *Breaching the German Dams* 32–4
7. Appendix B to Order No. B.976, PRO AIR 14/844.

A number of copies of the order are present in the National Archives.

8. Arthur 122
9. Foster 102
10. Falconer 59
11. Arthur 130
12. Euler 40. The original 'Most Secret and Most Immediate' documents may be viewed at PRO AIR 8/1234.
13. Morris 162
14. Ward and Lee 55
15. See PRO AIR 14/844. The order was relayed from Bomber Command to 5 Group HQ shortly after 1455 on 15 May when the 'message form' ordering that it be passed on was completed.
16. PRO AIR 14/2036
17. Morris in *Breaching the German Dams* 16
18. Bateman 16
19. Dildy 27–8
20. Humphries 1
21. Ottoway 108

Chapter 5

1. A copy may be found at PRO AIR 14/844
2. The detailed orders are reproduced in full in Humphries 22–7
3. Hobday, Les Knight's navigator, in Arthur 107.
4. PRO AIR 14/2036
5. Humphries 7
6. Shannon in Arthur 141
7. In Flower 49
8. Sweetman 148
9. Flower 49
10. Cooper 67
11. See, for example, Hobday in Arthur 146
12. Arthur 137
13. Arthur 147
14. Foster 107
15. Flower 51
16 Gibson 252
17. Probert 213
18. Humphries 10
19. Flower 51
20. Thorning 143
21. Flower 51
22. Details in Dildy 32
23. Euler 48

Chapter 6

1. Euler 50. The Very light was a pyrotechnic light fired off from a pistol.
2. Humphries 11
3. Gibson 251
4. Order B.976, quoted in Humphries 22
5. Arthur 209
6. Arthur 158
7. Flower 43

Chapter 7

1. Dated 7 April 1943, in PRO AIR 14/2036
2. Gibson 254
3. In Flower 53
4. Owen in *Breaching the German Dams* 30. The original document can be seen at PRO AIR 14/2036
5. Andreas Wachtel in Ward and Lee 64
6. Jones 27
7. Cooper 79
8. Euler 44
9. Gibson 259
10. Foster 109
11. Flower 62
12. Dildy 40
13. Euler 93
14. Further details at www. dambusters.org
15. Many years later, a tombstone was erected over the grave, which is still there, surrounded by iron railings, in the shadow of Gibson's office.

Chapter 8

1. *The Dambusters Raid* (2002) DVD
2. Ward and Lee 61
3. Brown in Arthur 209
4. Euler 55
5. Dildy 41
6. Wilson 175
7. Euler 94
8. Ibid 71
9. Ibid 68
10. Owen in *Breaching the German Dams* 32
11. Gibson 260
12. Various speeds are given in accounts of the raid, with 230 mph also mentioned. However, the official order B.976 gives a target speed of 220 mph.
13. Thorning 141
14. In Arthur 143
15. Made by Assistant Chief of the Air Staff John ('Jack') Slessor; see HP H59
16. Arthur 181
17. Gibson 261
18. In Morris 152
19. Cooper 132
20. Ward and Lee 52
21. Schütte in Arthur 229
22. Arthur 232

Chapter 9

1. Flower 67
2. Euler 67
3. Arthur 233
4. Ibid 234
5. Flower 55
6. Burcher in Arthur 174
7. Gibson 263
8. http://www.doncaster.gov. uk/db/enews/article.asp?A rchive=Y&CatID=31&Art =1046
9. Reproduced in full in Euler 62
10. Foster 111

11. Cooper 132
12. Ward and Lee 69
13. Cooper 87
14. Ibid
15. Amongst those supporting the use of it were Gibson, Martin, Townsend and Anderson. McCarthy, Knight and Brown were against it. Shannon was lukewarm, describing it as 'rather dazzling but gunner likes it'. See answers to questionnaires in the appendices to this book.
16. See Jones 23
17. Arthur 176
18. Foster 112
19. Gibson 264
20. Euler 68
21. Arthur 232
22. Euler 68
23. Arthur 234
24. Euler 71
25. Ibid 65
26. Gibson 265
27. From the Operation Records Book of 617 Squadron in Ward and Lee 70.
28. Arthur 203
29. Dildy 51
30. Euler 94
31. Cooper 93
32. Flower 58
33. Cooper 91
34. Ibid 105
35. Arthur 183
36. Ibid 293

37. Foster 115
38. Cooper 89
39. Gibson 266
40. Euler 120
41. Flower 68

Chapter 10

1. Arthur 237
2. Cooper 103
3. Arthur 238
4. Euler 121
5. Amongst the iconic sites that the Cistercians founded in Britain are Fountains and Tintern abbeys.
6. Euler 119
7. Flower 68
8. Cooper 103
9. Euler 119
10. Cooper 105
11. Euler 123
12. Ibid 128
13. Ibid 130
14. Ibid 125
15. Arthur 240
16. Euler 125
17. Arthur 244
18. Flower 68
19. In Arthur 250
20. Jones 22
21. This was Gibson's own verdict; see Gibson 267
22. Dildy 51
23. In Thorning 146–7
24. Dildy 55
25. Thorning 147

Chapter 11

1. Arthur 247
2. Ibid 192
3. Grayston in Dildy 54
4. In Flower 60
5. Dildy 54
6. Arthur 191
7. Thorning 147
8. Knight's flight engineer Raymond Grayston in Arthur 187
9. Cooper 96
10. Euler 77
11. Flower 69
12. Dildy 55
13. Gibson 269
14. Hobday in Arthur 190
15. Flower 60
16. Dildy 58
17. *The Dambusters Raid* (2002) DVD
18. Arthur 214 and 211 respectively.

Chapter 12

1. Arthur 253
2. Ibid 256
3. Euler 79
4. Cooper 96
5. Euler 75
6. Ibid 83
7. Arthur 222
8. Navigator Lance Howard in Arthur 222
9. Gibson 270
10. Ibid
11. Ibid

12. Quoted in Morris 65
13. See Morris 139
14. Flower 61
15. Dildy 59
16. Ibid
17. Ward 87
18. Dildy 64
19. Dildy 65
20. Thorning 121
21. Arthur 248
22. See Euler 171–3
23. Arthur 249

Chapter 13

1. Dildy 63
2. Arthur 266
3. Dildy 61
4. Arthur 215
5. Responses to these questionnaires are reproduced as Appendix 4 of this book. The original documents can be found at PRO 14/2087.
6. This figure was quoted in Cochrane's post-raid report – PRO AIR 14/2087. However, this is contradicted in the same report, which later suggests an impact of 200 feet.
7. Euler 94
8. Ibid 97
9. Dildy 70
10. Wilson 176
11. Ibid 172
12. Cooper 98

13. Arthur 223
14. Wireless operator George Chalmers in Arthur 224
15. Ibid 225
16. An explosion was recorded on the seismograph at Göttingen at 0338 which, allowing for time lag, suggests that the bomb was dropped at 0337/0338.
17. Jones 29
18. In Arthur 225
19. Euler 109
20. In Arthur 224
21. Sweetman 223
22. Euler 68

Chapter 14

1. Euler 102
2. Dildy 66
3. Chalmers in Arthur
4. Dildy 66
5. Ibid 66
6. Heal in Arthur 220
7. Dildy 65
8. Speer 384
9. Dildy 71
10. Probert 210
11. From www.dambusters.org.uk
12. HP H59
13. Arthur 268
14. Foster 117
15. PRO AIR 19/304
16. Cooper 100
17. PRO AIR 19/383
18. Euler 147

19. Humphries 39
20. Arthur 269
21. Ibid 273
22. Ibid 279
23. Ibid 288
24. Ibid 285
25. In Euler 116. The allusion to the Sorpe demonstrates that the British still hoped that the Sorpe, with its different dam design, might still crack with its structure seriously weakened.
26. Arthur 278
27. Ibid 282
28. Probert 199
29. Euler 236
30. Cooper 10
31. Foster 117
32. Feneron in Arthur 267
33. Humphries 40
34. Foster 117; Euler 110

Chapter 15

1. Cooper 106
2. Gibson 275–6
3. Falconer 123. The allusion to 'scrambled egg' was RAF slang vocabulary for a senior officer.
4. PRO AIR 14/2088. This message was telephoned in from 5 Group HQ to Scampton at 1615 on 17 May.
5. Cooper 110
6. Ibid 107

7. Ibid 105
8. Flower 73
9. Euler 93
10. Ibid 94
11. Ibid 191
12. Cooper 131–4
13. Ibid 106
14. Ibid 106
15. Euler 125
16. Cooper 107
17. Humphries 39
18. Ward and Lee 82
19. PRO 8/1234
20. PRO Cab 65
21. Cooper 109
22. Probert 190
23. HP H48
24. 5 Group newsletter for May 1943 – PRO AIR 14/2088
25. Euler 142
26. Reproduced in Ward and Lee 84
27. Humphries 42
28. See correspondence in PRO AIR 14/595; also in HP H49
29. See http://www.dailymail.co.uk/news/article-1323193/Nurse-says-marriage-RAF-Dambusters-hero-Guy-Gibson-Evelyn-Moore-broken.html. Originally broadcast in the BBC documentary *Dambusters: Declassified*. The story in the press in 2010 reads as if it were a new discovery but in fact the story of Margaret North (as she was then) is told in detail in Morris 124–34
30. For further information see Ghiringhelli: www.petergh.f2s.com/medals.htm
31. This situation was amended in 1973 and any of the current gallantry awards can be made posthumously. I am grateful to both Stephen Stratford and the Air Historical Branch for information on the awarding of medals.
32. PRO AIR 14/2215
33. Arthur 136
34. The plans for the visit can be seen at the National Archives: PRO 14/2215. Amongst the more unlikely details included in the briefing notes prepared was the fact that Scampton had always taken a keen interest in food production and had won the Station Garden Trophy for 1941/42.
35. An expression attributed to King Louis XV of France or alternatively his lover the famous Madame de Pompadour.
36. Humphries 44
37. Ibid 48

38. Ibid 52
39. Arthur 296
40. Reproduced in Ward and Lee 87
41. Cochrane to Harris in HP H59
42. From Sir Robert Thompson's autobiography *Make for the Hills: Memories of Far Eastern Wars*, L. Cooper (1989) 36
43. Further information in *Breaching the German Dams* 18
44. Both items of correspondence are in HP H59.
45. The towers that can be seen now at the Möhne dam were finished in 1952.
46. See PRO AIR 19/383
47. Ward and Lee 234

Chapter 16

1. Euler 3
2. *The Lancaster at War* (2009) documentary
3. See PRO AIR 14/2087
4. *Das Deutsche Reich und der Zweite Weltkrieg*, Bd. 9/1, 460
5. Estimates by the American historian John W. Dower in *War Without Mercy* (1986) 297–9
6. Ward and Lee, 21 and 20 respectively
7. See Bomber Command War Diary, May 1943; this and other monthly diaries can be found at http://www.raf.mod.uk/bombercommand/
8. Bomber Command diaries for April 1943.
9. Dildy 69
10. See PRO AIR 8/1234 dated 27 May 1943. There was not even unanimity about how to spell the name of this mythical dam. A note on the raids prepared by Cochrane on 7 June (see PRO AIR 14/2087) called it the 'Schwelme'.
11. See map in PRO AIR 19/383
12. HP H49
13. Speer 385
14. Ibid 386
15. See the *Telegraph* of 15 August 2009; see also HP H47
16. HP H77
17. HP H136
18. Dildy 68
19. Euler 85
20. In Flower 71; and Speer 468
21. Ward and Lee 90
22. Gibson 273
23. Adam Tooze, *The Wages of Destruction: The Making and Breaking of the Nazi Economy* (2007) 597–8

24. HP H49
25. Reproduced in Euler 116
26. PRO AIR 14/2088
27. Euler 116
28. Arthur 291
29. Ibid 299
30. Euler 117
31. Ibid 117
32. PRO AIR 14/2088
33. PRO AIR 19/383
34. PRO AIR 8/1239
35. HP H51
36. Euler 173
37. Flower 71
38. Reproduced in Euler 175
39. Flower 72
40. It was discussed in a letter from Squadron Leader G. Alan Morris, Air Attaché in Washington, to Harris on 31 July 1943, with 9-foot models of Lancasters costing £150,000 which would actually fly; HP H51
41. Morris (320–1) gives a balanced assessment of Gibson's strengths and weaknesses as a man and a leader.
42. Morris 290
43. Detailed 'Most Secret' information concerning the potential deployment of Highball in the Pacific may be seen in PRO AIR 8/1234. However, these demonstrate that in October 1943 trials with the weapon were still not complete. The actions of American forces in the Pacific in 1944 effectively removed the Japanese fleet as a serious threat without the need to resort to special weapons.
44. PRO AIR 14/595
45. A number of documents relating to those fears can be examined in PRO AIR 14/1636.
46. See http://www.lancaster-archive.com/bc_damsraid6.htm
47. PRO AIR 14/841
48. Probert 350
49. See Bruce Barry Halpenny, *Ghost Stations Lincolnshire* (2008) 39–42

Select Bibliography

Arthur, Max *Dambusters: A Landmark Oral History*, Virgin Books, London, 2008: an excellent compendium of eyewitness accounts of the raids, with a few black-and-white illustrations.

Bateman, Alex *No. 617 'Dambuster' Squadron*, Osprey, Oxford, 2009: well-written account of the raids, with a number of photographs and original drawings.

Bowman, Martin W. *The Dam Busters: A Pocket History*, Amberley, Stroud, 2009: heavily illustrated booklet on the raids.

Brickhill, Paul *The Dam Busters*, The Companion Book Club, London, 1952: the original 'classic' on the raids, though some key facts were unknown when the book was written as documents were still classified; a few illustrations.

Cooper, Alan *The Men Who Breached the Dams*, Airlife Publishing, Shrewsbury, 2002: an interesting account of the raids, with a number of black-and-white illustrations.

Dildy, Douglas C. *Dambusters: Operation Chastise 1943*, Osprey, Oxford, 2010: interesting account of the raids, with a number of photographs and plans.

Euler, Helmuth *The Dams Raid Through the Lens*, Battle of Britain International Limited, London, 2001 (translated from German): magnificently illustrated, with copious black-and-white photographs of the damage caused by the raids – the definitive guide to the story from the German perspective.

Falconer, Jonathan *The Dam Busters Story*, Sutton, Stroud, 2007: heavily illustrated booklet on the raids.

Falconer, Jonathan *The Dam Busters: Breaking the Great Dams of Western Germany*, Sutton, Stroud, 2003: the definitive pictorialised (mainly black-and-white) account of the raids from the British perspective.

Flower, Stephen *Barnes Wallis' Bombs*, Amberley, Stroud, 2010: definitive guide to the scientific development of the weapons used in the raids, with a number of black-and-white illustrations.

Foster, Charles *Breaking the Dams: The Story of Dambuster David Maltby & His Crew*, Pen & Sword Aviation, Barnsley, 2008: a biography of Maltby, concentrating on the war years, with black-and-white illustrations.

Gibson, Guy *Enemy Coast Ahead Uncensored*, Crécy Publishing Limited, Manchester, 2010 edition: key reading for background to the raids, though Gibson occasionally gets his facts wrong, perhaps in the interests of secrecy. Black-and-white illustrations.

Holland, P. and Holland, M. *Winds of the Storm: The Legend of the Dambusters*, Timeless Images, undated: a short booklet, with a number of impressive black-and-white and colour illustrations.

Humphries, Harry *Living With Heroes: The Dam Busters*, The Erskine Press, Norwich, 2008 edition: a fascinating insight into the role of one of Gibson's key assistants at Scampton, giving some interesting insights into the raids from a different perspective. Some black-and-white illustrations.

McKinstry, Leo *Lancaster: The Second World War's Greatest Bomber*, John Murray, London, 2009: an interesting insight into the role and development of the Lancaster, including a chapter on the dams' raids. Black-and-white illustrations.

Morris, Richard (with Dobinson, Colin) *Guy Gibson,* Viking, London, 1994: the definitive biography of Gibson. Black-and-white illustrations.

Morris, Richard (ed.) *Breaching the German Dams: Flying Into History*, Royal Air Force Museum, London, 2008: a fascinating range of articles on the raids. A number of illustrations (mainly black-and-white).

Ottoway, Susan *Dambuster: The Life of Guy Gibson VC DSO DFC*, Pen & Sword Aviation, Barnsley, 2007: a good biography of Gibson, with a number of black-and-white illustrations.

Parry, Simon *Spitfire Hunters*, Red Kite, Walton-on-Thames, 2010: despite its title this illustrated book has an interesting chapter on the rediscovery of Lancaster ED825.

Probert, Henry *Bomber Harris: His Life and Times*, Greenhill Books, London, 2003: a brilliant insight into the role of Harris in the war, including his part in the raids. Black-and-white illustrations.

Speer, Albert *Inside the Third Reich*, Phoenix, London, 2003 re-issue: an interesting insight into Speer's assessment of the raids and their potential impact. The raids form only a small part in the book, but it is nevertheless an amazing and unique insight into the mindset of the Nazi high command in the war. Some black-and-white illustrations.

Sweetman, John *The Dambusters Raid*, Cassell, London, 2002: another much-respected book on the raids, with a number of black-and-white illustrations.

Thorning, Arthur *The Dambuster Who Cracked the Dam: The Story of Melvin 'Dinghy' Young*, Pen & Sword Aviation, Barnsley, 2008: fascinating insight into the life of 'Dinghy' Young, well supplied with black-and-white illustrations.

Ward, Chris and Lee, Andy (with Wachtel, Andreas) *Dambusters: The Definitive History of 617 Squadron at War*, Red Kite, Walton-on-Thames, 2008: a raid-by-raid account of 617 Squadron in the Second World War, with many black-and-white illustrations.

Ward, Chris and Wachtel, Andreas *Dambuster Crash Sites*, Pen & Sword Aviation, Barnsley, 2007: an invaluable guide to the crash sites of the bombers that were lost – very useful to those wishing to find the sites. A number of black-and-white illustrations.

Wilson, Kevin *Bomber Boys: The Ruhr, the Dambusters and Bloody Berlin*, Weidenfeld & Nicholson, London, 2005: includes an interesting chapter on the dam raids, with a few illustrations.

A number of records at the National Archives at Kew have been examined in the course of preparing this book. They are referenced in the text by the abbreviation 'PRO'. The Harris Papers at the RAF Museum have also been extensively referred to and are referenced with the abbreviation 'HP'.

Other Media
Dambuster: Wing Commander Guy Gibson VC, CD 41 Recordings, 2009: a re-recording of Gibson's wartime *Desert Island Discs* recording, with most of the words spoken by the actor Richard Todd, using Gibson's own words.
Dambusters Declassified, BBC, TV documentary, 2010
The Dambusters Raid, Delta and Laserlight DVD, 2002
Last of the Dambusters, Atypical Media production in association with The History Channel, TV documentary, 2008
The Lancaster at War, The History Channel, TV documentary, 2009

Acknowledgements

I would like to acknowledge the help and support of family and friends who have supported me with this book. First of all, to those dedicated people who look after national archival treasures at both the Public Records Office at Kew and the Harris Collection at Hendon who were always courteous, helpful and accommodating. Also to the enthusiasts who give freely of their time and talents at the RAF Museum at Scampton, unsung heroes all.

Then of course to the talented publishing staff, especially Jonathan Reeve at Amberley who have helped get this book, so to speak, off the ground.

Finally to my family and my good friend, Pete Scriven (an aerospace man himself), who have accompanied me on scoping missions around the UK and across to Germany; thanks for your company and I hope you had some good memories along the way.

Lastly we should not forget that thousands of people lost their lives because of the raid from both sides of the conflict. I have tried to recognise the bravery, skill and perseverance of the aircrews whilst also acknowledging the resultant loss of life amongst ordinary civilians in Germany in terrifying circumstances. I hope this book does their memory justice.

Thanks in particular to my daughter Deyna who took a number of the photos in the book and helped me in my research.

List of Illustrations

Battle of Britain Books from Amberley Publishing

Also available from Amberley Publishing

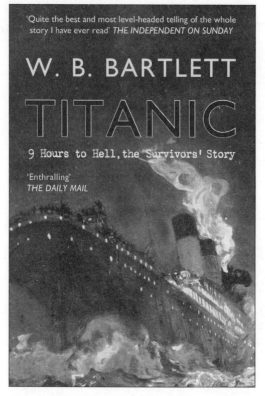

A major new history of the disaster that weaves into the narrative the first-hand accounts of those who survived

'Enthralling' THE DAILY MAIL

'Quite the best and most level-headed telling of the whole story I have ever read'
THE INDEPENDENT ON SUNDAY

It was twenty minutes to midnight on Sunday 14 April, when Jack Thayer felt the Titanic lurch to port, a motion followed by the slightest of shocks. Seven-year old Eva Hart barely noticed anything was wrong. For Stoker Fred Barrett, shovelling coal down below, it was somewhat different; the side of the ship where he was working caved in. For the next nine hours, Jack, Eva and Fred faced death and survived. 1600 people did not. This is the story told through the eyes of Jack, Eva, Fred and over a hundred others of those who survived and recorded their experiences.

£9.99 Paperback
72 illustrations (14 colour)
368 pages
978-1-4456-0482-4

Available from all good bookshops or to order direct
Please call **01453–847–800**
www.amberleybooks.com

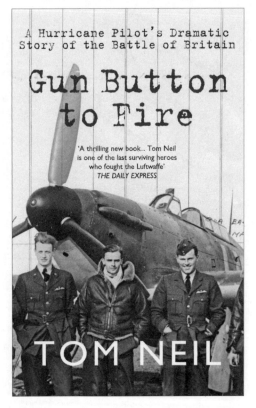

Index

Index